Illuminating, entertaining, and insightful.

—Chicago Tribune

Shapiro [has] done his homework, seeming to know the books as well as their authors do. He elicits philosophies of travel (Jan Morris says, "Grin like a dog and run about the city") as well as homely advice (Tim Cahill: "Never go shark diving with a guy that's only got one arm").

—Washington Post

Hearing some of the great travel writers talk about their craft is certainly instructive for readers and writers alike. Most enjoyable are [Shapiro's] interviews with some of the standard-bearers: Arthur Frommer, Eric Newby, Peter Matthiessen and Jan Morris.

—The New York Times Book Review

Big-minded, big-hearted, progressive and compassionate.

—San Francisco Chronicle

I enjoyed A Sense of Place down to the last drop. This is a wonderful book, full of literary and experiential allusions, a fascinating read.

—Keith Bellows, former editor, National Geographic Traveler

I've never thought of us so-called travel writers as forming a comradeship, but in this innovative book, Shapiro brings our motley crew into a single focus by surveying eighteen of us, as writers and as people, through a single pair of perceptive, generous, and imaginative eyes.

—Jan Morris, author of Trieste and the Meaning of Nowhere

Shapiro's descriptions of each writer are miniature masterpieces, I felt, every one, in part because each is so different. He evokes the very special and unique atmosphere of Isabel Allende showering her kindness on everyone, Tim Cahill and his open heart, Jan Morris with her wry compassion, Eric and Wanda Newby twinkling together.

—Pico Iyer, author of The Open Road

"Travel writer" is much too claustrophobic a label to hang on some of the finest nonfiction writers of our generation, and Michael Shapiro coaxes out fascinating insights into their journeys, their craft and the beloved places they leave behind.

—John Flinn, former travel editor, San Francisco Chronicle

Hooray for Michael Shapiro, for bringing us these sweet insightful visits with the great creators of contemporary travel literature. These are the writers who gave so many of us our longing for the road, our passion for place, who informed our own wanderings. I always wondered about their lives, and it took Michael Shapiro to track them down, get them talking, and share with us their perspectives on our world.

—Lynn Ferrin, former travel editor, Via magazine

Whether getting up at 4 a.m. to photograph the sunrise over Jerusalem, or prowling Waikiki Beach's Halloween madness, Michael Shapiro goes beyond the ordinary in his travels—and his writing. He brings a passion to his topics, digging beyond the surface to find deeper meanings and connections, but always with a sense of fun. And in the end, he and his readers are wiser for the effort.

—Larry Bleiberg, former travel editor, Dallas Morning News

A Sense of Place won a bronze medal in the ForeWord Magazine Book of the Year awards and was a finalist for the 2005 Independent Publisher Book Awards.

THE

CREATIVE SPARK

*How musicians, writers, explorers,
and other artists found their inner fire
and followed their dreams*

THE
CREATIVE SPARK

*How musicians, writers, explorers,
and other artists found their inner fire
and followed their dreams*

MICHAEL SHAPIRO

SOLAS HOUSE
PALO ALTO

Travelers' Tales and Solas House are trademarks of Solas House, Inc., Palo Alto, California. travelerstales.com | solashouse.com

Art Direction: Kimberly Nelson
Cover Design: Kimberly Nelson
Cover Art: Alex Brady
Interior Design and Page Layout: Howie Severson

Library of Congress Cataloging-in-Publication Data is available upon request

978-1-60952-176-9 (paperback)
978-1-60952-177-6 (ebook)
978-1-60952-178-3 (hard cover)

First Edition
Printed in the United States
10 9 8 7 6 5 4 3 2 1

*For my mother, Phyllis Shapiro, who encouraged me to be
curious and creative from my earliest days, and for my wife,
Jacqueline Yau, my teammate through life*

Life isn't about finding yourself or finding anything.
Life is about creating yourself and creating things.

—Bob Dylan

TABLE OF CONTENTS

INTRODUCTION

Emerging from the Chrysalis

Something magical happened as I completed this book. One evening just before sunset I was in our backyard watering the planter boxes. On a stem of parsley I noticed a startling pattern of color, concentric rings of orange and black dots. Looking closer I saw the segments of a swallowtail caterpillar and could identify its tiny feet. For the next few days the caterpillar chomped on the parsley plant, absorbing energy for the next stage of its life. I placed a stick in the pot, at an angle to give the caterpillar a place to hang its chrysalis.

The caterpillar's appearance felt like a message from the universe. For many months I'd been working on transforming interviews I'd conducted with some of the world's most creative people into a coherent set of chapters. I'd distilled the essence of these interviews into a tonic of ideas about the creative process. And I'd written biographical introductions that sought to put each person's life in perspective and offer insights about the sources of his or her art.

As I write this, on 2019's summer solstice, our adopted caterpillar (my wife has given it the gender-neutral name Jordan) is undergoing a miraculous transformation into a butterfly. During the past week, we've watched the caterpillar turn into a chrysalis that matches the color of the branch from which it hangs, its striated brown camouflage the antithesis of the colorful creature it was just a few days ago. Yet it's what is happening inside the chrysalis that is truly astonishing.

The caterpillar is dissolving, using enzymes to digest itself. It's being broken down into nonspecific cells that can be used for any part of the butterfly. Yet some "highly organized groups of cells known as imaginal discs survive the digestive process," according to Scientific American. Each of these constellations of cells is programmed to build a specific part of the butterfly. There are imaginal discs for wings, for eyes, for legs, for every part of the butterfly. Typically, after about two weeks, a yellow-and-black swallowtail butterfly will crack open the chrysalis, dry its wings in the morning sun, and fly off seeking nectar.

Why bring up a caterpillar in a book about creativity? First, because it offers such a rich metaphor, and the name "imaginal discs" suggests that making art depends on imagination. And to prepare for its transformation, the caterpillar needs to first feed itself, just as a musician or author must absorb the thoughts and influences that come from songs, books, conversations, memories, and observations. Then many creative people seek to isolate themselves, cocoon-like, to escape the relentless drumbeat of popular culture so they can hear their own voices.

"What I noticed at an early stage was that the writers I admire are living a long way from the world," the author Pico Iyer told me. "The great originals are originals because they're living outside the received conversation, outside secondhand words and secondhand ideas, to some extent living in a space of their own where they're able to hear their deeper self and come up with things completely outside the norm. I think that's why they really shake us."

Isn't that what we crave in this era of information overload: songs or stories that really shake us and offer new ways of seeing the world, of hearing ourselves, of feeling, on a soul level, our deepest truths? That's why I've chosen the 31 creative people in this book. They're original, pioneering, dynamic, and insatiably curious. The authors, musicians, and others profiled in these pages could coast on their earlier accomplishments, but every one has continued to seek adventurous new avenues for igniting their creative spark. And those who are now deceased, such as Joan Rivers and Sharon Jones, worked until virtually the day they died.

Of course, seeking solitude to hear one's inner voice doesn't mean we should shut out those who came before us. As Iowa folk singer Greg Brown says, "I feel links back to a time that not much is known about. Songs, poetry, whatever you want to call it, that urge, it just goes way, way, way back there. And that's a good connection to feel to life. It's hard for me to imagine life without that."

Which takes us back to butterflies. As author Barbara Kingsolver notes, monarch butterflies that travel from Appalachia down to Mexico may live for just a few weeks. During a migration, one generation dies and the next is born—several times. That means a butterfly "returning" from Mexico to Kentucky could be the great-great-grandchild of the one that departed months before. And yet it returns to the exact spot from which its ancestors departed. Scientists don't fully understand this phenomenon, but perhaps the butterflies' internal compass is cellular. To consider this in human terms: the knowledge, dreams, hopes, and prayers of our ancestors reside within us.

Glancing at the list of people interviewed in *The Creative Spark*, you might wonder about some of the selections. Beyond well-known musicians like Smokey Robinson and heralded authors such as Frances Mayes are a number of names you probably haven't heard. People like storied musician Richard Thompson or the intrepid Irish travel writer Dervla Murphy, who are equally worthy of our attention. That's one of the goals of this book, to introduce voices that deserve a wider audience.

One of the most gratifying comments about *The Creative Spark* came from its publisher, James O'Reilly, in an email after he read the Lucinda Williams chapter. "I went straight to listen to her album, *Down Where the Spirit Meets the Bone*. Wow. I must have been living under a rock to not know her. I love her voice and music and intensity." He summed up: "This book is all about meeting people you'll love who you never knew, or who you thought you knew but didn't."

Another affirming response came from the book's editor, Larry Habegger, after he read all the chapters: "I've been asking myself, why did I let music drift out of my life? I used to be completely tuned in to the music scene, but I haven't followed it in years and hardly know these musicians or their music. I'm going to start listening again," he wrote in an email.

"The cumulative effect is really much bigger than a bunch of individual interviews," Habegger said about the book as a whole. "I feel filled up, not overfull, but satisfied and moved by all of these people and their collective experiences. It's really a portrait of life writ large, with the compelling undercurrent that these 'famous people' are real people like the rest of us. These are people living their lives, pursuing what most profoundly interests them, and by doing so, marvelous stuff happens. It's like alchemy; something magical occurs. Something real gets created and shared, and we're all the better for it."

Also in these pages are people some may not view as being artistically creative. You may wonder: Why is Jane Goodall in the book? The answer is simple: because of her original approach to studying animals and her dexterity in writing about the natural world. Same goes for oceanographer Sylvia Earle, who refused to let sexism stop her from pursuing a career in science. How about Warren Hellman, wasn't he an investment banker? Well, yes, he was, but he was much more gratified by becoming a capable banjo player late in life and founding Hardly Strictly Bluegrass, an annual free music festival in San Francisco's Golden Gate Park.

There are other potentially surprising names here, such as former Major League Baseball pitcher Mike Krukow who has become one of the most inventive color commentators in broadcasting. And there's San Francisco keyboardist Melvin Seals who leapt from a church music background into the psychedelic underworld of the Jerry Garcia Band.

I profile two chefs, both of whom run top-shelf restaurants in areas that were hit by recent disasters. Juan José Cuevas of 1919 restaurant in San Juan, Puerto Rico, turned his attention to feeding thousands of refugees after Hurricane Maria. And in Northern California, Kyle Connaughton, the chef and co-owner of Healdsburg's SingleThread, briefly closed his restaurant in October 2017 and employed his team to feed fire victims in Sonoma County and beyond. These efforts grew out of on-the-fly ingenuity motivated by a desire to help people in need.

There are two polio survivors, Francis Ford Coppola and Judy Collins. Both noted that the illness led to long periods of bed rest when they were children, during which they engaged in artistic endeavors. Coppola directed his own puppet shows. Collins, the singer and songwriter, turned to books: "For me, polio was like a vacation—I could read all the time," she told the Wall Street Journal.

Most of the interviews in this book were conducted during the past decade for magazines including The Saturday Evening Post, The Sun, and The Explorers Journal. Others were done for newspapers such as the San Francisco Chronicle or The Press Democrat (Santa Rosa, California). And some were done expressly for *The Creative Spark*—among them the conversations with Pico Iyer and Phil Cousineau. Naturally one book can't cover even a fraction of the worthy creative people, so this volume includes musicians, authors, and other innovators who have inspired me; it's a personal selection. Yet my sense is that their appeal is universal.

I've edited the interviews to present their most illuminating aspects, those most germane to creativity. And while this is not a how-to book, it has lots of useful nuggets that could inspire anyone seeking to follow a novel path. Listen to Amy Tan on why she writes: "Every single moment I've had is not a lost past; it is completely a continuum of who I am . . . Writing fiction is finding the meaning of my life, what I think, what I feel I have to remember, what I know about myself."

These artists would not suggest that anyone else try to follow their exact footsteps. Instead they say: Find your own path and pursue it passionately. "I think Einstein said something like: I have no special talents; I am only passionately curious," noted Pico Iyer. "And that's probably the definition of what it is to be creative: always to be asking questions and not even needing the answers."

Cousineau, who taps into the power of words by digging down to their roots, told me something similar: "I had to look up the word create, which goes back to the old French *créer,* to grow, and the secondary meaning is to find order where there's chaos. And that's part of the beauty of being someone creative. I don't start a story or a film or a radio show with all the answers. Those tend not to go anywhere. I pursue things that I would say I'm haunted by, provoked by. And if I can put my heart and soul into that, you as the reader or viewer, you're going to feel some of that charge."

Another question that may arise in readers' minds: why didn't you interview visual artists? Well, that's not my specialty—in journalistic terms, not my beat. I love and appreciate visual art, and in the past few months have gone to see the landmark Pieter Bruegel exhibition in Vienna and the Monet show in San Francisco. But I don't understand art the way I do songs or books, so I've focused mostly on authors and musicians.

Let's not forget humor. I had the great pleasure of interviewing the uproariously funny David Sedaris, who will talk about anything in his books in understated, pitch-perfect prose. And shortly before she died, I spoke with the brilliant Joan Rivers, a shining example of how laughter can help transcend the most painful of human tragedies, in Rivers' case, her husband's suicide.

So many priceless moments come to mind when I think back on these interviews. When I asked Smokey Robinson what he was most proud of, he said, "This moment," because a journalist (me) was still interested in his work more than 50 years after he began writing songs. And when I interviewed Warren Hellman about launching the Hardly Strictly Bluegrass festival, his eyes sparkled and he started talking faster, saying, "God I love talking about this." But for enigmatic concision, Merle Haggard wins. When I asked him about his album, *I Am What I Am*, he said: "It is what it is."

Some common themes came up among performers as different as Joan Rivers and California guitarist and songwriter Dave Alvin. Here's one: Ignore the rules. Inspired by Lenny Bruce, Rivers traversed comedic territory that no one had explored before, which was all the more shocking when she came up in the conventional 1950s and early '60s because she was a woman. Dave Alvin, who became known during the late '70s and early '80s playing with his brother Phil in The Blasters, said: "There are no rules in songwriting anymore." (Dave Alvin has gone solo; The Blasters are now led by Phil Alvin.)

Another common theme is that most of the artists in this book didn't chase commercial success; they stayed true to themselves. "There's just no reason to go downtown in the music industry," Dave Alvin has said, "because that's where Britney Spears lives . . . You have a longer career working the outskirts." Asked about commercial success, Greg Brown laughed and said: "That just never mattered to me." And when Francis Ford Coppola couldn't get studio funding, he risked the millions of dollars he'd earned from the Godfather films, as well as his home and office, to make the daring *Apocalypse Now.*

Ultimately, cancer survivor Melissa Etheridge told me, it comes down to "loving" what she does. "That's the most important thing; I think people could absolutely tell if I didn't love what I created because it wouldn't have the spark in it. That's what people relate to. The most important thing is for me to be in love and feel that the music has a place inside of myself."

For these artists, the pursuit of creativity is ultimately about expressing their humanity. Perhaps there's nothing more human than the desire to make art. For thousands of years, we have banged on drums, painted on cave walls, told stories, and sung to one another around a campfire. What's so remarkable about so many of our creative endeavors is that none at first glance appears essential to our survival. We need food, water, and shelter—but these necessities alone don't make for a rich and satisfying human life. We want music and art and stories—these are what echo and elevate our souls and help us better understand ourselves and the world. Perhaps they are essential after all.

Coming together to celebrate something original fosters community. Think about how thousands of people at a Melissa Etheridge concert share the sheer joy of music, or how a book such as Amy Tan's *The Joy Luck Club* can change a society's view of immigrants. Or how a David Sedaris reading, in the great oral tradition of Mark Twain, can unite a theater of people from all sorts of backgrounds in knowing laughter.

Innovative people have a brightness in their eyes, an inquisitive way of looking at the world, a desire to create things, even if those things are not tangible. But that spark doesn't reside solely in people you may view as artists. It's in all of us. "Surely something wonderful is sheltered inside you," writes Elizabeth Gilbert in her book, *Big Magic: Creative Living Beyond Fear.* "I say this with all confidence, because I happen to believe we are all walking repositories of buried treasure."

Most of the people profiled in these pages had a moment when they made a creative leap, a commitment to make something new. They took a chance. As a whitewater rafting guide, I think of that moment when my boat drops into a rapid—there's no turning back. You just have to navigate the rapids as best you can. That's what it's been like for many inventive people. They've pursued their passion, not knowing where it would take them. They made a commitment and stuck to it, day after day, until the song was written or the book complete.

"To get there takes work," notes Cousineau, author of *The Art of Pilgrimage.* "Inspiration moves you out of the ordinary moment, but it's the actual work, going back and trying to get to the essence of the thing. The famous image of Michelangelo looking at the block of marble and saying: I stare at it until I can see the finished statue—then I just cut away everything else. It's something like that with the story too."

During these interviews, I didn't always ask people directly about creativity. I let the musicians, writers, and others talk about experiences that shaped them and how they pursued their passions. Rather than seek to cover their entire careers, the interviews are snapshots of where each person is when we spoke: what they're working on, where they hope to go next.

By "snapshot" I certainly don't mean the profiles are superficial. In the interviews, I did my best to be curious and nonjudgmental, opening space for these artists to go deep. Moments into my conversation with Lucinda Williams, for example, she told me how decisions made about her mother's funeral led to fissures in her family. From this achingly personal conversation, readers can glean fresh insights into why Lucinda has such a devoted following and how her songs crack open listeners' hearts.

Ultimately, *The Creative Spark* stands as a testament to the highest aspirations of human beings, showing how creativity enlivens our souls and enriches our world. And how it resides in each and every one of us, just waiting to break out.

—Michael Shapiro
Sonoma County, California
June 21, 2019

Traveler's Mind
PICO IYER

Because his writing is so fresh, original, and penetrating, Pico Iyer is one of the most beguiling authors of our time. He simultaneously manages to capture a moment while his transcendent prose speaks to changeless truths. And nobody has written more eloquently or insightfully about one of the defining themes of our era: the unprecedented mingling of cultures, traditions, and heritages—and how they influence one another. Born in England to Indian parents in 1957, Iyer moved to California when he was seven and was educated at Eton, Oxford, and Harvard. (I wanted to ask if these were his safety schools but resisted that temptation.)

In his first book, *Video Night in Kathmandu: And Other Reports from the Not-So-Far East*, written when he was in his mid-twenties, Iyer's whirlwind travels take him to 10 countries; in each he spends about three weeks. He writes about how Japan, for example, created a Disneyland that reflects the traditional country's worldview. "It took what is known in American Disneyland as Main Street and turned it into World Bazaar," Iyer writes, "where all the products and all the possibilities of all the continents in the world are together in one synthetic complex that was wholly Japanese."

His next book, *The Lady and the Monk: Four Seasons in Kyoto*, could be described as the yin in counterpoint to the kinetic yang of *Video Night*. Iyer's second book is a meditative and introspective work about his intention to spend a year in a Kyoto monastery, but that lasts just a week before his curiosity leads him out of the monastery and into the ancient city. On that trip Iyer meets the woman who would become his wife; they've been together for more than 30 years.

In a career that started with a staff job at Time magazine, Iyer has written thousands of travel stories and essays, including the widely cited "Why We Travel," originally delivered as a lecture at the Smithsonian in 1996. The essay celebrates traveling with what Buddhists might call beginner's mind. "For me the first great joy of traveling is simply the luxury of leaving all my beliefs and certainties at home, and seeing everything I thought I knew in a different light, and from a crooked angle," he writes in that essay.

From the beginning of his literary career, Iyer creatively staked out a territory that few had explored: how one culture makes another's exports its own. He's written about how adored Kentucky Fried Chicken was in China and how baseball has been adapted in Cuba and Japan (where arguments are virtually non-existent). For more than a quarter-century, he has contributed essays to the New York Times, New York Review of Books, and Harper's, among more than 200 other periodicals.

His 2014 book, a slender volume published by TED Books called *The Art of Stillness: Adventures in Going Nowhere*, celebrates solitude, reflection, and quiet spaces. It is a handbook for remaining sane and grounded in a world of constant distraction and stimulation. Considering Iyer's peripatetic past,

The Art of Stillness may have surprised some people. Its author had, after all, spent the past three decades traveling nearly incessantly, visiting more than 80 countries, and prolifically, sometimes feverishly, writing about his adventures.

Yet those who know Iyer and his work weren't surprised. A close associate of the Dalai Lama—Iyer's father and His Holiness were friends, and Iyer typically accompanies the Dalai Lama on his trips through Japan—Iyer wrote the revelatory *The Open Road: The Global Journey of the Fourteenth Dalai Lama*. And he has chosen for decades to live quietly (during interludes between trips) in a nondescript suburb about 30 miles south of Kyoto. Iyer says he barely speaks Japanese, and whether at home or away, he doesn't use a cell phone or engage with Instagram or Facebook.

Given the remarkable range of Iyer's work, it was arresting to hear him make the following statement during a 2012 interview in San Francisco with travel writer Don George. "All writers write the same book again and again . . . Fundamentally, we have the same single question driving or guiding us through our lives. At some level, I'm just writing the same book many times over, but more imperfectly each time." When I interviewed Iyer nearly seven years later he told me, "Every time I write a book, I want the next book to be as different as possible and to come at my abiding obsessions from a radically different angle. After the next book, I'll try to go in a completely different direction."

On the surface these comments appear contradictory, but ultimately they're not, Iyer assured me in a follow-up email. "The seeming contradiction in what I said to Don and to you is, I think, the same point seen from opposite sides. Precisely because every book is more or less the same book each time, one tries to dress it up in different costumes, to come at the same story from different angles, to make the abiding obsessions look fresh, the way one might sometimes surprise a friend by greeting her in a three-piece suit and sometimes in a Grateful Dead

T-shirt. It's always the same person underneath, but a writer's job is partly to keep the reader off-guard and surprised."

Later in that email Iyer observed: "Bruce Springsteen followed the dark and deeply lonely, haunted *Nebraska* with the affirmative-sounding *Born in the U.S.A.* (though for him the two were so much the same that he'd actually considered including the song 'Born in the U.S.A.' on *Nebraska*). I suspect all of us function in this way."

Iyer published two books about Japan in 2019. The first, *Autumn Light: Season of Fire and Farewells*, is an appreciation of the ephemeral beauty and frailty of life. The second book is *A Beginner's Guide to Japan: Observations and Provocations,* which Iyer described as an outsider's look at his adopted home, where he'd lived for 31 years, half his lifespan at the time of its publication.

I spoke to Iyer by phone during the summer of 2018. As always, his sentences tumbled out in rapid-fire succession, each thought remarkably developed, every sentence polished. Iyer speaks quickly and eloquently; each concept offers so much to be considered, but there's no time to linger. Fortunately, I recorded the conversation.

Similar to the Dalai Lama, Iyer's religion appears to be kindness. He thanked me for asking original questions and complimented my "conscientiousness and precision." I'd felt slightly off my game when we spoke—I'd learned the day before our interview that my cousin had died suddenly. Yet after spending an hour on the phone with Iyer, I felt lighter and clearer, and somehow more hopeful about the world.

≈≈ ≈≈ ≈≈

In your writing you've talked about the circumstances of your birth and that you live outside the mainstream culture; you're not necessarily British or Indian or Californian. I wonder if you feel this gave you an opportunity to be more creative?

I think looking back I realize I was given three sets of eyes, three different perspectives to bring to any situation. Without consciously being aware of that, I think I quickly seized upon it as an advantage. I realized that if I was walking down the street in Santa Barbara, I could see it through semi-Californian eyes or (more interestingly) through English eyes, or (even more interestingly) through English eyes with some Indian blood in the background.

And I think I also noticed that I could bring these different perspectives together into fresh combinations. It's very common now, but in those days not so many people, if they traveled to Thailand, say, would be seeing it partly with the eyes of somebody whose blood was Asian and partly through the eyes of somebody who had grown-up entirely in the West. As Orhan Pamuk wonderfully says, two souls are better than one; in this context, it's not necessarily a recipe for schizophrenia, but rather for a multitude of choices. Very quickly I realized I had three palettes, in some ways, and it was maybe a little easier to live and to think and to look outside conventional categories.

One of the things that intrigued me when we spoke for A Sense of Place *was the formation of an inward home or an internal base. And that is an act of creation; I don't think that just happens. Could you talk about the creation of that internal home and what it's meant to you throughout your life?*

Yes, and it has evolved with every few years; it's an ongoing process that probably will never conclude. I didn't feel when I was born that I was given a whole set of answers to the basic questions: "What's your neighborhood? What's your country? What's your religion?" As you say, I would have to craft them together in collage form. Although that's a challenge, I did see it very much as an opportunity to define myself, not by where I came from but by where I was heading. So my home would probably be the people and places that really ground and accompany me at the deepest level.

I've chosen to live for 31 years in Japan even though I have no formal affiliation with it. That's a kind of creation, certainly a choice based on intuition and nothing rational. And I think the creative impulse is really whatever takes place in the subconscious, in those mysterious areas deeper and truer than the brain. So if at the age of 31, someone had asked me, "Where's your home?" I would have said Japan even though I had no official connection with it, and I'm still there on a tourist visa.

I never guessed as a little boy that this would soon become so common; to me it's the signature of the 21st century. So many people, especially people much younger than I am, are permanently creating and re-creating their home and their sense of home. In doing so, they are re-creating the world, and they're re-creating America. This country is much more interesting because it's filled with many-homed people.

You anticipated one of my questions about the 21st-century act of choosing one's tribe. Do you think this intermingling of cultures has made the world a more creative place?

It's made the world a much fresher and more dynamic and exciting and unexpected place. I think of London, which when I grew up was the dullest, dreariest, rainiest place on earth. The shops never opened on Sundays. Everybody seemed very much from the same tribe—and hostile to anyone from another tribe. Here, only two generations later, it's one of the youngest, fizziest, most international places on Earth, a real magnet for creative young people, partly because the average person you meet on the streets of London today is what used to be known as a foreigner, somebody born in another country.

Toronto, the same. When I was in grad school we used to talk of "Toronto the Gray," and now it's the most multi-cultural city on Earth, according to the United Nations. You literally find Indo-Pakistani-Chinese restaurants there. Of course this same sense of disruption plays out among refugees, those pushed out of home rather than choosing to move. And they should always remain our foremost concern in the global arena. But for the fortunate among us, it's an invitation to think outside of boxes because we were born outside those outdated categories.

I'm thinking, for example, of our last president, Mr. Obama, who couldn't see things in black-and-white terms, because he was neither black nor white. Or he was both. So he had a much broader global perspective than any president we've had before. I was talking about how I have three sets of eyes, but I feel that Mr. Obama could to some degree see any situation through the eyes of Indonesia, Kenya, Hawaii, and Kansas. It made him a richer and more sensitive and more nuanced leader than we've had before.

Meghan Markle is moving into the House of Windsor, and it's going to be a different place because she also stands outside those binary distinctions. In the field of writing, one of the most exciting essayists in the younger generation for me is Zadie Smith because she's outside race and outside class and increasingly outside nationality. You never know where she's going to land. She probably doesn't either, which means everything is in play and there's much more at stake.

One of the most popular nonfiction writers, Malcolm Gladwell, enjoys the same combination—half Jamaican, half English. The world is moving quickly in that direction. Anything that moves towards unpredictability is moving towards life. It's definitely a step in the right direction.

So let's talk about writing as a creative act. You're taking a blank page and turning it into something. If I were to read your very early work, such as Video Night in Kathmandu *or* The Lady and the Monk, *and compare those works to some of your more recent books, I might not know it's the same writer. Could you trace the arc of your career and how you view its evolution?*

I'd be delighted to, especially because no one has asked me that before. I think when you and I spoke for your last book, you introduced to me this wonderful phrase: "beginner's mind." And I was thinking that probably I approach the world through traveler's mind, which is to say I'm not so interested in going to other countries, but I am interested in exploring new terrain and looking around the corner to places where I haven't been before, inwardly and creatively at my desk as well as geographically.

Every time I write a book, I want the next book to be as different as possible and to come at my abiding obsessions from a radically different angle. After the next book, I'll try to go in some completely different direction. In terms of scenes and texture and coloring, I would agree with you, and I take it as a compliment that you wouldn't imagine each book was written by the same person.

It's like being an actor; with each book I am taking on a fresh persona. I'm creating a character or a version of myself to drive that book along. Once I've played a madcap zany, I want to play at being more methodical in the next, and perhaps an invisible tape recorder in the next. In the book after that I will try to turn myself into a tortured Graham Greene protagonist. That's the fun, that's how I try to keep the writing fresh, because every writer and every person knows that the biggest dangers are repeating yourself and becoming a caricature of yourself, or deploying the same tricks again and again.

All of us essentially carry one abiding question through life. And most of the writers I love reading are doing that, but they come at it from completely different perspectives. So Philip Roth will write one book, *Sabbath's Theater*, about the completely unhinged id, and then the next book, *American Pastoral*, about an extremely conventional upholder of the order. He's going at exactly the same issue, keeping himself alive by coming from left field in one case and right field in the other.

I think a part of me has followed that impulse. *Video Night* was written very quickly and catchily, so I thought, "Well, I've done that, I tried out that guise, why don't I do something different?" So in my next book, I deliberately was trying to stay in one place, and to write a travel book about being in one town. The friends who bore us are the ones who speak in the same voice every time. The book I just completed is deliberately a complement to *The Lady and the Monk* but set in autumn rather than spring. So, the same characters and same places but probably the pacing and the feel of it will be very different, which is my hope.

Indeed, to try to keep myself alive, I just wrote two books, both nonfiction and both about the same subject, Japan, and as completely different from one another as they could be. I suggested to my publisher we bring out both books at the same time, almost as a brother and sister—or husband and wife. They were more sensible and suggested staggering the publication by a few months. The first book is called *Autumn Light*, and it's about being in the midst of a Japanese neighborhood. I see it as a narrative written from the heart, about trying to absorb sympathetically the lives around one.

Right after that, I'll bring out a book called *A Beginner's Guide to Japan*, which is driven by an outsider's judgmental, rather analytical perspective. It's a series of sentences, each of which is a mad provocation, and a sequence of sweeping generalizations or strange quotes about Japan. I want to explode a sense of binaries, as Japan does so hauntingly, and write from a Japanese awareness that every truth is provisional, every moment the product of a mood that will change a moment later.

Regarding the second one, are you concerned you might get some kind of blowback from readers who don't understand what you're doing?

Yes, because I find that I don't express clearly enough what I'm trying to do in any case, so I always get that blowback. But that's fine; I don't think I mind too much about what the reader's response is. Of course I try to make the books as clear as possible, but I think the writer's job, often, is to unsettle, shock, or challenge the reader. A writer, like any person, has to remain on guard against pleasing a reader or an audience too much because that's another way of falling into a ditch from which it's very hard to extricate yourself.

That's always been the case, but we do live in an entertainment culture now, beyond anything we could have imagined 20 years ago. And if a reader is seeking diversion or fun, there are so many amazing ways of getting that today that I think a writer has to approach things differently. I can't compete with YouTube or an iPhone for amusement or diversion. So I have to offer the reader something she's not going to find anywhere else. We're much more spoiled nowadays when we can sit in our rooms and the whole world comes to us through our smartphones. So a writer's job may be to give a reader a hard time.

In your book, The Global Soul *(2000), you talk about how jet lag is a phenomenon we'd experienced for only about 50 years. Now we are closely connected to devices that distance us from direct experience. Do you feel we risk losing our creativity by being attached to our phones and our computers and our TVs?*

Very much, because I think as long as you're looking at the small screen, you can't really see the larger picture. In the course of my writing career, we've gone very quickly from having too little information about the world—which was the case when I began *Video Night in Kathmandu* in 1985—to having much too much.

What I noticed at an early stage was that the writers I admire are living a long way from the world. We are not seeing them on the Late Show, whether it's Cormac McCarthy or Thomas Pynchon or Annie Dillard or Don DeLillo; the great originals are originals because they're living outside the received conversation, outside secondhand words and secondhand ideas, to some extent living in a space of their own where they're able to hear their deeper self and come up with things completely outside the norm. I think that's why they really shake us.

Anybody who's too caught up in the moment probably can't see the perspective of eternity but also can't really think outside the terms that we've been given by CNN or Facebook or MSNBC. I think that's why we're all suffering from a collective headache.

When you talk about *The Global Soul*, two other things come to my mind. The first is that book is a perfect example of what I was describing. I wanted to make the reader feel seasick and jet-lagged and dizzy. There's an incredible bombardment of data and details on every page of the first half of that book, which makes you feel like you're in an airport where there are a hundred TV screens blaring at you all at once, and people are racing backwards and forwards.

It's a very unpleasant feeling. I could have brought up the same themes by writing something calm, but I thought I ought to convey the sense of jangledness so that the reader feels the ache to escape and the longing to be free of all this, which is what the end point of that book was meant to be. So it was a case of confronting the reader with something unpleasant to push her towards recalling what truly sustains her and what she cherishes.

For me jet lag is an affliction that those of us lucky enough to travel spend much of our lives in the thick of, so the challenge there is to see jet lag as something creative and a chance to do something new. Whenever I fly back to Santa Barbara, I really try hard to go out for lunch at four in the morning when I can smell the kelp [from the nearby ocean] at the hamburger stand and see all the people on the graveyard shift, aspects of my hometown I don't normally see.

When I arrive in a foreign country—Singapore, say—I try to walk around at three in the morning, and I'll see the kind of subconscious and uncensored Singapore I would never see in the daylight hours. Jet lag is a good example of something that no human had known until about 60 years ago that we have to live with and therefore turn into a creative possibility. I don't drink, and I don't really do drugs, so jet lag has been my closest equivalent to plumbing some netherworld of the subconscious.

I'd like to talk about a set of dueling ideas about travel and creativity. On the one hand, when I read your work, I think about this idea that what we find outside the self has to be inside the self. But there's also the concept that when you travel, you can completely open yourself to a place and potentially let it shape you. I know you travel in search of re-creation not recreation; I'm trying to make a distinction between travel writing that embodies a sense of self but at the same time reveals a willingness to let go of yourself. Is that paradox?

I think the point of travel is much more the second, to be free of yourself; more important than leaving your home is leaving your habits behind. Even if I go to the other side of Santa Barbara today, which I barely visit, that can be a very

significant kind of travel because I'm out of my routine and
my set responses.

I think of travel as a way much more of leaving oneself
and therefore one's defenses at home, and, as you say, of being
shaped by the world. I head off on any trip hoping to be a
slightly different person when I come back, and I can only
be a different person by emptying myself out. For me, a fun-
damental principle of creativity is that it's not about always
filling yourself up but rather emptying yourself out, so that
you can be filled by everything around you. In that sense, it's
an act of surrender. And that's how new things come into you.

Travel for me is a way of putting yourself in a very different situation so that your self is different or hollowed out. And
that's where the change comes. It's the shedding of self that's
more important than just encountering a foreign culture. It
reminds me of two things in answer to your earlier questions.
You and I are old friends, so you probably know that because
of my diverse background, very early on I decided to assume
as many different roles and pursue as many different interests
as possible, whether those were sports or movies or religion
or different cultures. My sense was that I could play them off
against one another and try to make one plus one equal three.

In *Video Night in Kathmandu*, in my very first chapter on
Bali, I thought, "Well, so many people have written about Bali,
and so many more have written about Shakespeare before. But
how about bringing my interest in Shakespeare and *The Tem-
pest* together with Bali and pushing those two things together?
Some kind of sparks may emerge from that. Shakespeare's
play may open up a way of approaching Bali that not so many
people have enjoyed before. And Bali might show me how
Shakespeare's play is not just about 17th-century England but
Indonesia right now.

And I think that's partly what my writing has always been
about. If I'm writing about the Dalai Lama, I'll come to him

through D.H. Lawrence. But if I'm writing about Proust, I'll come to him through Buddhism, trying to bring two very disparate things together in the hope that they'll throw light on one another.

To go back to your previous question about the arc of my career or my writing: living in Japan has taught me that creativity is a lot about taking things out. In Japan, they'll make a room as empty as possible. So that there is only one flower and one scroll left, and that means you have to bring all your attention to that scroll and that flower. That means you see everything you need—and more—there. The creative activity in Japan is really about sifting and minimalizing, making things as spare as possible, partly because that is how you spark creativity in a reader.

So for example, *Video Night in Kathmandu*, I would describe as a maximalist book. It's like a Bollywood stage set, like a house that's too bright and cluttered and full of everything, 10 times more than you need. More and more, as I spend time in Japan, my pages are about nothing at all. There's a lot of blank space in the two books I am bringing out. So it's a different form of creativity that's aimed at inviting the reader in. It's about listening more than lecturing.

In *Video Night in Kathmandu*, the page is so full that there's very little room for the reader. He or she had to just take in this guy onstage throwing a million things out, whereas now my books are meant to sound more like somebody at the back of the stage, whispering. That draws the reader in. The hope is that it makes for greater intimacy but also as in a haiku or in a brush painting, that the reader has to complete the work herself. It's a collaboration. And she is creative because the fewer words that are on the page, the more she has to complete the sentence.

So it's definitely a very different approach, and if my writing has changed it's partly the result of having moved from very verbal New York City to very quiet suburban Japan. But I'm glad my sense of creativity keeps changing and evolving, and that what I thought was an interesting way to address an audience in 1988 is now a very different one, 30 years on.

I'm glad you brought up the Dalai Lama. I know you accompany him when he visits Japan; I wonder if his life seems to you as an entire work of creativity. Here's a man who had to flee his country and then re-create not just a home for himself but a home for his people in Dharamsala.

That's an amazing question and you're absolutely right that that is the single most creative thing you can do, to fashion a whole culture outside its traditional borders. He's almost unique in having been given the challenge of doing that single-handedly. One of the most striking things that I learnt when I wrote my book on him was that, the minute he stepped into exile in 1959 in India, he turned to his younger brother who had accompanied him on that flight and said, "Now we are free."

I think he didn't mean just that he was free from the pursuers who were trying to capture him, but that now he was free to create a whole new and better Tibet. So long as he was in Tibet, he was surrounded by centuries of ritual and precedent and formalism—and it would be difficult to effect reform. Once he was outside, and as you said re-creating Tibet from scratch in India, he could do all kinds of things—like allowing women in his community to become abbesses and to practice ritual debating, as they had never been allowed to before. And bringing Western science to his monks' curriculum. And finally bringing democracy to his people, as they had never had before.

He's both a realist and a radical. One of the things I admire about the Dalai Lama, which is what makes him so creative, is his readiness to dispense with everything superficial to create a kind of transformation. He will often tell Tibetans in India: "Get rid of your Tibetan clothes—they're not made for a tropical country. You will not be less Tibetan if you start wearing Indian clothes."

He has this clear sense of what is fleeting and what is abiding. He nowadays says: "No more need for the Dalai Lama institution. It served its purpose and that time has gone. It was useful when we were all united in one Tibet, but now we need a different kind of leadership." I admire the fact he's ready to get rid of so much in the service of a vision that remains changeless. As you say, that's a great form of creativity because it's spontaneously drafting something using human possibility rather than just a pen.

In my travels I noticed that some of the most impoverished places, at least materially, are some of the most creative places. I think of Cuba, where there is music and art everywhere. Or southern Africa, where they take old telephone wire of different colors and create these beautiful works of art. I wonder if sometimes in the wealthier countries we get complacent, and if the lack of material wealth in other places can foster an abundance of creative wealth. Have you seen that in your travels?

Absolutely, in India, Haiti, so many countries. I think if the newcomer arrives in India tomorrow, she may well be shocked, but she won't be depressed. Just as you say about Havana, for example, in the midst of these difficult conditions and collapsing buildings there is such a sense of vitality and engagement and energy and dynamism.

The Dalai Lama often finds himself in Beverly Hills at big fundraisers full of billionaires and movie stars, and nearly always people will ask him: "How do you manage to survive in a country as impoverished as India?" He'll look around the room and see people on their sixth or seventh marriages and paying a therapist a huge amount for a session every day, and he'll say: "There's poverty, and there's poverty." He would say material poverty is a terrible thing, and he devotes a lot of his energy to trying to rectify the imbalance between the rich and the poor. But spiritual poverty is no less disabling.

One of the things that impresses me about the Dalai Lama is that he always travels as a student, rather than a teacher. When he goes somewhere, he wants to learn from it, especially having grown up completely secluded from the world in Lhasa. He's a very enthusiastic student of everybody he meets, always asking questions. If somebody asks the Dalai Lama to be his or her teacher, the Dalai Lama says: "No, I don't think I can be your teacher but I can be your spiritual friend." And if somebody as wise and grounded as he refuses to be a teacher, it's an interesting model for the rest of us. I think this speaks to what it is to be creative, how the creative spirit gets sustained even when you're 83 years old.

I think Einstein said something like: I have no special talents; I am only passionately curious. That's probably the definition of what it is to be creative, always to be asking questions and not even needing the answers. That goes to your earlier question about people like me, of whom there are so many now. Being given lots of different backgrounds and worlds that we're part of, our whole life would be about asking questions rather than needing to sit on answers.

You certainly adopted the Dalai Lama's approach; during our visits you are perpetually asking questions.

You're not the only one, Michael! I feel bad because I think a lot of friends and strangers who meet me come away with that same feeling. I'm just going to bombard you with questions because this is my chance to get to know you. Of course your life is much more interesting to me than my life. It can be an ungenerosity on my part but it flows from genuine curiosity.

Yet many people prefer to speak about themselves than inquire about others.

My guess is that the Traveler, with a big T, and the creative person are the ones asking questions. Somebody asked the great designer Philippe Starck: "How do you come up with these terrific ideas?" He said something like: "I spend three months every summer in a little house in the countryside. I don't read the newspaper; I don't hear the chatter; I'm not going to dinner parties. So inevitably what comes out of me is something completely fresh and different from what everybody else is doing and thinking."

When I chose to move to suburban Japan from New York, that was part of my thinking. As long as I was in New York, I was surrounded by everyone talking about what was in the New York Times yesterday and the latest New Yorker piece. As soon as I am in suburban Japan, where I barely speak the language, I have a much wider margin to my life, a huge open space. I'm learning from books and memories and what happens when I walk around a new corner in Kyoto. So I think an important part of creativity is just placing yourself away from the crowd, away from distraction, and away from what everybody else is talking about.

That distraction is ubiquitous now. Through mobile phones and tablets and the internet, the whole world has become like Times Square. Things are flashing at you and there are all these distractions: sports scores here, stock quotes there, weather forecasts. The instrument we work on, the computer, is our primary source of distraction. I know you had a great response to your book, The Art of Stillness. *Would you say those moments of stillness are a foundation of your creativity?*

I would say so. When we were planning this phone call, I know you were surprised to hear that I still have never used a cell phone. I barely know what social media is. I can't speak much Japanese, and where we live in Japan, we have no newspapers, magazines, [or] television that I can understand. So it seems like every day lasts a thousand hours and every thought coming to me is something fresh. I'm hanging out with unmet writers that I love—I often feel in Japan that my great pals are Emily Dickinson and Proust and Edith Wharton and Zadie Smith—and my neighbors who always have something unusual to say because I'm not on top of their culture in any sense.

It's not something I recommend for anyone else, but I am happiest when I'm really absorbed in something. And I'm least happy when I'm all over the place, distracted and fragmented. So I made a fairly radical move to try to put myself out of the range of distraction because I don't trust myself. The problem is not the machines; it's somebody like me, who can't resist the machines. So when my wife is telling me about her girlhood in Japan, I will listen to her for four hours. And there will never be a beep coming in. I won't be worrying about taking the car in for a smog check because we don't have a car. We have very, very few things in our two-room apartment, which means very few things to worry about and very few things to be distracted by.

So that's my personal form of luxury, being in a place where I can hear myself think and, most of all, remember what I care about, what's most important to me. The trouble with a crowded mind or crowded schedule is the same as with a cluttered desk, which is that there's so much stuff there that when you really need something you can't put your hands on it. The trivial and the essential are all mixed up.

So I've tried to create a life where there's much less of that. And of course being free of all that stuff means I get a lot of writing done when I am in Japan. And on this side of the Pacific, I go to a hermitage where the main blessing is being free of an internet or cell-phone connection. It's amazing how even 72 hours in silence can completely clear you out. I often notice now that in airports we have so many recharging stations for our devices but very few for ourselves. And it's really ourselves that need the recharging. The good thing about information overload is that it's moved many people to think afresh about how to get away from information by taking long hikes or going on retreat or whatever.

You see ads for remote lodges trumpeting the fact that they are beyond the reach of cell phone service.

Yes, people spend hundreds of dollars a night for the privilege of handing over their cell phones and laptops on arrival.

What strikes me is that you've constructed your home life to give you the space that one often finds only when one travels, the escape from distractions, leisure time. That must do wonders for your ability to be creative.

I think you put your finger on why I've lived for 31 years in a very foreign country on a tourist visa. I still live on a tourist visa, by choice. I could have a spousal visa since my wife is Japanese, but I feel like a tourist there. On some subliminal level, I've chosen to be a foreigner and a tourist. I'm happy to trade familiarity for simplicity. Living in Japan on a tourist visa, we have to live in a very small apartment and have a very stripped-down life, just as when you're traveling you're living out of a suitcase in a pretty small space. But I'm more than happy to do that because every time I go to the supermarket I don't know what I'm going to meet. Every day brings many new things that I can't begin to understand, and the longer I am in Japan the less I feel I'll get to the bottom of it.

Which is another reason why I think my writing is very different now. When I was in my twenties, writing my first two books, I really felt I knew it all, which is not a great thing in any regard. In *Video Night in Kathmandu*, I went to Japan for two weeks and I summed up the whole country in 40 pages. Now I've been there 31 years, and I can barely compose a haiku about Japan. That space of unknowing in my head means there's much more negative space, empty space on each page. It's much more about fumbling in the dark than sitting on top of something.

You've cited Milan Kundera's line about seeing the world as a question rather than going abroad thinking you have all the answers.

I'd forgotten that quote—I haven't cited that for ages and I should. It's a perfect one.

In 2012, you published a book called, The Man Within My Head. *Is that man a creation of your ideal father figure, maybe some combination of your actual father and Graham Greene?*

It's a very strange and curious and disturbing book in some ways, again deliberately. We all have these artistic figures—or distant unmet figures—we feel very close to and one of them for me is Graham Greene. So I was trying to figure out what it is about Graham Greene that tears at me so much, because on the surface, his circumstances couldn't be more different from my own. And some of his travel books, I think, are the worst travel books ever written, especially the one about Mexico.

And yet I will pick up one of his novels and I feel he knows me better than my friends and family do. So what's going on? Some people feel this way about Joni Mitchell or Henry James. I wanted to explore that and then I wanted to think why I would want to take Graham Greene, who is not always an admirable person, as a father figure when I have a very impressive and charismatic father of my own, and play those two off one another. In relation to creativity, one of the things I did with that book—and it took me a very long time—was to keep changing the subtitle so you don't know if it's fiction or nonfiction. To me it kind of hovers in some nowhere zone between fiction and nonfiction.

It's certainly not a memoir, but it's certainly not a novel entirely. It was my way of trying to create something a little different for myself: to occupy that place in my head and in the reader's head which isn't really sure about things. It's much more to do with the subconscious because I think part of the creative process is about seeing the future rather than the past. So often in my life I will be walking down the street in Havana or Saigon and everything around me is straight from the Graham Greene novel that I've been reading all these years. Is that because I am projecting the novel onto the sights around me? Is it because Greene was able to tell my future? I couldn't tell you but it's an interesting question to ask.

One great idea I stole from my wise writer friend Richard Rodriguez: he said that whenever he completed a book he didn't send it to his editor for 12 or 18 months. He would lay it aside and go about his life and start on his next projects, but while he was working on his next projects, maybe nine months later, suddenly something would come to him about the book he had finished that would effect a change. I've taken to doing that. So in the book about the Dalai Lama, I completed it and set it aside. One day I was walking down a road in Big Sur and suddenly thought, "Well, I have eight chapters about the Dalai Lama, how about if I make it nine?"

Suddenly I'd got three sections of three chapters each and that gave it a nice shape. I didn't change a single word in the manuscript, but somehow that little change seemed to make everything come to focus. It was quite a dramatic transformation, the kind of thing I could never have seen when I was in the thick of the project or at my desk or organizing my notes. It's only by being many, many miles and months away from the project that you can make those larger changes. With the Graham Greene book, I kept on working on the subtitle so it would be as unfactual as possible. There are funny ways in which the creative impulse works if you give the subconscious enough space to feed on the material.

A final question: for me a great appeal of travel has been pitching myself into situations, not knowing how things will turn out. I still find that to be a theme in my life. In summer 2016, I rowed a raft down the Colorado River through the Grand Canyon on a 16-day whitewater trip with my wife, as scared as I'd ever been that I couldn't meet a challenge. Yet I love that sense of nervous expectation that travel and adventure can engender. Can you talk about how a leap into the unknown can spark creativity?

Actually, the unknown is all around us, and it's up to us to claim it. We can do so only by being jolted out of our habits. I did a piece recently about how I was flying back to Japan one day, and I missed my plane so I had to spend 24 hours at the San Francisco airport, more specifically in an airport hotel in Millbrae. I would never dream of going to Millbrae. Millbrae is a place to pass through quickly. Silicon Valley is 20 minutes to the south and beautiful San Francisco is 20 minutes to the north; why would anyone want to be in Millbrae?

But suddenly by virtue of missing my flight I was there for almost 24 hours. I had nothing to do. Nobody knew I was there, and I had one of the richest days of my life. I saw a movie I'd missed at the cinema; I got to see an NFL playoff game on a huge screen in a hotel lobby with 80 people cheering, a much more exciting environment than usual. I walked along San Francisco Bay, and the bay in Millbrae is much prettier than in San Francisco because there's almost nobody there. As I was walking back to my airport hotel, the lights were coming on around the hills, and I noticed that it was much more beautiful than Osaka, the rather ugly industrial city I was flying to. It wasn't a choice, but circumstance threw me into Millbrae for 23 unwanted hours, and that became one of the most interesting experiences of the year to me. Because I was not doing the kind of thing I normally do.

I apologize for constant digressions, but that's the state of my mind. That's why I have to work so long in taking things out of my prose! You were talking about how materially impoverished places are often very creative. Certainly they're extremely resourceful. One of the really happy developments in my lifetime is that Haiti and India and Nigeria are now all around us in California and London and everywhere. It's made our food, our friendships, our classrooms, our literature and culture so much more exciting than they were before. When talking about English literature now, much of the most striking literature is written by people from China and Vietnam and Ethiopia and Guatemala and India, bringing us their stories and perspectives.

The world is moving ahead so exhilaratingly in all these ways. The whole world is becoming more creative just because different cultures are being thrown together at a speed and with a volume that's never been known before. I feel very lucky to be alive at a time when cities and countries are becoming so much more mingled and so much more exciting.

Thanks so much Pico—that's a nice coda. Is there anything you'd like to add?

I thought I would want to add something but, for once, not. That's an unexpected note on which to end, the world as a creative spirit.

World of Wonder

BARBARA KINGSOLVER

Novelist, environmental activist, and poet Barbara Kingsolver came oh so close to never publishing her first novel, *The Bean Trees*. She'd left a comfortable job as a science writer at the University of Arizona, and in 1985, her first year as a freelancer, earned just $6,000. "I learned to live on it," Kingsolver says. "I never looked back." She wrote *The Bean Trees* for herself, she says on her website in a section called Barbara Kingsolver Revealed, never imagining that anyone else would want to read it.

She was "embarrassed" to tell her agent that she was working on a novel, a book she'd written in a closet to avoid waking her husband, during "the insomniac nights of my first pregnancy." As her pregnancy neared its conclusion, Kingsolver cleaned out the one-room house she shared with her husband and considered dumping the manuscript in a trash can. Somehow she mustered enough belief in herself to send it to her agent, with a note saying, "I'm sorry, you probably don't want this. I think it's a novel." Though she was hesitant and tinged with doubt, that may have been the most important creative leap in Kingsolver's life, the moment that led to all her success as a writer.

The story of a woman who travels from rural Kentucky to Arizona and finds solace in community reflects Kingsolver's own journey. As her agent told her, dispelling her doubts, it certainly is a novel. Thanks to the support of independent booksellers, who recommended *The Bean Trees* to their customers, the book made Kingsolver a beloved and widely appreciated author. She followed her initial success with *Animal Dreams*, also to literary acclaim.

In 1993, Kingsolver's novel, *Pigs in Heaven*, was her first book to appear on the New York Times bestseller list, but her marriage had faltered and she divorced. Not long after, Kingsolver was offered a fellowship inviting her to travel for a writer's residency. Then a single mother, she hardly had time to watch a movie, she says, let alone go to another state for a visiting-writer residency. The Wallace Foundation allowed her to take her residency in southwestern Virginia so her extended family in nearby Kentucky could help watch her daughter. At Emory & Henry College, Kingsolver gave lectures and met biology professor Steven Hopp. Soon they were married.

In 1998, Kingsolver published *The Poisonwood Bible* about an evangelical Baptist who takes his family to the Belgian Congo in 1959, as the African nation struggles for independence. Subsequent books, including *Prodigal Summer,* and the National Humanities Medal, awarded by President Bill Clinton, vaulted Kingsolver into the numinous world of revered authors, but celebrity was never her goal. "All public exposure is hard work for introverts like me," she says, "especially in a culture that treats celebrities (even lower-order, literary ones) as objects rather than humans with feelings and families."

In 2004, after living for a quarter century in Arizona, Kingsolver and her family moved to the Appalachian region of Virginia. Three years later she published *Animal, Vegetable, Miracle* (2007), co-written with her husband and young daughter, Camille, about living for nearly a year on food that they either grew or raised, or that was procured locally. *The Lacuna* (2009), which Kingsolver calls a "contemplation of . . . history, collective memory, American identity, and the ways nationalism can be weaponized" grew out of opinion pieces she'd written in newspapers after the 9/11 attacks. She'd received hate mail that she alchemically transformed into literature. "It was the hardest and most satisfying work I'd ever done," she says.

Kingsolver's most recent work, *Unsheltered* (2018), examines the lives of a hardworking couple who despite following the recipe for achieving the American dream are left destitute. The book was written as Donald Trump occupied the White House, which led Kingsolver to ask: "Is the world as we've known it just over? Fear and polarization rule; familiar shelter is failing us."

I interviewed Kingsolver in 2012, as she prepared for a tour to promote *Flight Behavior,* a book set in her home region of Appalachia that examines the paradox of climate change hitting farmers extremely hard while they continue to deny that weather patterns are transforming. Monarch butterflies are the central symbol of the book, as they possess both fragility and wisdom we can't comprehend. It takes several generations of monarchs to migrate from their spawning grounds, so the butterflies that "return" to Appalachia each year are seeing their summer homeland for the first time.

Today Kingsolver lives on her Virginia farm, tending to an expansive vegetable garden, canning tomatoes, raising Icelandic sheep, and occasionally pulling a breeched lamb into the world. She's held firm to her belief that life is much improved by good books, communal and family ties, and adventures. "I work every day to represent Appalachia honestly and honorably, to a world that mostly underestimates this place and my good neighbors," she writes on her site.

Kingsolver kept her writing "secret for decades" because she "doubted its worth." Despite her success and renown, her doubts haven't evaporated. "Every time I begin a new book I relive that moment when confidence hangs in the balance, wondering again if readers will really want to follow me down this road," she says. And every time, Kingsolver finds a way to overcome that doubt, to sit down and write. Her readers, myself included, continue to travel with Kingsolver through the worlds she imagines. And like all the best travels, through Kingsolver's books, we learn, we grow, we find delight and challenge, and in the end we're better for it.

✎ ✎ ✎

How does the title of your book, Flight Behavior, *apply to the central character as well as to the butterflies?*

What I love about a good title is that it can function as a kind of key that can unlock every important door in the book. That's my requirement, and until I have that title, I'm not happy. So I'm very happy. I was well into the novel before I thought of this title, but I knew it was the right one. This is about flight behavior at every level, as in flying away, as in fight or flight, because this is really a novel about denial. It's about how every one of us in some way or another tends to fly away from what we don't want to look at square in the eye, the reasons for that, and the consequences of it.

When you get into the realm of politics or climate change, do some people say they don't want you to be focused on that and instead want you to concentrate on art? Do you risk getting called preachy?

If you preach in a book, you're not an artist. I wouldn't dream of preaching in a book. I couldn't preach if I tried because I don't always know what the hell I believe in. I'm about the last person on Earth who could preach. What I do is ask questions. That's what I think all good art can do: It can invoke questions in the reader whose answers are maybe unknown.

Sometimes the questions may be a little uncomfortable; ideally they are because good art can move us into emotional and intellectual territory that is new to us. It can be uncomfortable, or it can be exciting. When people talk about political art, I don't actually know what they mean. That has always been baffling to me because I think all the best art in the world could be called political in that it addresses questions of civic responsibility.

If you look at the Nobel Prize for literature, it always goes to writers who ask questions that are of consequence to the human condition. I just consider myself an artist; I go into a book with profound respect for the craft, and I spend my days working on good sentences and constructing a compelling narrative. I've heard people say that I preach in novels. I find that hilarious. There's nothing in this novel that tells you what to think. This novel does one thing: It asks what you think. Preaching presupposes confidence in one's rightness that I do not possess.

I think back to your first two books, The Bean Trees *and* Animal Dreams. *I was living on an intentional community near the Mendocino [northern California] coast, and part of what appealed to me so much about your books was a sense of importance of place and community.*

This [*Flight Behavior*] is very much a novel of place. It happens to be set in the place where I live. It came out of an interesting dilemma that I see. I really love southern Appalachia. I have a lot of respect for its people, culture, and traditions. Southern

Appalachia is not well represented in the world. We so-called hillbillies might be the last social-economic group in America that people get to laugh at on television. If the word "Tennessee" is mentioned on a talk show, it's sure to be a laugh line.

So it was pretty important to me to invoke this place realistically and respectfully with full awareness both of its beauty and of its problems. I live in a community of farmers; I live among rural people, among farmers who are already suffering great consequences from climate change. In our last 10 years, almost every year has been disastrous because of new kinds of unpredictable weather: tornados, which we've never had before; hailstorms, the likes of which we've never had before.

Rural people are already bearing more than their fair share of the damage of climate change. And rural, conservative farmers are the least likely Americans to really understand or believe in climate change. That presents a fascinating dilemma to me, and I thought it was worthy of a novel. I chose a very unworldly protagonist in Dellarobia because she is the most place-anchored character I've ever created. The whole novel takes place essentially on one farm. She got pregnant at 17, gave up her own plans such as they were as a high school kid, and married this very limited life on a farm. And she's never been anywhere. Even though she wishes she could go somewhere, she has no idea where that might be.

Yes, it seems that she hasn't found her place yet. When I think of butterflies, I think of transformation and metamorphosis, and she hasn't had that early in the novel.

Right, she got stuck as many people do. And it's perfectly possible for someone in her position never to change, never to progress or metamorphose, but that wouldn't make a very interesting novel.

I was recently in your adopted state of Arizona writing a story about Frank Lloyd Wright. He reinvented himself with every building he imagined. Every time I read one of your books, I find something distinctive, but also revelatory, something unexpected or something you've never done before. In Flight Behavior, *what's new or where did you challenge yourself? What was the biggest risk you took?*

I love that question. You're exactly right; it's really important to me never to write the same book twice, not even close. What gets me to my desk every day is the thrill of doing something absolutely new that I'm not at all sure I can really pull off, because it's exciting. You'd be amazed at how many requests I get from readers to write a sequel to this book or that book. I appreciate their attachment to the characters, but I would not do that in a million years. I have no interest in the sequel, in doing the same book over again.

Every time I construct the architecture of a new novel, I stretch myself in a new way and there's always something that seems impossible. Nobody's ever asked me that before, but I could go through all 14 books and tell you the impossible thing, or the thing that seems impossible to me at the outset, the thing that scares the dickens out of me. In this one, the scary, difficult thing was not the research or the characters; I know these characters very well.

The challenge was to write about climate change, and more fundamentally to write about science, and convey in an artistic way the scientific fundamentals that a person really needs to understand in order to understand what climate change is. You need some basic physics; you need to understand scientific method, how science works and how it doesn't. You need to understand the difference between correlation and causation. Sadly most Americans are profoundly ignorant about basic science. It's something that really sets us apart from the rest of the developed world, our malignant ignorance of science.

I recently read that nearly half the people in this country say that they don't believe in evolution, which is really like saying you don't believe in gravity. Evolution is that important to understanding absolutely everything about biology. I'm sorry this is the case, and I don't necessarily blame people for their ignorance, but that's what we're dealing with. As a person trained in science, I feel this is in some way mission work, to carry the important ideas of science that people really need to know. So that was the challenge, the scary one. In the beginning I had no idea how I was going to succeed at that. And at the end, I felt, by golly, that I did.

You've spoken about the challenges of being a celebrity writer, which you never sought. But it seems people today look to writers almost as spiritual leaders to validate or reflect their beliefs or tell them what they should think. I wonder what you think about that because you have such a devoted following.

That's an interesting question. I like what you said about people looking to writers as new spiritual leaders among people who have left organized religion. I think it's probably true. Now and through the ages people have looked to novels for wisdom. When I think about a novel that has rocked my world and ask myself what it gave me, the answer really is wisdom, some deeper understanding of the world than I had before, some new fresh way looking at challenges, at problems, at difficulties.

And I think about that as a writer too, that this is the best of what I can give people, if I can possibly muster it myself. One interesting thing about that is that it means writers tend to improve as we age, unlike athletes and dancers and fashion models. We're automatically going to get better if we can stay alive and keep our eyes open through several decades, and produce something that's worth passing on, not just in terms of craft but in terms of life experience. I think you're right that in this secular age it might become more true than ever that people are looking to writers as their spiritual mentors.

However, when I think of myself in that way, that's scary (laughs). The minute I said those words, "mission work," I regretted it because it squarely contradicts what I said earlier, that I don't preach. So that was probably a badly chosen metaphor. And I don't want to condescend. Mission work implies that I'm taking light into the darkness, and I already wrote a whole novel [*The Poisonwood Bible*] about why that's a bad idea. I didn't really mean spreading the gospel.

I guess a better way to put it is that I am so lucky that I live in two worlds intellectually. I was trained as a scientist, so I was lucky enough to acquire the skills to understand the world in a scientific way. And yet, by an amazing stroke of luck, I get to do what I love best, which is to write literature. There are very, very few of us literary fiction writers who were trained in science, so few that you could kind of count them on one hand. A better way to put it is that I have a sense of obligation to do something that might be unique. So I have written about science in several of my novels. I think probably in all of them there's at least a subtext of scientific analysis.

Even if it's not overt, it gives you a foundation or a background for writing from a more informed perspective because you have that scientific knowledge.

Right, and I gravitate toward scientific metaphors. For example, *The Bean Trees*, that metaphor has to do with the rhizobia, the visible bacteria that are in the roots of certain plants that allow them to thrive in barren places. That was my starting point for that novel. When I saw the leguminous vine covered with beans, I thought of the phrase "bean trees." I thought about how human communities could be like that too, that there are all these resources that might not be apparent that have to do with symbiosis, with community rather than individual survival. So even then, even in the first novel, when I thought about that, I was still in graduate school as a biologist with no idea I would ever get to write that novel, and that it would be used in AP [Advanced Placement] English classes (laughs).

I've read that you came close to tossing that book because you didn't think it was worthy of sending to an agent. Was it really a close call; did you almost throw away The Bean Trees?

It really was because I had no frame of reference. It was my first novel, and even saying that suggests that I knew there would be more. I did not. I knew it was important to me, but I had no way of knowing that it could matter to anyone else. I really was working in solitary confinement as a writer at that time. I didn't take writing classes in school; I didn't go through an MFA program—I had no community of writers who would give me feedback. There was never a teacher who took my writing and said, "Oh wow, you're really good; you could be a writer someday." I didn't dream I could be a writer.

And the context of my upbringing was it would have been immodest and even ridiculous to think you could have been that important in the world, that you could distinguish yourself that remarkably. I grew up loving books and thinking that they were written by the gods. Charles Dickens, he was a god. And John Steinbeck, he was a god. And I was a clay-footed girl. Even when I was 31 or 32 years old writing that book, it still seemed like a magnificent indulgence. I didn't do it for other people. I did it because I had to do it. And it was a great risk for me, a great leap of faith for me to give it to someone and say: "Here, I think this would be important for other people to read too."

That was almost impossible for me to do. I kind of had to do it by squeezing my eyes shut and just putting the thing in an envelope and throwing it in a mailbox. Which is exactly what I did. I remember it so well. It was a public mailbox that you don't see anymore, at a shopping mall in a parking lot. I was like nine and a half months pregnant, and I got out of the car and waddled over and said: Here you go, goodbye. It felt kind of like throwing it in the trash can to tell you the truth (laughs). I was pretty sure the results would be exactly the same. That was my state of mind. It still astonishes me every day that I get to do this. I still can't believe how lucky I am that I get to do this really fun thing for a living and that it matters to other people. I'm so happy about that.

And that comes through talking to you and in your work. Since you started writing, about half of independent bookstores closed. You've credited these stores for helping sell your first books. Do you have an affinity for independent bookshops?

There are a handful of professions that I would canonize for sainthood: high school English teacher, librarian, and independent bookseller. I am grateful to them, not just personally and selfishly, not just for helping my books to find their way to audiences and helping me to become a writer. I'm very grateful for that, but I also love community. That's something I write about a lot. I tend to think of the world in terms of communities. I think of communities as the basic unit of human survival. I've had the great good fortune of traveling around the country and seeing all these bookstores that were the beating heart of intellectual and spiritual communities. To continue the image that you posited earlier, about writers being spiritual leaders, that makes bookstores a kind of church.

Exactly.

People enter them with that kind of reverence and excitement. They look around and see their congregation. They see the names on the signs that are going to give them joy and relief. I do think of them as churches of the modern era. And I'm very sad to see them close. I understand that the way people get books is changing very radically right now, and it's not entirely a bad thing. I'm a full participant in this—the majority of books now, I read electronically—I love that I can hear or read about a book that interests me and buy it in 10 seconds, and I think there are good things about that.

But I really miss booksellers and hope that in the new world of reading that the dynamic of bookstores will not be lost. Chat rooms can only go so far in replacing the local bookseller. I wish them well. It's true that half of them have closed. I don't know the exact statistics, but the amazing thing is that half of them are still open. And when I go into tabernacles like The Tattered Cover in Denver, like Book Passage (in Corte Madera just north of San Francisco), like Politics and Prose (Washington, D.C.), when I go into these great and enduring bookstores, I look around and say: Wow, something here is working. Something here is indispensable. There's something about this place that people know they need. That's pretty reassuring because that will persist.

I've done some work as a travel writer and am very interested in how travel shapes people. Could you tell me how going to a very remote, undeveloped place such as the Congo as a child with your family shaped you and informed your life and work?

Instead of second grade, I went to the Congo. That's a question that's impossible to answer because as we would say in science, there's no control group. There's no Barbara that didn't go live in the Congo when she was seven years old. I have no idea of the person I would have been without that experience. I think it's safe to say that travel does shape people. I know that was formative to me. I know that I came home from the Congo to southern Appalachia with my eyes wide to see my more familiar world in a whole new way. Some kids might grow up complaining that they didn't have the newest fashion in shoes or book bag, and I never could forget the kids I played with who maybe had one shirt, and if they did they had it on every day. They would never have a book bag because they would never own a book.

I've always had a wanderlust. I got it from my dad. We didn't just live in the Congo; we lived on the island of St. Lucia for a while. We spent some time up in Canada on some land. We lived in a lot of places. The minute I graduated from college—I didn't even stick around for graduation—I was already on an airplane. I bought a $200 one-way ticket to Europe and got any job I could for several years. I lived in France, in Greece, in England; later on I lived in Spain and in the Canary Islands.

I've done some travel writing too. For a while I had regular stints with the New York Times travel magazine to do some more conventional travel pieces, although I could never quite manage to write a conventional travel piece (laughs). My editor was always saying: "But you are not telling us where to eat and where to stay." And I was thinking, there's always interesting stuff going on in this cooperative. I did my best.

I think travel has made me a different kind of citizen. Living in Europe, for example, [showed] me that we really need a better healthcare system in this country. We could have it—we don't have to invent it. My kids got sick in Spain, and I saw how wonderfully it [the healthcare system] works there. For better or worse, travel has made me love some things about my country more, and it has made me impatient with other things about my country because I know we could do so much better. I think education [especially science] is one of those things, and I think healthcare is another.

Could you tell me about the PEN/Bellwether Prize for Socially Engaged Fiction that you established and funded?

This goes for an unpublished first novel, so it's a career-founding event. The prize is $25,000 and guaranteed publication so that brings someone from obscurity as a writer into significant publication. Now that there's a legion of these books, they have a certain following so the books are published to some notice. What these writers have done with that has been so gratifying to me because they take this as a doorway into more courageous writing. Every one of those writers (Bellwether Prize winners) has proven to be inspiring—they all have done other very courageous and beautiful things as writers. That's exactly what I wanted. I wanted to foster courage.

That's fantastic—and that gives people the thing that you didn't have starting out, an established writer saying: Your work is worthy and it deserves to be seen by the world.

Well, that's exactly what I wanted to do.

Down Where the Spirit Meets the Bone
LUCINDA WILLIAMS

There's something about the way Lucinda Williams sings—her songs just tear open your heart. It's everything from her lyrics to her languid Southern phrasing to the emotion, longing, and desire in her voice. Ultimately it's Lucinda's authenticity that resonates with her fans, a legion that's been building steadily since she released her eponymous album, *Lucinda Williams*, in 1988.

Though she'd put out a couple of albums nearly a decade earlier, it doesn't seem coincidental that she titled her 1988 record with her name. That album announced Lucinda to the world with the defiant "Changed the Locks" (covered years later by Tom Petty), the plaintive "Night's Too Long," and the upbeat "Passionate Kisses," which became a global hit and earned her a Grammy for Best Country Song in 1994, after Mary Chapin Carpenter covered it.

Lucinda—most fans call her by her distinctive first name—is often seen as a pioneering Americana artist, blazing a trail for many who've followed. Yet to categorize her music would be to diminish her art. You know within seconds that Lucinda's songs must be hers—she sounds like no one else.

Her breakthrough album was 1998's *Car Wheels on a Gravel Road,* which won the Grammy in the Best Contemporary Folk Album category and which Rolling Stone called a "home-grown masterpiece." It includes "Lake Charles," a song about an old boyfriend who still held a place in her heart, and "Drunken Angel," about a songwriter friend of hers who was shot to death in a bar fight. Both have become linchpins of her live sets. She views her 2016 album, *The Ghosts of Highway 20*, as a sequel. In *Car Wheels,* Lucinda is the kid in the back seat looking out the window, she told me, and in *Ghosts,* "I'm driving the car, looking out the window and looking back, thinking of the losses."

On her album *Blessed*, Lucinda included a companion disc of raw early versions of the songs as she was working them up. It was like seeing an artist's sketches before she paints, alongside the finished work. Many of her best songs have a deep sense of place—Southern locations, such as Slidell and Lake Pontchartrain, add texture to her songs.

I first saw Lucinda play in a small San Francisco nightclub in 1993—I had a girlfriend from the South who said we had to go see her favorite singer. The smoky club was packed—we climbed a stairway to get a better view of the petite firebrand as she set the hazy room ablaze with her singing and guitar playing. Between songs Lucinda would speak confessionally to the audience as if they were long-lost friends. My interviews with Lucinda, first in 2011 then in 2016, confirmed how genuinely open she is.

Midway through our more recent interview, which was scheduled to be a half hour but lasted nearly an hour,

Lucinda told me about a family controversy that surrounded her mother's burial. It was almost like she was confiding in me as though I were a friend, which in hindsight felt ironic because though we'd never met, I felt like she was a companion because her music tapped into my deepest emotions and meant so much to me.

Lucinda Williams was born in 1953 in Lake Charles, Louisiana. Her father, Miller Williams, was a poet and itinerant literature professor, her mother an amateur pianist. Her songs reflect a Southern gothic literary sensibility; in 2016 she told Rolling Stone: "I related to Flannery O'Connor at a young age. My mother's father was a fire-and-brimstone Methodist preacher. I saw a lot of that kind of thing growing up, and I read about it in O'Connor. Her writing was really dark but also ironic and humorous. It informs a lot of my songs."

In 2017, Lucinda succeeded in doing something few artists could successfully pull off. She re-recorded her 1992 album *Sweet Old World*, which she felt hadn't received the attention it deserved, on its 25th anniversary. The new album, *This Sweet Old World,* illuminates Williams' growth as an artist. She's more confident now though her vulnerability still shines through on songs such as "Something About What Happens When We Talk." Her voice sounds better than ever, aged and mellowed like a fine bourbon, on compositions such as the re-make of "Sidewalks of the City," an overlooked gem.

Most recently, I saw Lucinda play at The Fillmore in San Francisco. My wife and I had spent the afternoon in the city at the Women's March, a day after the January 2017 inauguration of President Trump. It rained heavily and we were drenched, but Lucinda lit up the steamy room. When we arrived we'd felt desolate about the political future of our country, but spending the evening with Lucinda was the perfect tonic. Her show was part protest rally, part revival meeting, and all no-holds-barred kickass rock show.

She opened the concert with the encouraging "Walk On," and later played "Are You Down" and "Protection"—followed by an encore set that included covers of David Bowie's "Rebel Rebel" and Sam Cooke's "A Change Is Gonna Come." It was exactly what we needed to hear. Lucinda didn't sugar-coat anything, but her presence helped a roomful of dispa-rate souls come together and believe that someday everything would be all right.

≈ ≈ ≈

Could you speak about being so open about your emotions?

Well, I consider myself an artist first. It's self-expression, which is what art is meant to be, is supposed to be. That explains why I'm able to put out that kind of depth with all that feeling and everything. Like an artist who's painting or a photographer, I look at it in the same way. I do it for myself first to deal with it, to deal with the pain and deal with the situation and circumstances and all. It's very cathartic and therapeutic. So it starts there and then comes out in the song and goes to other people. I just never felt self-conscious about doing that—maybe because I grew up around poets and writ-ers and short-story writers. In the writing world, it's done all the time. In other artistic worlds, nobody really questions that. I guess I'm kind of an anomaly in a way.

But isn't there something more visceral about music that gets in your soul?

I totally agree. People don't question the depth and all that as much in books and poetry. My dad's writing, of course, really influenced me. I'm realizing that more and more, the older I get, now that he's gone. I've turned two of his poems into songs, which was very challenging, and now I'm excited because I feel like, Wow, this is a whole new thing here, making a poem into a song really does show you the difference between poems and songs.

His creative writing students would say when Bob Dylan first came out: "Bob Dylan's a poet." And my dad would say: "No, he's a songwriter." When I took my dad's poems and tried to turn them into songs, I understood what he was saying. He would write a poem about anything from a cat sleeping in a windowsill to a wreck on a highway. He has this one poem he wrote about passing a wreck on the highway on his way to meet with this woman—he has this dying need to be with this woman, and he passes this wreck and gets out. Later he feels guilty because he didn't stay to help. This is really a tense poem.

My dad used to always say: "Never censor yourself." I'm fortunate in that regard—I was very blessed because my father was a poet and sort of a mentor to me. I've always been somewhat of a rebel; it's kind of in my blood. I like to push people's buttons a little bit. I want people to be moved.

When we spoke years ago you suggested that the main similarity between poetry and songwriting is making every word count.

Exactly. Yes that's it, and not sugarcoating things. There's a place for those kinds of songs. I love great pop music—don't get me wrong. But we're talking about something else. Every single song doesn't have to be this cathartic narrative. I saw Bob Dylan going through that. I saw him put out that album (in 1997) *Time Out of Mind,* that Daniel Lanois produced. I love that album. In the 1960s, half of us didn't know what he was singing half the time. *Time Out of Mind* is more about feeling. I am not embarrassed to admit that Bob Dylan was my hero starting from when I was 12 years old in 1965. I just fell madly in love with him and his music and everything.

Right about the time that album came out, I was trying to put songs together for the *Essence* album. I had just come out of the success of *Car Wheels,* and *Essence* ended up being a whole different thing. I gave myself permission to come up with songs like "Are You Down." At first I thought, I can't put this out—it doesn't have all of that lyrical intensity that people are used to, like "Lake Charles" and "Drunken Angel."

Another folk singer who comes to mind when we are talking about sharing feeling through song and using words poetically is Greg Brown.

He's great. Why don't more people know who this guy is?

In 1994, he released an album that was lyrically beautiful and his fans wanted his next album to be similar, but he was inspired to do something quite different.

The only way to deal with that is just do what you're in, and do it well. That's one reason I feel blessed because I've been able—I've kind of worked on that. Like Bob Dylan and Neil Young, you can still be yourself and write good songs and just try and move around a little bit and let it move slooooowww. But some people get stuck and keep doing the same thing over and over. Some people call it the sophomore jinx. You put out one album, and it's really well-received; then you get kind of stuck. You gotta write through that.

Do you feel that tension between expectations and artistic creativity and freedom?

Not anymore. But I felt it during that period after *Car Wheels* came out and the next couple of albums. I saw the reviews, and some of the fans' responses; it was sort of a bumpy road I had to go through and get past. At some point, my fans just went, OK, I get it. This is who she is—she's going to do this, she's going to do that, whatever, but it's still her.

When *Essence* came out, Robert Christgau (longtime music editor for The Village Voice) who was a huge fan, he was just like, "I don't get it." And then Robert Hilburn in L.A. (pop critic for the Los Angeles Times) wrote a glowing review of *Essence* at which point Robert Christgau went back and re-listened to it and then came out with a better review. It just had to sink in—it was just the shock of it all at first. I knew I was taking a chance—I just hadn't written songs like that before, like (the song) "Essence." I was kind of allowing the music to guide the songs more than I'd done before. I was just growing.

I've grown to the point where this is a good place to be. I am who I am. Oh God, I just quoted Popeye! (laughs). I am who I am and that's all that I am.

I'd like to talk about the Ghosts of Highway 20 *album because it's so moving. I was in the South recently on Highway 20, so I'd like to ask you about the connection between road and place and memory.*

What I've realized is that the song, "The Ghosts of Highway 20," is like the song "Car Wheels on a Gravel Road" part two. In "Car Wheels" I was the child in the back seat looking out the window, and in "Ghosts of Highway 20" it's 40 or 50 years later. I'm driving the car, looking out the window and looking back. I'm kind of looking at the same thing, but in "Car Wheels" my parents are in the front seat driving, I hear the low rumble of their conversation, and I'm describing all these things. In "Ghosts of Highway 20," I'm older. Now I'm an adult and I'm driving through and thinking of the losses.

What initiated that song was I'd gone back to Macon, Georgia, to play at the old Cox Theater, which had been recently renovated. That's where the Allman Brothers used to play. I was amazed at how little had changed in the town. Macon is where I started school in the early '60s. It's where my dad took me downtown to hear this blind preacher street fair guy by the name of Blind Pearly Brown. He used to play on the street corner in downtown Macon. I was probably about six years old. That's where we lived when he took me to meet Flannery O'Connor, who lived in Milledgeville, Georgia. We drove to her house, so all this stuff happened there. That part of my life was all around in that area there.

I realized later that Highway 20 runs through Jackson, Mississippi, where my sister was born. My dad was teaching at Millsaps College in 1957. And Vicksburg, Mississippi, where my brother was born. We moved around a lot when I was growing up. My dad was teaching, and he finally achieved tenure at the University of Arkansas, but that wasn't until 1971. From the time I was born in 1953 until we moved to Fayetteville, Arkansas, in 1971, he taught for a year or two here, and a year or two there. LSU in Baton Rouge, Louisiana, is a big part of my life too, but those very early years were in that real deep Civil War area, also where a lot of blues artists were born and died. It's just such a rich area.

How have you seen the road change?

When I was writing "The Ghosts of Highway 20," I was imagining the roads that we would drive down then, which were two-lane blacktops. You don't see a lot of those things that I describe, like the signs along the highway that say, "Repent now. The end is coming." The dinosaur or the snake ranch, we'd stop and go in and look at these weird things. That's a change that is hard to deal with because on the one hand it's a lot easier to travel now. You have freeways and all that. I miss that time. I guess it's easy to look back and romanticize it; I miss that part of the South. It's still there, but you gotta look for it now. Macon looks like it's stuck in time almost.

I need to visit my mother's grave in Monroe, Louisiana, which also runs off of Highway 20. We were going to have a cremation and a memorial service. Her side of the family was completely different than my dad's side of the family. Her father was a minister, and they moved around all over Louisiana. She had four brothers—she was the only girl— they didn't like my dad. He was college educated and a poet. That's a whole 'nother story. Her brother and his wife came, drove to Arkansas, which is where she passed away. I was in charge, being the oldest child; it was left up to me to organize everything.

Long story short, she ended up being buried in her family's plot in Monroe, which I could tell you right now is not where she wanted to be. I didn't even know there was a family plot. It's a cemetery, is it going to be overgrown with weeds? I was so upset I didn't even go to the funeral so of course I've been dealing with that guilt ever since then. I told Tom (Overby), my husband: "We need to take a road trip, go to Monroe."

Do you feel like church and gospel music has influenced you?

On *Blessed* is a song called, "A Little More Faith and Grace."
That was a song that Mississippi Fred McDowell recorded; I
changed the words, and I took the Jesus out of it. I didn't want
it to be Christian; I just wanted it to be spiritual. Both of my
grandfathers were Methodist preachers. My dad's father was
a Christian in the true sense of the word. He was for equal
rights and women's rights.

One of my dad's brothers, he was married, beautiful
woman, two beautiful kids. He came out, this was back in
the '80s when it was not a comfortable place to be. My dad
used to love this story: He said my uncle Travis sat down
with my grandmother and said, "Mother, I have something
to tell you." She said, "OK, what is it son?" And he said, "I'm
a homosexual." She said, "Oh lord, I thought you were going
to tell me you're a Republican." That's my dad's side of the
family, hardcore Democrat. My grandfather was described as
a socialist Democrat.

Like Bernie Sanders?

Exactly like Bernie. That's why I loved Bernie. He reminded
me of my grandfather on my dad's side. Gospel music is just
beautiful, the old hymns. That's what inspired that song I
wrote for my dad after he went, "(Let Me Know) If There's
a Heaven."

*That's an amazing song. You have another song, "If My Love
Could Kill."*

I had that line, if my love could kill, and I was trying to work
it into a song somewhere because I just love the imagery of
that. I don't remember if I wrote it right before my father

died or right after that, but it was pretty close to the time of his death.

We watched Alzheimer's consume my grandfather, and it was like watching somebody die while they are still alive.

Yes, it's horrible. It's the most horrific disease because that's exactly what happens. Your body shuts down eventually, but it's not as if our dad was in bad physical health. He was in great physical health, and then that happens. It's just tragic. It seems to happen to the most brilliant minds. I love performing that song. It feels good.

Does it make you feel reconnected to your father?

Yes, the other one I love to perform and that everybody's really been taken with is "Dust," the one that I did from his poem. People just love that. People have really embraced that song.

Do most people know it comes from your father's poetry?

Yes, I tell them.

What's the other song based on your father's poetry?

It's called "Compassion" from the album, *Down Where the Spirit Meets the Bone*. "Ghosts of Highway 20" was the last song I wrote for this album. "Dust" was written kind of towards the end.

How about "Louisiana Story"—what's that song about?

I've been working on that for years. That's kind of "Bus to Baton Rouge" part two. I'm reimagining my grandmother's house in Baton Rouge, my grandparents on my mother's side, the last place they lived.

You refer to ghosts often. Are they family or friends or places?

The ghosts are just part of my childhood, remaining memories. The ghosts are kind of like the spirits of my memory or something. You could say it literally, like my mother is buried in Monroe, and she's gone now. But also just losing your childhood, that kind of loss too. You could also point to the Delta blues artists I grew up listening to and loved and who inspired me and influenced my music so much, who are from that area and buried around there. And you can also look at it like we were talking about the loss and change in the South with the advent of the modern highways and how it obscures a lot of that stuff that you used to see when you would drive.

Would you name a couple of Delta blues artists who influenced you over the years?

Pretty much all of them. Memphis Minnie, Robert Johnson of course, Skip James, Muddy Waters, Howlin' Wolf.

Can you offer insight into the process of how you write a song?

Whenever I'm writing songs to get ready to make a record, I write by myself, my guitar and me, for my benefit. I record them into a tape recorder. I can't write music so I got to get it down on tape so I can remember the melody and stuff. I work by myself, and I play it for Tom—he's my best critic. You need to have a sounding board—there's nothing like that feeling of finishing a new song. I take it up to Tom, and he listens to it. I wait for him to come back down from his office. I can tell by the look on his face, OK, does he like it? He'll have a big smile on his face and say: "It's great honey. It's great." And I go, "Really, you like it?" That's the process.

You covered Bruce Springsteen's song "Factory." What led you to do that?

I met him before and consider him certainly an acquaintance. He sat in with us one time when we played in London. I worked that song up during the Occupy Wall Street movement. We were playing at The Fillmore. Tom came up with the idea of putting together a group of songs as a tribute to the workers, the working class. And that was one of the songs, "Factory," which Tom turned me on to. It's not one of Bruce's more well-known songs. I just loved it. I loved the simplicity of it, what it said, the lines in it, the melody.

We wanted to put it on the album as a tribute to Tom's dad because Tom grew up, believe it or not, in the small working-class town of Austin, Minnesota, where his dad worked at the Hormel meatpacking plant for 30-plus years. That line, "I've seen men walk through these gates with death in their eyes." And Tom said, "I've seen those men. My dad was one of those guys, and he got out." Usually in those towns it's a very generational thing—if your dad worked in the factory, you worked in the factory. And Tom lost his dad a couple of months before mine.

Is "Can't Close the Door on Love" autobiographical, and is that about Tom as well?

You know, yeah, I mean kind of, yeah. That was one I started a few years before and never did finish. That was probably one of those days when we had a big argument or something.

Well, like all your songs, it's honest.

Yeah.

One last question: your writing has a strong sense of place . . .

It just comes out, that's just attention to detail. I did move around a lot when I was growing up, and I've always enjoyed the character of different towns and different feels and different accents. The names of towns, it just adds so much more interest to the song.

Front Porch Songs

LYLE LOVETT &
ROBERT EARL KEEN

In 1976, Lyle Lovett and Robert Earl Keen, a couple of Texas A&M students with a fondness for playing music, got to know each other. Here's how Keen remembers it, as he was speaking at the ASCAP Country Music Awards in 2012: "I met Lyle Lovett in 1976 in College Station, Texas, the home of Texas A&M University. I used to hang out on this old porch with my ragtag bunch of buddies, pickers, ne'er-do-wells, [and] wannabes. All of a sudden one day, this really cool guy with a ton of hair and a really nice bicycle drove up on the lawn. I thought, this guy has style and poise. I didn't even know what style and poise was back then, but I knew he had it." He also had "really good manners and stuff and said, 'I like what you're playing . . . I'd like to play a song with you.' It was kinda like if Kelsey Grammer walked into *Hee Haw*. It was a little different."

Lovett, an only child, and Keen have been close friends, maybe more like brothers, ever since. They've spent much of their time together, Keen said, "talking about the merit of a good song, or a great song. That's where it all begins. And if there's anybody who knows a great song and has written a great song, it's Lyle Lovett."

Over the next four decades, Keen and Lovett became two of the most beloved and respected American songwriters of our time. They both have an uncanny ability to tell stories through song and to evoke emotion in listeners. They can take what seems to be a unique or unusual experience and frame it in a way that makes it universal. Lovett is known for his Large Band, with 14 or 15 people onstage, including backup vocalists and a horn section. Keen typically performs with a six-man outfit; some band members have been touring with him since the 1990s.

Though Keen and Lovett may not live at the top of the Billboard charts, they have legions of devoted fans who know most of their songs and sing along at their concerts. And both, with different styles, have carved out tremendously successful careers without trying to fit into any music category. Each has remained true to himself, played what his heart called forth, and become known for crafting songs that no one else could have created. Over the course of more than four decades, they've shown how friendship, encouragement, and under-standing can nurture creativity.

"When I'm with Robert, when I'm with this man here, I find that I think of things that I wouldn't think of unless I was sitting with him—whether it's in conversation or writ-ing a song," Lovett told Texas Monthly in 2015. "He has that effect on me. He's a catalyst in that way. That's a rare thing in life. There's something about the Texas mind-set: People like to tell stories, make stuff up. That's part of our heritage." Another aspect of the Texas sensibility, Lovett said, is that a Texan would rather write his own song than cover another art-ist's work. "If I have a chance at being interesting to someone," he told the magazine, "I need to have my own point of view."

Keen and Lovett's earliest collaboration may be a song titled "This Old Porch" by Lovett, and "The Front Porch Song" by Keen, which they co-wrote about their days kicking back and playing music at Texas A&M. Each man recorded his own version after Lovett recognized that the ever-humble Keen didn't put enough of himself into the song. So Lovett remedied that by adding a verse to complete what has become known in songwriter circles as a masterpiece.

Here's one verse: "And this old porch is like a weathered, gray-haired, seventy years of Texas / Who's doing all he can, not to give in to the city / And he always takes the rent late, so long as I run his cattle / And he picks me up at dinnertime, and I listen to him rattle." And here's the defiant final verse, which Lovett added as a rebuke to those who doubted him and Keen: "This old porch is just a long time, of waiting and forgetting / And remembering the coming back, and not crying about the leaving / And remembering the falling down, and the laughter of the curse of luck / From all of those sons of bitches, who said we'd never get back up."

Lovett and Keen are now among the best known and most successful Aggies, and there's been talk locally of installing a statue of them in College Station that re-creates the front porch scene. Keen told me he thinks of the porch as his and Lovett's Walden Pond, a touchstone where the two college students found solace, dreamed big, and laid the foundation for their future.

Lyle Lovett was born in 1957 and grew up in Houston. His music career began with songwriting, but soon he got in front of the microphone, releasing his first album in 1986. Though rooted in the tradition of country music—his work has been called alt-country and Americana—his music defies categorization. Many of his songs have elements of folk, blues, gospel, or jazz—or often some combination of those styles. Among his best known songs are "If I Had a Boat," "She's No Lady," "Here I Am," "Church," and "Don't Touch My Hat."

Lovett's appeal has carried over to the big screen. Similar to Tom Waits, he has a quirky mystique that intrigues directors and film buffs. Lovett has appeared in several Robert Altman films, including *The Player* and *Short Cuts*. During filming of *The Player*, Lovett met Julia Roberts; after a whirlwind courtship, they wed in 1993. But citing the intense demands of their careers, they divorced two years later. In my interview with Lovett, I apologetically said I had to ask him about someone he hung out with in the '90s. Even over the phone it seemed like he was steeling himself for the inevitable Julia Roberts question, but I had no interest in that. I asked him instead about a song he recorded with a soul music legend who became a reverend, a collaboration that earned a Grammy award, one of four that Lovett has won.

Keen was born in 1956 and also came of age in Houston. After college he moved to Austin, where he wrote songs and played in clubs. His signature song, "The Road Goes On Forever," which ends with the line "and the party never ends," has become an anthem among his live-large fans. For a couple of years in the late '80s, Keen lived in Nashville but soon returned home to Texas where he's fashioned a successful career and lived the life he's wanted. Keen never aspired to be a "big star," he says on his website. "I thought of it in terms of having a really, really good career and writing some good songs, and getting onstage and having a really good time." And that's exactly what he's done.

An early highlight for Keen was winning the Kerrville Folk Festival's prestigious New Folk songwriting competition in 1983. He toured in 1989 with music legends Townes Van Zandt and Guy Clark, the ideal graduate school for a singer/songwriter. At the end of 1999, he hosted a millennial celebration in Austin that drew 200,000 people. In 2012, Keen was inducted to the Texas Heritage Songwriters Hall of Fame with Lovett and the late Van Zandt. Among Keen's most popular songs are "Feelin' Good Again," "I'm Comin' Home," "Gringo Honeymoon," and "Merry Christmas from the Family."

As Keen's and Lovett's careers took off they found they spent less time together than they did in college, so they began playing acoustic shows together, just the two of them with their guitars, in between tours with their own bands. In a way, they're taking their Texas front porch on the road and sharing the conversation with thousands of listeners.

I interviewed Keen and Lovett separately by phone in advance of their 2016 shows together in San Rafael and Santa Cruz, California. It was refreshing to ask each of them about the other's work, as they could share effusive praise without worrying about sounding immodest. For these remarkably humble musicians, it was probably easier for them to speak about a good friend's art and humanity than to talk about themselves.

～ ～ ～

Lyle, could you give me an example of a song that says: "This is who I am"?

Lovett: "This Old Porch" or "The Front Porch Song." It's just one of those songs that represented exactly how I felt at that time. Anytime you can do that in a song, anytime you can represent how you feel accurately, I am always proud of those kinds of songs. Robert wrote the first three verses, and that was the song. I loved the pictures that he painted, and I got him to teach it to me. Then I started to think about Robert and his relationship with his landlord. He painted these great pictures, but he was always so good-natured that I felt like he kind of left himself out of it. So my objective was to put him in the song.

In the summer of 1980 we knew we wanted to play music, but we both wondered if it was possible. We had received varying degrees of support from our professors in school or people who were trying to guide us. Some people were really encouraging, and some people said: "Don't throw your life away; don't be foolish about this." So it was a mixture of feeling encouraged and discouraged, and feeling lots of insecurity. That's where that last verse comes from. I am as proud of that last verse in "This Old Porch" as anything I've ever written.

Robert, would you tell me how you decided to tour with Lyle?

Keen: Lyle is one of the first friends I made in college, and we have stayed in contact all these years. We have played shows on different occasions, but we hadn't done shows where you swap songs and sit on the stage and just have a good time.

Lyle, why is it so special when you guys get together, and how does your understanding of one another's music make the collaboration better?

Lovett: Robert and I are friends, actual friends, since 1976. Gosh, I just enjoy being around Robert; I always have. Over these last few years, we've booked dates together as a way to spend time together because otherwise we're both going in different directions and don't get to see one another very often. I love his music. When I think of Robert, I think of him as my friend Robert, I don't think of him first as singer/songwriter Robert Earl Keen. Robert is one of those people, he knows me well enough—he knows my family well enough— I can talk to Robert about anything that's going on in my life and vice versa. I love his sense of humor. Knowing Robert for so long, I love seeing him express parts of himself that I saw in

1976 when I first met him. I love seeing those parts of Robert come out in songs.

Robert, you've said that it's a joy to be understood, since the very early days when you and Lyle played together on the porch. Could you talk about how it enhances the musical experience to play with somebody you feel just gets you?

Keen: I've done things like this before in a smaller setting. You sit on the edge of your seat waiting for the other person to do something, and by and large they don't ever do what you expect. You want a show where people are really feeling like there's great communication and the songs follow one another. With Lyle, I don't really have to do any guesswork. He is going to challenge me on one hand and then he's going to just lob a few over the plate every now and then. So it's a really good dynamic.

When you play together, I imagine you guys don't script anything, that you have a natural conversation.

Keen: That's how it works. And we don't play the same thing every night. For my own shows, and I know Lyle does this too, I write a different setlist every night. You hit the high spots, but you always dig down and try to find stuff that you haven't played in a long time that might be really good for the area that you're in. We don't want to repeat ourselves over and over. The format is we come out and I talk a little bit and then Lyle introduces the show. Then one of us starts to play a song—it's almost like a coin toss—then the other one plays a song. Then we talk about some more stuff. It's pretty personal, a lively conversation about music and songs and our life together.

It almost seems like you're long-lost brothers. How has your friendship evolved?

Keen: Well, I think it just grows by virtue of the fact that we've stayed together all these years. I always feel the same; every time I see Lyle, I get a smile on my face. I get a kick out of what he's got to say. I always thought it was a really deep relationship from the beginning. It hasn't changed a whole lot. The only difference is we don't spend the time that we spent together. When we were in school, we literally spent all day every day into late night and then started again the next day—we had just an incredible synergy.

Lyle, how do you see your songs and songwriting as similar to Robert's approach, and what's different?

Lovett: The similarities are that we really do appreciate the same things in people, in life, and in the world. I think that comes through in our songs. We both appreciate narrative and imagery. We both appreciate songwriters like Guy Clark and Townes Van Zandt who tell stories by painting pictures that allow a listener to imagine the story rather than just explaining every word. The difference between us is just the difference in the way each of us speaks; it would be the same difference in a conversation. So I do think we are more similar than we are different, and that comes from our values and a sense of what we appreciate.

I like that you let the listener fill in the gaps with imagination.

Lovett: When we write, we have an intended narrative, but it's up to the listener to sort of piece it together and figure it out. Those are the kinds of songs that I'm drawn to, not to figure out the narrative so much, but to figure out the reason for the narrative or the emotion behind it.

Both you and Robert have songs that pack an emotional impact. I sometimes wonder why certain songwriters just hit me. There are people who put together the writing and the playing, but it also has a lot to do with the voice. When I think about Robert, I think about a song like, "I'm Coming Home." Though I'm certainly not a rock star on the road, when I hear "I'm Coming Home," I can relate. I wonder if you could speak to the universality of songwriting and the feeling one can evoke through music.

Lovett: Robert's context is he's playing a show somewhere, and he's on his way home. That might not be universal, but that idea of wanting to get back home to where your heart really is, that's a universal feeling. That's a very powerful song. I usually jump in and sing with him on that one.

Robert, would you say that you and Lyle are ambassadors for the cool side of Texas?

Keen: I don't know, but I'll take it. We have vastly different styles, but we come from the same place. We like visuals in our songs, and our visual is generally what we grew up with and what we experience today. Both Lyle and I went out to Nashville and spent a lot of time working in publishing companies and record companies up there, but we have always lived here [in Texas]. Our experience and our interest as far as songs and songwriters has to do with people that are more like the Southern gothic novel, people who want to impart a story and give you a feel for the landscape.

Lyle, would you discuss how it's different to play with one other person as opposed to playing with your large band?

Lovett: I enjoy doing it all different ways. It's a great thrill for me to be onstage with the band, to stand in the middle of those great musicians and to be able to play the arrangements that we record, to play my songs in the way that I imagine them when I go into the recording studio. That's really gratifying, really fun. Since it requires a little more organization than just going out by yourself, there's a little less flexibility and a little less spontaneity in that show.

These songwriter-in-the-round shows, they are just the polar opposite. These shows are only spontaneous and unstructured. We don't ever discuss what we're going to do, and it really makes it fun. You go out there; you don't know what's going to happen. It's sort of a stream of consciousness; one song suggests another song. There is ultimate flexibility because no one else is depending on you, so you can just sort of play whatever you want. This kind of show is so conversational that people in the audience seem to more easily take part in the conversation. Spontaneity is the really fun part of these kinds of shows. And Robert always surprises me in conversation, always says something I don't expect him to. He's so dang funny.

Robert, could you say how you and Lyle are similar as musicians and how you are different?

Keen: Lyle is brilliant about the study of people and language, especially his songs that have speaking parts. I can never get my head totally around them because they are so great and the dialogue that he puts in there is so dead-on. He has a great ear for speech and a certain feel for the way the characters move in his songs. My characters—if it's a song with characters, whether it's a first-person song or a third-person song—my characters are much more linear than his are. His are somewhat more mysterious, enigmatic. The similarities have to do with the local color that we draw from. We never really worry about: Is this subject matter songworthy? He writes songs about penguins and I write songs about, I don't know, somebody vomiting.

So you wouldn't write a song about having lunch with a bear? (This is a reference to Lovett's song, "Bears," in which he urges listeners to "meet a bear and take him out to lunch with you.")

Keen: Not necessarily (laughs).

But there are some supernatural elements in your songs, like old musicians rising from the dead. (In Keen's 2005 song, "The Great Hank," he imagines Hank Williams coming back from the dead and appearing in Philadelphia.)

Keen: I do like that. I think it's really fun. It allows you sometimes to speak in a very truthful way. I heard someone explain, it may have been John Updike, that he likes fiction because in fiction people are basically telling the truth disguised as a story, and in nonfiction people are trying to make a story out of something that might not be story-worthy, so they have to lie a bit. I love fiction because you're able to create these characters that can really tell a truth that I normally wouldn't because I play my cards pretty close to my chest about my real feelings about certain subjects.

Lyle, I wonder if anyone ever said to you: "If you're going to be country, be country. If you're going to play folk, play folk. And if you want to be a rock star, just rock."

Lovett: Conventional wisdom says it's better to fit neatly into one category or another. I've been really lucky over the course of my career to have worked with people who have not required that of me. Being a singer-songwriter and recording the songs that I write, I'm not sure that I would have been able to. Thankfully the people I work with were nice enough to let me record whatever I wanted. From a marketing standpoint, it was only my first three records that came from the Nashville part of MCA. Those first three records, because they were released from Nashville, were in the country bins. The records from there forward were usually in the pop bins. So people had to search out the records, which is never ideal. But I was just glad they were anywhere in the store.

The reason I went to Nashville originally was I got to a point in my life—in 1984, I turned 26—and said, I really need to figure out if this can be a viable way to make a living, or if I need to get serious about finding a real job. So I went to Nashville because I knew people in Nashville were interested in songs. My initial thought was to go to Nashville and see if I could get a publishing company interested in my songs and try to get other people to record my songs.

You and Robert have a deep sense of place. Would you talk about how your rootedness in Texas informs your songwriting?

Lovett: It's just writing about things that you know. Everyone has a sense of place. If I am writing about Texas, somebody from Ohio might not think about Texas but might think about his own home. The importance of a sense of place is to try to communicate the emotional connection to that place. If you do that, then that can become universal. I'm not trying to write jingles for the Texas Board of Tourism, although I was thrilled that years ago they used, "That's Right (You're Not from Texas)" in a little TV spot. But I'm not selling my own experience as much as I am trying to talk about what it means to me. My hope is someone else can identify his or her feelings about that same thing.

Robert, could you discuss how you tell such vivid and memorable stories in the short time frame of a song?

Keen: The music is the engine that keeps it rolling, and then the words are the landscape that you're seeing through the windshield, cruising down the road. I try to get as much good imagery [as possible] going with the words and have the music pull you along. Whereas if you were trying to write a really good piece of prose you might feel the necessity to fill in a lot of the gaps, or a lot of the spaces that would put things together in a narrative form. The music connects a lot of the stuff, without [the listener] even thinking about it. So I like to make sure that all the images are really, really strong, and anything that's transitional, I'll drop it. The music drives the story, and then I do a lot of editing.

You've said: "It doesn't matter if the stories are true as long as they're good."

Keen: I'm always a little bit put off by, "This is based on a true story." Well, so is everything; give me a break. The difference between fiction and nonfiction is that in fiction you can disguise the truth all you want to, with all kinds of lies and fantasies. You don't have to worry about lying—you can lie all you want. In nonfiction, you have to stick with the truth regardless of how boring it might be. I've always been drawn to fiction.

And the Latin word, fictia, *as the author Jonathan Raban has said, means "to give shape to" not to lie. Isn't that what an artist does, gives a story shape?*

Keen: That makes sense to me. One of my songs, "Whenever Kindness Fails," starts out: "I crossed the desert on a dining car." That part was totally true, and everything else is just blown-out-of-the-water fiction. So I gave shape to that particular thing, and the rest of it was just my own made-up story.

Lyle, you worked for The Battalion, the student newspaper at Texas A&M. Did your training as a journalist inform your songwriting?

Lovett: I was a history major and loved history. Then I thought: I just like writing so that's why I got into journalism. I enjoyed journalism because it made me realize how little I'd paid attention to usage in the past. Learning German helped me really learn English too, parts of speech. When you're learning a foreign language, you do break it down, and I was able to apply that to English too. My regular beat was the city council in Bryan, Texas.

A lot of times I'd have to take my own pictures too. I would work all night in the darkroom many times. It's a similar thing in the recording studio, where you set up all night doing one more mix of the song just trying to get it as right as you can. All that really prepared me for what I do in the music business. In terms of songwriting, you think about everything that you've ever learned when you're trying to write a song. You try to trick yourself into writing something good any way you can. You start with the lead and see what happens. Songs are slippery; writing songs is the hardest part of everything.

I saw a quotation where you said, "Songs are sort of sacred ground, . . . a place where you can actually tell the truth." Would you elaborate on that?

Lovett: Oh man, I wonder what I was thinking when I said that, but it is true. A song is a place where you can get away with telling the truth in an unvarnished way and people seem to accept it. But the kind of songs that I am drawn to, like Guy's songs and Robert's songs and Townes' songs, you feel that you're hearing something that is true and genuine and sincere. It's that element of sincerity that I must have been speaking to. It's the difference between a song that might be a clever, even catchy, contrivance and the way a song impacts you. Townes Van Zandt's famous quote is: "There are two kinds of music: the blues and Zip-a-Dee-Doo-Dah." The kind of music that really sticks with you has the element of sincerity.

Robert, at this stage of your life, is the road different than it was 20 or 25 years ago?

Keen: Definitely. There are things that I really avoid. I don't play as many honky-tonk places. I like to play fundraisers for places that make a difference. There are quite a few places in the world that are just there to sell beer. Years ago, I thought all that was a stepping-stone to something else, but some of it is not stepping-stone. It becomes *Groundhog Day*. As you get older, you slow down. It's a little bit of a struggle, getting up and down every day, driving 500 miles a day. You don't have quite the energy. Or you have to work harder at getting the energy. The road kind of zaps you; it's kryptonite on wheels sucking all the Superman juice out of you. I've gotten to where all I really look forward to is the playing and being onstage.

When you wrote, "The Road Goes On Forever" in the late 1980s, did you imagine that you'd still be touring as much as you do?

Keen: Never, ever. It never even crossed my mind. It was such a pinch to write that song that I was just glad that I finished it. I didn't really think about the merit of it.

Would you say it's become your theme song?

Keen: Oh yeah. People don't even shout that one out because they know that I'm gonna play it. On the few occasions that I've decided not to play it, people are incredulous. I'm connected to that [song], body and soul.

Lyle, I'd like to ask about a famous person you hung out with in the early '90s, The Reverend Al Green. What was it like to collaborate with him on "Funny How Time Slips Away"?

Lovett: It was so cool to play with Al Green. Carlos Vega played drums and Billy Preston played organ; just to be in the room with Billy Preston was incredible. I rode to and from the studio with Al Green, and that was cool. I asked him questions—it was really fun to interview The Reverend Al Green. The only other time I got to work with him was on Letterman. He is really an amazing force of nature.

By any measure, Lyle, you've had a successful career. How would you define success?

Lovett: For me, being successful is getting to do something that you love in the way that you love to do it. It's easy to ruin something you love by doing it the wrong way. You have to be very careful about who you work with, because the people you work with ultimately become a huge part of your life. The people you work with are the people you spend as much time with as the people you live with. But if you do something you love the way you want to do it, you're in a position to be around people whose company you enjoy, and they will enrich your life in ways you can't even anticipate.

Reason for Hope
JANE GOODALL

"Oooh, Oooh, Ooooooh, Oooooooooh, Ooh, Oh, OOH!"
What sounds like the call of an excited chimp startles
hundreds of nearby primates and brings them to rapt attention. But this is not in the heart of the Tanzanian jungle where
Jane Goodall conducted her groundbreaking chimpanzee
studies. It's the National Arts Club in Manhattan where Dr.
Goodall is beginning a lecture. "That's the sound you'd hear if
you came with me into Gombe National Park," she says.

Goodall was born in 1934 and was spending up to 300 days
a year traveling the world, into her mid-eighties, to advocate
for planetary consciousness and humane treatment of animals. She appears onstage with a chimp she calls Mr. H. The
stuffed animal has traveled with her to 59 countries and been
"cuddled" by Mikhail Gorbachev, Kofi Annan, and thousands
of schoolchildren. Mr. H. isn't the first toy animal Goodall has
received. When she was one year old, her mother gave her a
stuffed chimpanzee named Jubilee.

"Most of my mother's friends were horrified and predicted that the ghastly creature would give a small child nightmares, but Jubilee was my most loved possession and accompanied me on all my childhood travels," Goodall writes in *In the Shadow of Man*, her seminal study of chimpanzees, published in 1971. Goodall showed an early affinity for observing animals. One day when she was four, she disappeared for hours, causing her panicked mother to call the police and report her missing. Where was she? Crouching in a henhouse trying to see how a hen laid an egg.

By the time she was eight, Goodall says she'd decided she wanted to go to Africa someday and live among wild animals. Like Doctor Doolittle, she wanted a parrot called Polynesia to teach her to talk to animals. "For a long time I pretended to my friends that I could understand them. I interpreted the squirrels and the dogs and the birds, and my friends believed me." And she fell "passionately in love" with Tarzan, who "married that other wimpy Jane," Goodall says. "I would have made a better mate for Tarzan myself."

Her parents divorced when she was 12, and when she graduated high school the family didn't have the funds to send her to university. But her mother, Vanne, recognized her daughter's fierce intelligence and intense desire to explore the world, so she encouraged Jane to attend secretarial school because secretaries could find jobs anywhere.

Shortly after she completed her studies, a school friend invited Goodall to visit her family's farm in Kenya. The day Goodall received the invitation, she quit a promising job at a documentary film studio and returned to her hometown of Bournemouth, where she worked as a waitress to save money for her passage to Africa. In Kenya, Goodall visited Dr. Louis Leakey, the paleontologist who was director of the national museum in Nairobi and overseeing a dig at the Olduvai Gorge. Goodall landed a job as a secretary for Leakey and spent hours each day under the searing African sun digging for the remains of humankind's forebears.

After a few months, Leakey began speaking with Goodall about studying a group of chimpanzees living in the Gombe reserve near Lake Tanganyika. The young secretary was astonished because she had no university training, but she approached the assignment with tenacity and endurance. "Can you imagine what this was like for a young girl who loves animals, who dreamed about this all her life, to wake up not out of a dream but into a dream? It was magic."

At first local guides accompanied Goodall into the forests of Gombe, a reserve about half the size of Manhattan, but when government officials allowed her to explore by herself, she set off alone. For the first few months the chimps wouldn't let Goodall get closer than about 500 yards, but she followed them until they became accustomed to her presence. She began to recognize many of the chimpanzees she routinely observed. Goodall gave them names: One was called Olly after an old auntie, another Leakey for her mentor. A chimp that reminded her of the gardener in *The Tale of Peter Rabbit* was called Mr. McGregor. And a pair of males she often saw together were named David Graybeard and Goliath.

Many scientists criticized Goodall's personal approach, but she was undeterred, writing in *In the Shadow of Man*: "Some scientists feel that animals should be labeled by numbers— that to name them is anthropomorphic—but I have always been interested in the *differences* between individuals, and a name is not only more individual than a number but also far easier to remember." Goodall's study was funded for only six months. She feared that if she didn't make a significant discovery, she wouldn't be able to continue her research. Near the end of the study's trial period, she came upon a group of chimpanzees eating a piglet. Until then chimps were thought to be primarily vegetarians who didn't eat large mammals.

Soon she made a much more profound discovery. Goodall found David Graybeard squatting by a termite mound. The chimp was inserting a long grass stem into the mound and eating termites that clamped onto the stalk. This was the first documentation of tool use by chimpanzees. Even better: Goodall watched as David prepared stalks by stripping off the leaves before using them to fetch termites. This was not just tool use, but rudimentary toolmaking, one of the first recorded examples of a wild animal fashioning a tool. The study that Goodall started in 1960 is the longest field study of any animal species in its natural habitat and was recognized by Guinness World Records.

"She was the one who showed everyone how to do it. No one before her knew how to study primates," said her biographer Dale Peterson, recognizing Goodall's creative spark. "Before, people went with 30 African porters and spent a month in the field. No one realized that you had to get them used to you. Wild chimps are emotional, volatile, and several times stronger than humans, but Jane had courage, patience, and longevity." During her decades in Tanzania, Goodall deepened her research and showed that chimpanzees, which share about 98 percent of humankind's genetic makeup, are more like us than we thought possible. She documented everything from brutal tribal warfare to close familial bonds; chimps who haven't seen one another for days hug and leap for joy when reunited. And she observed mothers grieving over deceased infants.

Goodall married a National Geographic photographer in 1964 and had a son in 1967. But her first marriage ended in divorce, and she lost her second husband to cancer. In 1986, Goodall left Gombe to advocate for preservation of wild chimpanzees and the forests they call home. Since then she's broadened her advocacy through the Jane Goodall Institute and the Roots & Shoots youth program. Once derided for her unconventional methodology as National Geographic's "cover girl," Goodall has been awarded the Society's Hubbard Medal and received one of England's highest honors, Dame of the British Empire. France awarded her the Legion of Honor, and she was recognized by the United Nations as a Messenger of Peace.

While discouraged by the assault on the enviroment and its inhabitants, Goodall remains hopeful. In a Dec. 1, 2017, opinion piece in the New York Times, she wrote: "The lust for greed and power has destroyed the beauty we inherited, but altruism, compassion and love have not been destroyed. All that is beautiful in humanity has not been destroyed. The beauty of our planet is not dead but lying dormant, like the seeds of a dead tree. We shall have another chance."

I met Goodall on a chilly March day at a New York City hotel. She wore a red turtleneck and no makeup, looking remarkably fit and spry. Despite her hectic schedule, she gave me her undivided attention for the duration of our interview, emanating serenity and equanimity.

≈ ≈ ≈

One of your first books was called, In the Shadow of Man, *and Dale Peterson's biography is entitled,* Jane Goodall: The Woman Who Redefined Man. *Do those two titles describe the arc of your life so far or perhaps the evolution of who you've become?*

When I first saw chimpanzees using tools and making tools, that was in 1960, it was amazing because at that time it was thought that only humans used and made tools. We were defined as "man the tool maker." And so Louis Leakey, my mentor, when I told him about it, he said, "Now we have to redefine man, redefine tool, or accept chimpanzees as human." We haven't accepted chimpanzees as human so we redefined man. That's not quite the way people will read the title, so it's fun.

You really did change the way that scientists viewed primates, bringing them from other to us. Would you elaborate on what was so significant about this and what it meant for the way we look at primates and animals in general?

First of all, we have to qualify it and say "some scientists" because some scientists still think the same old way—possibly for some of them it's because they're working in situations where they're doing invasive, sometimes painful things to primates, and it's more convenient that they're not considered thinking, feeling beings with personalities and lives of their own. But the whole thing here is really difficult because although scientists at Cambridge told me I shouldn't be talking about animal personality, mind, and feeling, I cannot believe they really felt that. If you have shared your life in a meaningful way with an animal, how could you logically or from your heart believe that they didn't have personalities and minds and feelings? I just don't get it.

You credit your mother as a major influence and a strong source of support.

None of this could have happened if it weren't for my mother. I was a child dreaming of going to Africa when I was about 11 years old—at that time we didn't have any money; we couldn't afford a bicycle, let alone a car—and Africa was still known as the Dark Continent. It was a very faraway place; World War II was raging, and I was a girl. People laughed at me and said: "Jane, dream of something you can achieve." It was my mother who used to say: "If you really want something and you work hard, if you take advantage of opportunity and you never give up, you find a way." My mother's mother was a very strong person, and she had as her favorite text from the Bible, "As thy days, so shall thy strength be." That's taken me through all the toughest times in my life. We can all manage a day, and if we take it a day at a time then perhaps the next day will bring a slightly better picture. Not always, sadly, but it's a very helpful kind of philosophy.

Starting with your early work, it seemed as though you intuitively knew that the proper way to study chimpanzees was to go into the forest alone, get them used to you, and observe their behavior. How did you know to do that when scientific doctrine said everything about your approach was—

Was wrong. Well, first of all, I wasn't a scientist. I hadn't got a degree. I had an unbiased mind, which is why Leakey chose me, although he didn't tell me at the time. I mean, how else would you go in and study an animal? All the books I'd read about people being out in nature, all the early naturalists, they would wander off alone and see things. It just intuitively made sense, that where two or three people would be scary, one person would be less so. So just doing what came naturally, I didn't plan it, that's how it was.

Was your lack of a degree an obstacle?

I have a trait of being really obstinate. I wouldn't give up— those words of my mother stuck. I went to Cambridge University to get a Ph.D. because I had no degree of any sort when I went to Gombe. Louis Leakey wrote to me after a year and he said: "You know, I won't always be around to get money for you; you're going to have to stand on your own two feet; you have to get a degree. But we haven't got time to mess with a B.A. You have to go straight for a PhD."

I was very nervous, as you can imagine. There were all these professors, and it was very shocking to be told that I had done everything wrong. I'd been out in the field a year, and of course I got to know some of the chimpanzees, and I had given them names: David Graybeard and Goliath and Flo and Fifi and Mike and all the rest. They told me I shouldn't have done that—I should have given the chimpanzees numbers. That would have been scientific.

So if I was talking about number 12 and 6 and 29, you wouldn't know who I was talking about. They also told me that I couldn't talk about chimpanzees having personalities. The fact that they all had their own vivid personalities didn't mean a thing, that only humans were supposed to have personality. In the same way I couldn't talk about them having intellectual ability. [Conventional thinking believed that] they didn't have a brain capable of thinking; they didn't have a mind, and they absolutely didn't have emotion, nothing like despair or anger or fear and sadness or happiness. Those were unique to us. So there I was, very naive, but I had this obstinate nature, and I thought I was right.

I'd also had this amazing teacher when I was a child, a teacher who taught me so much about animal behavior: my dog Rusty, who gave me the courage to stand up for my convictions at Cambridge. I think any of us who have shared our lives in a meaningful way with an animal—a dog or cat or rabbit or maybe a horse—know that animals have minds and personalities and feelings. So why shouldn't they all have names? Why must they have numbers? That's what people in concentration camps had: numbers.

Your successes appear to be a result of intelligence, intuition, and persistence, yet you believe that luck was essential as well.

There is luck in all of this—it was luck that I went to Nairobi at the same time as Louis Leakey was in the natural history museum, and that somebody told me about him, and that I went to see him, and his secretary happened to be leaving, and he gave me a job. I was in the right place at the right time. So many things have happened. Maybe you want to do something that doesn't work out and you're terribly disappointed. Then maybe a few days, weeks, or months later you look back and you say: Well, of course it would have been really bad if that happened. Sometimes things that you really care about and want to do, you can't get them to happen, but then when the time is right, they suddenly do happen.

In your book, Reason for Hope: A Spiritual Journey, *you say chimpanzees have been among your best teachers. You even say you learned something about being a good mother from Flo.*

During all these years, of course my mother, my dog, Louis Leakey were tremendously important in shaping who I am, and also David Graybeard and Flo and some of those other extraordinary chimpanzees. Flo's successors are still roaming the hills of Gombe today. What an amazing family that's been. We've learned so much about infants, about good mothers and bad mothers, about the gradual development of the child, about the relationship between the mother and child and between brothers and sisters. It's a whole rich and unique collection of family histories.

What do you believe we can learn from chimpanzees and animals in general about being a better species ourselves?

One would be the mothering because that is something that is so clear to make such a difference in the child. Good chimpanzee mothers are models for any human mother. Indeed, many young women come and thank me for giving them the courage to be a mother, and they read very carefully about the good mothers and the bad mothers in my books; that's very rewarding for me. You need to provide children with a secure environment and not punish them until they understand that they've done something wrong. So at first preventing them from doing naughty things, and chimps do this beautifully by distracting them. They tickle them or something. That was something I practiced on my child. So once they understand it's naughty and deliberately do naughty things, you start with the discipline in a little bit more firm way.

Another thing that is very clear with the chimpanzees is that although they're quite violent, they hate the time between the attack and a reconciliation. There is an enormous desire on the part of the victim for reconciliation to improve the relationship and return social harmony. There's a little phrase in the Bible that my grandmother was always quoting to us as children: "Let not the sun set on my wrath." In other words you've got to say sorry—you shouldn't go to bed until you've made up. The chimps seem to have that built into them and that's something we could do a little bit more in our society. We could learn from them.

Initially you were required to bring a companion, and that was your mother.

The reason that Mom came was that the British government officials didn't want responsibility for a young woman alone. The sex thing came into it, I suppose, although nobody ever talked about it. You know, would I be raped? So I needed a companion basically. And it was good having her those first four months. She boosted my morale because the chimpanzees ran away day after day after day. I knew if I didn't see something exciting before the six months' money ran out, that would be the end.

In hindsight, what do you feel are the most important discoveries you made about chimpanzees? What do these discoveries say about chimpanzees and what do they say about us, the human cousins?

Well, the initial discovery of tool use and toolmaking was really, really important because it got us money, it woke up science, it was the first breaking down of the barrier between us and them, which was thought to be so solid at that time.

This was when you saw them with sticks taking termites out of mounds?

Yes, with straws, little blades of grass. And since then, it's been shown that in all different places where chimps have been studied there are different tool-using behaviors, different objects used for different things, and the young learn it from the adults by watching and imitating, which also was thought to be a human thing. So we can talk about primitive cultures and that's another great blow at this nonexistent wall between us and them.

I think showing that they have similar emotions, that they have personalities, that there are these long-term supportive bonds between mothers and offspring, and brothers and sisters, that they're capable of love and altruism on one hand, and brutality, violence, and war on the other: In all those ways they are so much more like us than anybody would have predicted. Because they're more like us than anything else, it helps you to see, when you compare the two, ways in which we are unique. It also perhaps gives us a window into human evolution, how we got to be the unique creature that we are. The one thing that strikes me most of all is that because chimps are so like us in so many ways, you can jump off and say: What is it that makes us different? What is the main thing other than how we look?

*So how would you answer that question? We have 98 percent
genetic commonality and a lot of social similarities—*

And the brain is almost identical except that theirs is smaller.
And they have tremendous cognitive ability and in captivity
they can be encouraged to stretch their minds and do extraordinary things just like we do.

And learn sign language.

And do amazing things on computers. There's so much they
can do, but nevertheless if you compare even the brightest
chimp with an average human then there isn't any compari-
son. Our intellect has leapt into a new realm, and I've always
believed that's because for some reason we developed a sophis-
ticated spoken language so we can teach children about things
that aren't there, learn from the past, plan for the far distant
future and discuss. If chimpanzees could do that, then they
wouldn't be disappearing at the rate they are today. Chimpanzees can do amazing things, but they can't give a lecture; they
can't build cathedrals, and they can't write books. They can't
send people to the moon, they can't make weapons of mass
destruction; they can't destroy forests. Only we can do that.
This highly developed intellect, this ability to communicate,
should put us in a position of responsibility to be good stewards to this amazing and extraordinary planet. And yet that's
not happening. We're destroying the planet.

*Was your view in the first couple of years of observation at Gombe
a bit more sanguine about the chimpanzees, that perhaps they represented in some way our better nature?*

Yes, I thought they were like us but nicer. Most of the real
violence takes place out on the boundaries, and I really wasn't

there in those early days. I couldn't follow them for long distances; they wouldn't tolerate it, so I didn't get to see them on those horrible boundary patrols.

In terms of your decision to leave Gombe in 1986, were you motivated by a desire to bring education and activism to people around the world in hopes of preserving Gombe, and perhaps the entire planet?

I didn't start off thinking about the entire planet (laughs). I started off thinking of chimpanzees in Africa and forests. I began in Africa. In 1986 I made the commitment to leave the forests and go on the road and try and spread a message of awareness, to try and help the chimpanzees languishing in five-foot-by-five-foot cages in medical research labs and help the chimps in bad zoos and circuses. Gradually, from that decision, as I began traveling in Africa, and then traveling around the world, I realized that everything was interconnected, that many of Africa's problems could be directly related to unsustainable lifestyles of the affluent communities, like us, around the world. So the mission of JGI [the Jane Goodall Institute] grew.

How do you stay hopeful in the wake of environmental devastation, chimpanzees in cages, and global warming? How do you remain so serene?

Well, I'm giving myself a big dose of medicine right now: The book, *Hope for Animals and Their World: How Endangered Species Are Being Rescued from the Brink* [2009] is about animals rescued from the brink of extinction, ecosystems restored that were totally destroyed. This is amazing. I'm really having fun with this. I'm meeting the most extraordinary people.

One bird species, the black robin in New Zealand, was down to two, one male and one female. Imagine! And this man wouldn't give up. He helped this pair, he would take eggs away, and they would hatch somewhere else and he would bring the babies back. Now there are 500. I'm meeting people all over the world who are doing this kind of thing. Nature is really resilient when you give her a chance. All around the world people are now beginning to admit that we're right—there is global warming. And everywhere I go there are these shining eyes saying we'd like to show Dr. Jane what we've done to make the world a better place. There's enthusiasm and commitment and courage. So you can't give up. There's all this horror, but with our backs to the wall we've always done pretty well as a species. So we either go under, but we'll jolly well go under fighting, or we'll get enough people woken in time to turn it around.

And what are the most important things we can do?

If everybody could spend a bit of time thinking about the consequences of the different choices that are made each day: what you buy—that means you have to learn about where it was made, how it was made, how many miles it traveled, what it's made of, which means more than most people have time to really learn. That's beginning to happen with labels [seals of approval]. So there are foods with certain labels—even if that's not always perfect, at least you're doing the right thing.

In 1991, I flew over Gombe, which is on the east shore of Lake Tanganyika. I saw that all the trees around the park had been cut down. So we started a project called TACARE (Take Care) [in 1994]. The key thing was that it involved putting together a team of Tanzanians, not white people, but Tanzanians from the area who went into the villages not to say, "We're going to do this and make life better for you," but to listen. "What is it you feel would make your lives better?" Was it conservation or planting trees? Not at all—it was to do with health and education. So TACARE was put together in a holistic way trying to address the needs and wants of the people, gradually introducing them to other components of the program.

Most important was working with groups of women, giving them the opportunity to take out tiny loans in a micro-credit program based on Muhammad Yunus' Grameen Bank. Today we are widening what we do by buying the best coffee from the high areas around Gombe from farmers who couldn't easily get that coffee to market. So the people love the TACARE program. They're offering 10 to 20 percent of their high land to regenerate for the chimps. Stumps that look dead—if you stop hacking at them for firewood—within five years they can regenerate and become a 30-foot tree. So TACARE forests are springing up. This is what we hope will give the chimps the chance to move in. We don't know if it's going to work, but we're trying.

Do you believe it usually takes a cataclysmic event before we wake up and pay attention?

We were discussing yesterday how to stop people from being so complacent. How do you get people to think that what they do matters? That's the key thing. I'm spending my whole life trying to reach as many people as possible saying that what you do every day makes a difference. You can't live through a day without making a difference. After reading my books, especially *In the Shadow of Man*, children say, you made me think of animals in a different way; I always loved animals but I didn't think of them as being personalities.

You mention indigenous peoples—I think often what they have that we lack is a sense of community and belonging.

Yah, and they think of animals as their brothers and sisters as did St. Francis. I know this Jesuit priest who spent a year going back as far as he could in the records to how people felt about animals at the time of Jesus. He found that back then there was absolutely nothing in the Christian doctrine that said humans had souls and animals didn't. The normal way of thinking about animals was more like St. Francis did—he thought of animals as his brothers and sisters. There are wonderful stories of him rescuing them and stopping little children from killing them.

I wonder if you ever see yourself retiring and what your idea of retirement would be.

My idea of retirement would be writing. (Laughs)

What do you think your next book might be?

I'm not going to tell anyone about it, I'm not going to have a deadline, I'm not going to have publishers breathing down my neck. I'll give you one story: In eastern Congo, for the people living near the forests, a wild animal is food. If it's edible, it's food. That's how they think—they're hunters. They don't have any domesticated animals. They have traditionally gone out and shot something. There's been a civil war, and there's more people so it's devastating the environment. They're going hunting illegally around there. There was a group of nine kids, about 10 years old. While they were looking for firewood they found a young bushbuck fawn, that's about the size of a baby goat.

Ah, food! So they caught it and were taking it home to kill it, but three of them, three out of nine, belonged to Roots & Shoots. They said: But we shouldn't be doing this—it's not legal. And the others said, Well, we've always done it. And they said, Yes but this animal has a right to its life. We don't need to eat this food. We are given food. So in the end they took it back and let it go. And the teacher who told me, the Congolese teacher, he was crying. He couldn't have imagined hearing this from a Congolese child. The little girl said I'd like to think that one day I'll be out in the forest, and the beautiful bushbuck will stand there and look at me and say thank you.

The same thing happened a few weeks later with a different group of kids with a tortoise. They argued and finally took the tortoise back. And because he'd been eating some wild mushrooms, they took their few pennies and went to the market and bought him some mushrooms. And now they go and feed him. So those are the stories that give hope. It shows that you can change. People say you can't change the culture. Well, you can. You have to start somewhere and hope that it spreads. If the time is right, it will. And if it doesn't, well, I'll be dead.

Timeless Love
SMOKEY ROBINSON

Wearing a translucent white shirt and white pants, Smokey Robinson is commanding the stage at the Luther Burbank Center in Santa Rosa. The culmination of his set is "The Tracks of My Tears," a song he's sung thousands of times. Yet Smokey is singing like his life depends on it. He's throwing his body into the song, bending toward the audience one moment and clutching his heart the next. He invites the audience to sing with him then takes the song to a crescendo with the line "Baby, baby, baby, take a good look at me now," that brings everyone to their feet, especially the ladies. His falsetto notes, slender physique, and impossibly green eyes have many in the audience swooning.

It's a magical performance. We're not just seeing a living legend; we're seeing a performer who's at the top of his game at the age of 70. As this book was completed, nearly a decade later, Smokey was still touring at a time when most of his peers had retired.

Born William Robinson, Jr. in 1940 in Detroit, Smokey wrote his first song, "Goodnight, Little Children," for a school play when he was six. "At that point, I became Cole Porter to my mom," he told The Telegraph, a British newspaper. "She was in the audience nudging people, 'That's my son!' She had me singing on the phone to our relatives."

Smokey wasn't the only star-to-be in his neighborhood. Diana Ross lived four houses away and Aretha Franklin ("I've known her since I was eight years old") lived around the corner, Robinson said in an interview on Howard Stern's radio show. Robinson's mother died when he was 10; after the tragedy, an older sister with children of her own moved into the home, and the kids had to sleep three to a bed. As a teen, Smokey delivered telegrams on his bicycle and did exceedingly well in school. He always loved to sing but planned on studying electrical engineering at college because he "never thought singing was gonna work out."

When Robinson was 18, he met Berry Gordy, who a year later would launch Motown. Robinson's idol then was singer Jackie Wilson, whose songs were largely written by Gordy. Robinson auditioned for Wilson's manager, who didn't think much of his songs. But in one of those fortuitous encounters that foretold Robinson's success, Gordy was there that day and heard Smokey perform.

"He liked a couple of songs we sang and met us outside," Robinson told Stern. "He asked if we had any more songs, and I had about 100 songs in a loose-leaf notebook that I'd written during my school years. He just critiqued them. He was my mentor in teaching me how to write professionally." There's a saying attributed to the Roman philosopher Seneca that luck is what happens when preparation meets opportunity. Smokey was prepared. Though still very young, he'd worked diligently on his songcraft and had organized his work in a binder. When he met Gordy, he had something to show him. Shortly after Gordy started Motown, he brought in Robinson as a songwriter (for $5 a week) and soon signed his band, The Miracles. When Robinson was 21, he became a vice president at Motown.

A gifted hitmaker with a knack for crafting brilliant compositions, Robinson wrote songs that topped the charts for his band, The Miracles, and for other Motown singers as well. In 1960, The Miracles recorded their first hit, "Shop Around," which became Motown's first million-seller. A parade of sensational hits followed: "You've Really Got a Hold on Me," "I Second That Emotion," "Ooh Baby Baby," and "Going to a Go-Go," which was covered by the Rolling Stones in the early 1980s. Among the hits that Robinson wrote for other artists were "My Guy" for Mary Wells, "My Girl" and "Get Ready" for The Temptations, and "I'll Be Doggone" and "Ain't That Peculiar" for Marvin Gaye.

Robinson last performed with The Miracles in 1972 and launched his solo career with an album entitled *Smokey* in 1973. He remained an executive at Motown, which made it hard for him to focus on the creative side of his life. But he continued to produce occasional hits such as the seductive "Cruisin'" and the love song "Being with You." His songs took on a more jazzy feel on his 1975 album *The Quiet Storm*, which helped lay the foundation for the smooth jazz radio format.

Robinson has been inducted to both the Rock & Roll Hall of Fame and the Songwriters Hall of Fame. Astoundingly, he didn't win a Grammy award until 1988, for the song "Just to See Her." That same year Motown was sold to MCA and Robinson left his post as vice president. More recently, Robinson's 2014 *Smokey & Friends* album features many of his classic hits sung in duets with other top-shelf performers. Among the highlights are "The Tracks of My Tears" with Elton John, "You Really Got a Hold on Me" with Steven Tyler, and

"Quiet Storm" with John Legend. And the duet with Jessie J on "Cruisin'" is transcendent.

In advance of his 2010 appearances in the San Francisco Bay Area, I received an assignment to interview Robinson for The Press Democrat, a daily newspaper covering Sonoma County north of San Francisco. His manager offered me 15 minutes. "Can you do it at 7:15 on Friday morning?" Back then I typically played poker until the wee hours on Thursday nights, but I didn't hesitate for a second. "Of course, I'll be ready any time," I said.

I've interviewed many well-known people during my career, but I was a bit nervous as I prepared to speak with Robinson. That vanished the moment our conversation began; Robinson put me at ease by suggesting I call him Smokey, and his zest for life came through on the phone just as it always does onstage. Concluding the interview, when I asked him what he's most proud of, Robinson said something about appreciating the moment that has stayed with me through the years (see the Q+A section). Though I didn't have enough time to delve deeply into his creative process, my brief conversation with Smokey remains one of the most memorable of my career.

≈ ≈ ≈

You've been touring for 50 years or more. What keeps you on the road?

I'm feeling really good man, and what keeps me on the road is the love of doing this. I tried not being on the road a while ago, and it didn't work for me. I just love this. I love all aspects of my work; I'm very blessed because I get to live the life that I love; I love being in the studio; I love writing songs; I love producing records. But I think my favorite thing is to be on the road, doing concerts, in front of an audience where I get a chance to one-on-one with the fans and have a good time with them. I never do a show for people; I do a show with people. And we have a wonderful time every night. I just don't do it as much as I used to, of course. But I still do it because I love it.

I've seen you perform several times, most recently at Oakland's Paramount Theatre. You were bringing ladies up on the stage and completely enjoying yourself.

That's true, Mike. I really do have a good time every night.

I would like to go back to the Motown days. Something really special was happening in Detroit in the late 1950s and early '60s. When did you have a sense that there was magic going on with you and Berry Gordy and the amazing musicians at Motown in the early days?

I met Berry before he started Motown. Motown started out as a local label, and all of our records were a hit locally. So I had a sense that we were on to something great then, from the very first record we had out, a record called "Come to Me," by an artist named Marv Johnson. It broke so big locally that Berry couldn't handle it. So he went to New York and put Marv Johnson on national and international distribution with United Artists records.

He would do the same thing with The Miracles and me. We had records that would break out in Detroit, and then he put us with Chess Records out of Chicago for a while. One day The Miracles and I were going to come out with a record called "Way Over There." I told Berry that you may as well go national with this record yourself because we were having problems with the other labels paying and all that. So he did, and that's how it started to be a national and international label.

The first big hit you had for Motown was "Shop Around"—right?

Exactly. That was a hit across the board, a number-one record. It was the first million-seller that Motown ever had.

In the 1960s when everybody was writing protest songs, you always came back to love. Was that a conscious decision, or was it just what you wrote about?

I've written a couple of songs in my life that dealt with protest. But it was a conscious decision because if you write about protest or a car or a dance, those things come and go. They're passé the next year. But love is everlasting. I want to write everlasting songs. I want to write songs that if I had written them 50 years before they would have meant something, or 50 years from now they will mean something. Love will be around forever. I really, really pray and hope that as long as there are two people, love will exist. So that's why I do that.

You've been referred to as the poet laureate of love and Bob Dylan called you America's greatest living poet.

Yeah, Bob said that. Bob's my man; Bob's my brother. I've known Bob for many, many years. In fact I knew Bob when he said that, and I never expected him to say anything like that, but of course it was a very flattering statement from one of my peers, who is a great songwriter himself.

On your most recent albums, listeners will know right away it's you, but it's not the pop stuff you were doing decades ago. It sounds influenced by jazz. Could you tell me how you view your recent music?

The last one was a smooth jazz album because it had all those standard tunes: Gershwin and Cole Porter, those songs I've been singing basically all my life. I've been singing them in my live shows for 15 or 16 years and decided to record them.

You've done so much in your career. Is there anything else that you would still like to do?

Yeah, Mike, I would like to have a great part in a great movie. I don't need a starring role or anything like that. That's my aspiration, entertainment-wise, at this point.

What kind of part would you like to play?

Whatever part is good. It doesn't matter; I'm not going to restrict myself. When they send me something, or call for me to do something that's a great part, then that's it. I don't care what role it is. I don't have a role in mind where I'd say, Oh, this is the one I'm looking for. I get sent scripts, and the ones that I've been sent haven't been parts that I want to associate myself with, a pimp or something like that. I don't want to do that. When the right role comes along, and we in my camp say, "This is it," then I'm going to do it."

How did you meet your wife?

I've known Frances for 25 years. We had a great friendship. I am 12 years older than her, but we have the same birthday. So a bunch of our friends took us out for our birthday, about nine years ago, and we had a great time. As I was getting ready to leave town, we decided that we would go back to that restaurant and have some coconut shrimp and that just started the ball rolling. And we started to develop our love relationship from that time.

Does it feel good that people put on your songs during romantic times?

Yeah, people tell me that all the time, that they had some kids to my music. Or somebody will come up to me and say, "Hey man, I was born because of your music." I love that; that's great.

I heard the name Smokey came from your uncle who called you "Smokey Joe." How did that start?

I loved cowboys, and I loved the ones who sang: Gene Autry and Roy Rogers and cowboys like that. He would always take me to see cowboy movies, and he and I would play cowboys, so he had a cowboy name for me, Smokey Joe.

I read that you found the strength during the 1980s to overcome cocaine through Christianity, that you had a moment in a church that turned things around. Was that how it happened?

Like so many others, I was foolish. It wasn't like I did it at a time when I was a young man or anything like that. My career was going great. I was 39 or 40 years old before I got into anything like that. I was having fun with my friends, but it was detrimental to my life. Now I am a national spokesperson against drugs in the United States. I speak all over the country at rehab graduations and at schools and universities, and at business meetings and churches. The drug thing doesn't discriminate. It goes into every area of life. Some people think it's mostly in the ghetto with people whose lives are downtrodden, but no, no, no. I haven't done any drugs, at all, period, since May 1986. That was when I went to the church and was prayed for. I gave it to God. And He don't give it back unless you go back to get it.

You created a food company to support inner city youth. Could you tell me about that?

It was called Smokey Robinson Foods. We started off with seafood gumbo, and we made chicken gumbo because a lot of people can't eat seafood. And then we made red beans and rice. We were teaching kids the art of business because especially in the inner cities, and I'm not just talking black kids here, most of the kids in the inner city think that they have to be an entertainer or a sports figure or something like that in order to make it. We stress to them that there are all sorts of avenues open to them. They can be doctors and attorneys and senators, even president. We want them to be themselves. That was my key phrase to them: Be who you are.

Last question because I know our time is just about up: what would you say in your life or career that you're most proud of?

Right now, this very moment. And I mean that. I've been doing this for 51 years, and you're still interested in what I'm doing and interviewing me. You're going to print this, and the concerts are still packed. Right now, this moment is my proudest moment.

Wow, thank you Smokey. We look forward to your show in Santa Rosa.

All right man, take care.

King of California
DAVE ALVIN

The Los Angeles music scene in the late 1970s and early '80s was extraordinarily creative. After the predictable, staid music that dominated the charts in the mid-1970s, bands such as The Blasters, Los Lobos, and X brought vitality and authenticity to their music. The Blasters, led by brothers Phil and Dave Alvin, defied easy categorization—their songs were rooted in the blues, in some cases sounded like rockabilly, and had the anything-goes ethic of punk. There were no rules—anyone could do anything. Perhaps what defined the burgeoning L.A. beat back then was a sense of community.

"Everybody looked out for each other, you know. Everyone lent a helping hand," Dave Alvin recalled in a 2016 interview with Terry Gross on NPR's *Fresh Air.* "X helped The Blasters. The Blasters helped Los Lobos. The Germs helped X. You can go down the list. And what always amazed me was the huge variety of sounds that came out of the L.A. scene."

Something had been lost in music by the mid-70s, Alvin told Gross, "the sort of thing that made me turn up the radio when I was eight years old; you know, the car radio with my mom driving, that thing had disappeared from music."

In the late '70s, the nexus of this scene was a club called the Starwood that allowed all ages to see shows. "Kids could get in," Alvin recalled. "They could see The Germs. They could see The Blasters. They could see The Go-Go's. They could walk the gauntlet. They could get in fights. They could dance. They could fly through the air . . . Every night there was a different club with a great band playing, and the creativity was electric."

But, similar to the sweet moment of San Francisco's Summer of Love, the beauty was ephemeral. Hard-core punkers began turning mosh pits, which started as circles of free expression, into violent contact zones where people got hurt. And some of these punkers would get pissed off and direct their anger at band members. Someone once threw a bottle at Alvin's face, and he saved himself by raising his 1961 Fender Mustang guitar to take the blow. "There's about a six-inch-long, quarter-inch-deep gash in the Mustang to this day," he said.

Alvin grew up in Downey, California, just south of Los Angeles, where he and older brother Phil listened to what today is called roots music, everyone from country singer Merle Haggard to bluesman Big Bill Broonzy. Dave Alvin may be best known for The Blasters' up-tempo "Marie Marie," which was covered by Buckwheat Zydeco.

"The Blasters came straight outta Downey in the late '70s with an intoxicating mix of blues, vintage rock 'n' roll, country, folk, gospel and other bedrock idioms," the Los Angeles Times wrote. "They marked their ambitious territory right off the bat in their anthem 'American Music' (which goes) 'It's a howl from the desert. It's a scream from the slums. It's the Mississippi rollin' to the beat of the drums.'"

By 1986, Dave Alvin had left The Blasters. He briefly joined X, then struck out on his own. As a solo artist he found his voice with soulful ballads like "King of California," "Abilene," and "Fourth of July." He's toured extensively with his band, The Guilty Men, and a few years ago changed things up by putting together an all-female band called The Guilty Women. His 2011 album, *Eleven Eleven* (Alvin was born on Nov. 11, 1955) marked a return to his blues-rock roots.

In 2012, his brother Phil had a life-threatening heart condition and flatlined in a hospital in Spain. The old L.A. music community, including Los Lobos and X, came together for a 2013 fundraising concert to help Phil pay his medical bills. "All I did was pick up the phone, got a hold of John and Exene [of X] and said, can you help? . . . Called Los Lobos, can you help Phil? Everybody came. It was like 1982 again," Dave Alvin said on *Fresh Air*. "Everybody came because we were part of a tribe. And even though the tribe is scattered now, we still come together to help each other."

Phil's health scare led to a rapprochement between the brothers, and in 2014 they released an album of Big Bill Broonzy songs called *Common Ground*. The following year Dave and Phil collaborated on another set of blues covers, *Lost Time,* which includes songs written by Willie Dixon, Joe Turner, Rev. Thomas A. Dorsey, and James Brown. In 2018, Dave Alvin teamed up with Texas country musician Jimmie Dale Gilmore for a tour that led them to record the album, *Downey to Lubbock.*

Typically wearing a cowboy hat, white Western shirt, a red bandanna around his neck, silver rings, and leather boots, Dave Alvin looks like he could wrangle a steer if the need arose. Instead he puts pain to his guitar and has become one of rock's most accomplished performers. He has all the tools: astonishing guitar chops, a compelling voice, the ability to tell a heartfelt story in four minutes, and rock-star charisma. He's as comfortable and as committed playing in dive bars for 20 people as he is commanding a stage in front of 20,000 people at San Francisco's Hardly Strictly Bluegrass festival.

So why isn't Dave Alvin better known? Maybe because he's never chased fame. "There's just no reason to go downtown in the music industry," he told Sound Waves magazine years ago, "because that's where Britney Spears lives. There's just no reason to play the game. I just can't play it and win . . . You have a longer career working the outskirts. You know, you go downtown, you're gonna get jumped. I don't even bother with that. I just play the music that I like."

I spoke with Alvin in 2016 while he was on tour in New York in advance of his appearance at Hardly Strictly Bluegrass, the annual free festival that draws hundreds of thousands of people to San Francisco's Golden Gate Park.

~≈ ~≈ ~≈

What do you say to the people who wonder how much great music you could have created with your brother if you had stayed a Blaster?

Well, I know that my accountant would have been happier if I had stayed a Blaster. But the thing about any kind of roots music—whether it's blues, bluegrass, rockabilly, Western swing, whatever it is—if you're a band, the band has to be there with each other 100 percent, meaning everybody's into it. If you're a blues band, but you got a bass player who hates playing the blues, you might be good musicians, but it's not going to be that great of a band. With The Blasters, it got to a point where we were fighting too much. It's not fun, and you gotta have that fun element; you gotta have everybody on the same page. So it boiled down to psychologically I just couldn't do it anymore.

You refer to California music as diaspora music. How has that affected what you've done over the years?

My brother and I come from a little place called Downey, California, about 16 miles south of L.A. It was just about the last little town in L.A. County. It was a working people's area. All the little towns that surrounded Downey had bars. When we were kids and we started sneaking into bars, you could hear everything from blues to Norteño music to country and western to jazz. You could hear it live in a bar being played in a community. People came from the South or the Midwest or from Mexico or from Illinois or from the Northeast— everybody brought some bit of their culture, and it all got poured into the cultural melting pot of California. That didn't happen in a lot of other spots in the country—it's certainly true now everywhere. But back when we were kids it was California, Texas, Arizona maybe, Chicago, so it created a culture for native musicians.

I use the Grateful Dead as an example. You could go to a Grateful Dead show—and like them, hate them, love them, despise them—that's not the issue. The issue is: you can go to a Grateful Dead show, and they play a ragtime blues song followed by a country song followed by 30 minutes of outer-space music. It didn't matter because I think the California thing made all that acceptable. Sure, Merle Haggard and John Coltrane. Why not? It was a musical culture in California that, more than several others, was accepting of whatever works, whatever you liked.

A few years back (2006), I made a record called *West of the West*. It was all native California songwriters: everybody from John Stewart (the songwriter who wrote "Daydream Believer" for The Monkees and who was a member of the Kingston Trio), Jerry Garcia, Merle Haggard, and Brian Wilson. A lot of people don't consider Merle a California songwriter even though he was born, raised, and lived his whole life here. When I put that record out, people were like: "Merle Haggard is from California?" Yeah, not everybody lives in Beverly Hills. It's a big, complex state, and we have big, complex songwriters.

This makes me think of people like Richard Thompson, the British guitarist who played with Fairport Convention. After he came to California, he would shift from a hard-driving rock song to a heartbreaking ballad on the same album.

I have that in my career where there are people that like me when I play acoustic and hate me when I play electric. Because when I play electric, yes, it can get a little loud (laughs). And then there were people who were mad when I left The Blasters. When I play with my brother Phil now, they probably don't like it if in the middle of the show I pull out an acoustic guitar and play an acoustic song. It's a juggle, man.

Is it so hard to see that "Marie Marie" and "Abilene" are both great songs?

I understand all the viewpoints on that so when I do play a show I try to balance it out for everybody. I tend to do things organically in my career. Nothing I've ever done has been forced on me from above. It's hasn't been: Hey Dave you should make a disco record. People have tried, unsuccessfully. Everything I've done, no matter what it is, there's some element of the blues in there. I have a standard quote: "There are two types of folk music, loud folk music and quiet folk music, and I play both." And I think that extends to Richard Thompson and a few other people. If you're coming out of the folk tradition of murder ballads and blues and sacred songs, the way I view it is I can do whatever I want, as long as I'm inside that tradition.

Would you say that roots music is a good way to describe what you do?

Yeah, roots music is probably the way I'd define it. I don't like the term Americana; I don't know what that means anymore. Actually I do have an idea what it means; that's why I don't like it. And I don't like the term alt-country. Ever since The Blasters, whatever band I've been in, or records I've made, or music I've made, has been called everything from punkabilly, cowpunk, roots rock, Americana. To be honest, I'm just a blues guy. But I'm a songwriter so the songs that I write can be blues songs, but maybe they're not blues songs. I don't try to limit myself as a songwriter. Roots music, that's probably what it is. It's American roots and that encompasses international roots too.

You're a mainstay of San Francisco's Hardly Strictly Bluegrass festival. What's special about it and why do you keep coming back?

One reason I keep coming back is it's fun. Everybody there treats the musicians—here's a shocker—like they're almost human beings. And that'll bring you back every time. Also, it's a great audience. You're treated well; the stages and equipment are great; the audiences are accepting. A few years back, I did a thing called Dave Alvin and The Guilty Women. I called up various women who I'd worked with over the years. I just said, "Hey, do you want to do a gig—there's no time to rehearse." Everybody said yeah. We had me and I think eight women onstage. I just said: "Here's what songs we'll do," and we had a little run-through backstage. Then we went out and played for the first time ever in front of like 10,000 people. It was great, so that's just kind of the vibe of the festival. I've done everything there from playing with a big loud band to playing solo acoustic.

The very first time I played there was the third festival (October 2003) when they were starting to transition from Strictly (bluegrass only) to Hardly (all genres). I showed up with my full band and we plugged in. There's a great song-writer from Iowa named Greg Brown, and Greg was playing acoustic on some other stage when we kicked in. I forget what song we were doing but apparently it was one that Greg knew because he said to his audience, "Screw it," and he just started playing along with us and singing along. I loved that. They've since spaced the stages out more so that doesn't happen.

People like you and Greg Brown, I think why the hell don't more people know who these guys are—does being part of a festival like this help you connect with larger audiences?

Certainly. Let's say Elvis Costello and Jackson Browne are playing, and you're on the same stage a couple of hours earlier. That gives you a certain credibility with people because it's a way of saying: "This guy's good too." There are certainly frustrating aspects of doing this for a living, especially as long as I've done it, but on the other hand, I'm incredibly lucky. I have friends who are very talented who can't tour; they can't draw flies anywhere. They're probably more talented than me or as talented as the headliners at any given festival. But for whatever reason, it's just never clicked, and those reasons can be anything from bad management to a bad record label to having an idiosyncratic style that doesn't get played on the radio. So Hardly Strictly, . . . it doesn't hurt to get out in front of tens of thousands.

Back to the albums you made with your brother Phil. I've heard that you and your brother get along fine if you're doing other people's music, that you don't argue about Big Bill Broonzy.

(Laughs) It's a couple of different things. One, my brother had some health issues and we almost lost him, and I've lost a lot of my friends. So when my brother was able to perform and sing again it was just like well, let's do all the songs we should have done over 30 years. The first album (2014's *Common Ground*), we did Big Bill Broonzy songs. These are songs we've sung since we were 13, 14 years old. And it's much the same for the *Lost Time* album (2015). These are just songs that we should have cut in The Blasters. Now we've got a second chance— let's get it done—and my brother's voice is better than it ever was.

The other reason is we're musicians, and musicians make music. I never had a career plan to become a singer/ songwriter. I was a fry cook when we started The Blasters, and that was my career plan. Fortunately we started making enough money in The Blasters, more than I was making as a fry cook, so I quit. Now my career plan is if worst comes to worst, I'll go back to being a cook. What I'm trying to say is we're musicians—we play music. The versions that we did of these songs are different than the originals. It's just what we do. Probably my greatest strength is songwriting, but on the other hand I also consider myself a blues guitar player. It's all part of one big mess.

When you cover a song, especially a song from a long time ago, do you ask yourself what can we do that's original or different or innovative?

Yeah, between my brother's voice and whatever I bring to the picture, it's always gonna be different. We tried for these albums to find songs that hadn't been done a lot. Sometimes like with the Big Bill Broonzy record, it was unavoidable (to do a well-known song), like *Key to the Highway*. My plan was, OK, everybody's done this 18-minute-long jam, and we'd say, no it's pretty much just a swinging little number so let's just cut it that way. It's the same as if they were songs I have written. I sit down and say what is this song telling us and then you move from there and it winds up sounding like yourself.

It seems that you and your brother are strong personalities and have very distinct ideas about where you want to go musically. I can imagine that would make it hard to collaborate.

Yeah, we stayed brothers, but it was difficult to work together. There's a Bob Dylan line in "Tangled Up in Blue" that says it best: "We always did feel the same; we just saw it from a different point of view." And that's really what it boils down to.

Does literature inform your songwriting? It sounds like there's some Raymond Chandler influence in some of your songs.

I'd been influenced musically by a variety of blues and folk and country songwriters. So when I started writing songs my idea was: How do I put this and not sound pretentious? Gee, I wonder if Ernest Hemingway and Raymond Chandler started a band, what kind of songs would they have? I know Raymond Chandler was a classical music guy, and I think Hemingway liked Fats Waller. I just kind of pictured:

Let's take these very American musical forms and mix them up with certain American literary influences. Certainly Raymond Chandler, Dashiell Hammett, early Hemingway, they all could fit easily into a roots music format.

What do you have to do to tell a story so concisely in a song? You don't have 10,000 words . . .

Well, you could. To me there are no rules in songwriting anymore so you could (go long). Bob Dylan had "Sad-Eyed Lady of the Lowlands" (a full album side on *Blonde on Blonde*) but when I write songs, the thing is sometimes I will let it go long and other times I'm like, no, let's clean this up. Sort of like if you are writing a poem: What's important? What do I leave in; what do I leave out? Sometimes the stuff you leave out that you think at one point is mandatory, like I'm telling a story here; I got to talk about his pet dog, and when you play the song at a rehearsal you realize, well maybe that pet dog doesn't have to be in there, and maybe the mystery of the song can be deepened by not having the pet dog in there.

So leaving some space in there for the reader to imagine—

Kind of, there are no rules. "Louie Louie" is a great song. When Richard Berry wrote "Louie Louie" he wasn't thinking; he was just feeling. Is it the same kind of song as "Blowing in the Wind"? No, but it's a great song. The late Guy Clark was a guy who chiseled his songs. They're like Michelangelo sculptures. In a Guy Clark song, there is not a word or even a note that shouldn't be there. Other songs by other songwriters, maybe there's a few words you could get rid of, but goddamn that's a great song. To me it doesn't matter. You know a good song when you hear it, so there's no rules. I approach song-writing one way, and someone else will approach it another, and sometimes it works beautifully. That's all I gotta say.

Do you plan to record again with Phil?

I'm certainly going to do another album or two with my brother. I enjoy playing with him. It's given me a lot of joy over the past few years. I just stand onstage grinning like a goofball.

But in cowboy boots, right?

In cowboy boots. Who's that goofball in cowboy boots over there? Oh that's Alvin, yeah.

Fearless

MELISSA ETHERIDGE

I t was the kind of dream just about every rock star hopes will come true: an invitation to play during the Grammy Awards. In January 2005, Etheridge got a call from the executive producer of the show, inviting her to cover Janis Joplin's "Piece of My Heart." It was a golden opportunity, but Etheridge didn't know if she could do it. She was in the final stages of chemotherapy treatment for breast cancer, which had been diagnosed about five months earlier.

"My first thought was, Well, I don't want anyone else to sing it, you know? The second thought was, Oh, I'm going to be bald. Then I had to really think if I was going to have enough energy," Etheridge told Entertainment Weekly. At the time, Etheridge was spending most days in bed; a "good day" meant simply being able walk down some steps to her garden and back up to the house.

Ultimately Etheridge realized that performing at the Grammys was an opportunity "to step back into what I loved to do" and show people she was recovering. "I wanted to show people that . . . I've been through hell, yeah, this is awful, but I am not dying," she said. "I wanted to present myself as, 'I'm back. I'm not weak; this has made me stronger.' I just didn't want anyone to make fun of me."

Her surgeon suggested she wear a wig because "nobody wants to see a bald rock star," Etheridge said. (The surgeon must have somehow missed Sinead O'Connor.) Then Etheridge spoke to her friend Steven Spielberg who advised her to forget the wig and "walk out there proud." Which is exactly what she did on February 13, 2005. Singer Joss Stone started the medley by covering Joplin's "Cry Baby," then Etheridge walked out to a thunderous ovation and plunged herself into "Piece of My Heart."

When Etheridge sang the line, "I'm gonna show you, baby, that a woman can be tough," everybody in the audience was on their feet and some were in tears, but Etheridge, though she didn't show it, was running out of energy. She saved her strength for the song's crescendo, an exultant raspy howl that sent chills down the spines of the thousands of people at the Staples Center in Los Angeles and the millions watching on TV. The performance made news internationally as cancer survivors worldwide tossed away their wigs.

The Grammy performance wasn't the first time Etheridge stood up courageously for what she believed. In 1993, Etheridge came out as a lesbian and released her landmark album, Yes I Am, with mega-hits such as "I'm the Only One." Another blockbuster song from the album, "Come to My Window," speaks to the fierceness of her emotion: "But I'm the only one who'll walk across the fire for you / And I'm the only one who'll drown in my desire for you."

Born in 1961, Etheridge grew up in Leavenworth, Kansas, a suburb of Kansas City that hugs the Missouri River. As a girl she listened to Top 40 radio in the days when AM stations featured a wide variety of music. She picked up a guitar when she was about eight and played in country groups as a teen. Etheridge briefly attended the Berklee College of Music in Boston then left for Los Angeles to work in clubs. In the mid-1980s, Etheridge sent a demo tape to Olivia Records, a women's music label, but received a rejection letter. Eventually her music reached Chris Blackwell, the legendary head of Island Records, who offered Etheridge a publishing deal.

Her debut album in 1988, simply titled *Melissa Etheridge*, featured "Bring Me Some Water," which became a big hit and announced her ferocity as an artist. Etheridge won her first Grammy—Best Rock Vocal Performance, Female—for her song, "Ain't It Heavy" from her 1992 album *Never Enough*. In 2001, after a difficult breakup, she released *Skin,* which earned her another Grammy nomination for the song, "I Want to Be in Love."

In early fall of 2004, Etheridge was diagnosed with cancer, from which she's made a full and triumphant recovery. She's continued her work as an activist, supporting gay rights groups and hurricane victims. She believes fervently in the threat of climate change and contributed the song, "I Need to Wake Up," to Al Gore's 2006 documentary, *An Inconvenient Truth.* "Wake Up" won the Academy Award for Best Original Song in 2006.

In 2014, two days after Etheridge and her partner, Linda Wallem, turned 53—yes, they were born on the same day: May 29, 1961—they married. Wallem is a Hollywood producer who created the show *Nurse Jackie*, among other credits.

Etheridge's most recent album is 2019's *The Medicine Show*, a rollicking and raw collection of defiantly political anthems and starkly personal ballads. Without addressing the U.S. president by name, she voices her outrage about the state of the union. "This is not light listening, nor is it meant to be," says the magazine American Songwriter. "Etheridge sings every lyric like it's her last."

I spoke to Etheridge in mid-2018, in advance of her July show at Rodney Strong Vineyards, a winery near Healdsburg. The audience of mostly women greeted her with adulation, except for one moment, when she said, "How're you doin' Napa?" sparking howls of indignation from the Sonoma County crowd. Fully in command of the stage, Etheridge laughed about it and asked where she was—then she made a point throughout the show and emphasizing "Sonoma" whenever she spoke to the audience.

❧ ❧ ❧

You're celebrating the 25th anniversary of your landmark album, Yes I Am. *Can you tell me what the album meant to you at that time and what it means to you 25 years on?*

Back in 1992-93 when I was making the album, it was about me getting back to a rock 'n' roll song album that reflected where I was, emotionally and in my thoughts. So it was a real straightforward album. I got to do it with the amazing producer, Hugh Padgham, who just knew how to be invisible in his production and just have the song and the vocal be upfront. It was a wonderful experience. You always hope your albums are a success, but of course this one, once it got some air underneath it, it just went and went and went and wouldn't stop. It was such a delight—it had a long, long, long life and still does. It's that landmark album that everyone hopes they have. I'm just so grateful for it.

I've appreciated your music for many years, but perhaps my most indelible memory is when you came on the Grammys while you were recovering from chemotherapy after having breast cancer and sang Janis Joplin's "Piece of My Heart." Do you consider her a role model?

Definitely, a role model in her performance, not so much personally. I didn't want to end up like her. When she got onstage, she knew how to take her love of the blues, rhythm and blues, and soul music, and turn it into rock 'n' roll. I understood that's what we were all doing. So I would study her for how she was onstage, that fire and that power. I was so honored to sing a tribute to her on the Grammys and to do it while I was going through chemo. That was intense. I'll do that song at very special events, but I don't do it all the time.

Back to the Yes I Am *album, it sounded like—and please correct me if I am wrong—a coming out for you, not just about your sexuality but about who you are or who you were. I think it's hard for young people today to understand what a big deal that was. Could you give me a sense of what that meant for you at the time?*

One of my great joys is how it has become easier for people to be themselves, and for one to step up and say: "This is who I am." I think that saves lives, and it is a beautiful thing about where we've gone as a people. At the time, in the early '90s, I had put three albums out, and they were very personal albums. I was being asked personal questions. I had a big aversion to lying and didn't want to keep some sort of secret, so it was a big choice for me. I had to come to the conclusion that if someone wasn't going to buy my records, or boycott me, or go against me because I was gay, then they really weren't enjoying my music. They weren't really listening to it. I had to believe in my music and believe in the power of change. I did, and it certainly worked out just fine.

Did you get any blowback, for example, stores that wouldn't carry your music?

I did not hear about that from any stores; the only stories I heard were in the very beginning when the people who work the radio stations to try to get radio airplay, in the beginning when they got pushback—nah, we're not gonna play a gay person—bless my record company, Island Records, just looked at them and said: "You are not going to be the people who do that." Even if there were resisters, they eventually had to jump on; it was just a big wave. I went from selling about 1 million records per album to about 6 million on this [*Yes I Am*]. So I can't ever say that it [coming out] harmed me in any way.

What was it like growing up in the '60s in the Midwest, and what artists came through at that time that got you excited about music?

I was born in 1961 so the '60s and '70s were my childhood, and man that was such wonderful music. We had one radio station that we got in Kansas City in the '60s and that was WHB. The great thing about them is they played everything. They were top 40. Back then it was the top 40 songs of all genres so I could hear Tammy Wynette, then I could hear Marvin Gaye, then Led Zeppelin, then Tommy James and the Shondells. It was all different music, all kinds.

I never thought in my head that there was some border between them at all. In the '70s, when FM finally came in, we had a rock station KY102 (KCKC in Kansas City). As a teenager I just immersed myself in rock 'n' roll: Bruce Springsteen, discovering all different types of music. It was where my fantasies, my dreams were, in music. It's where all these dreams came from.

Were there any women during that time—like Linda Ronstadt, who was really big here in California—who made you think: Wow, I could do that too?

That's exactly who I was going to say, Linda Ronstadt. She had a big influence right there in the '70s, with songs like "You're

No Good," that California country rock sound. That's when I thought I could play the acoustic guitar and rock. And then there were all the soul women I admired, Aretha Franklin, Gladys Knight, it was a combination of all those women.

Because of your courage on so many levels, you've become a role model to a lot of people both in and out of music. Is that a responsibility, a privilege?

It keeps me in line. It keeps me understanding that the choices I make not only affect me but live on forever and affect others. It's OK with me because it keeps me honest; it keeps me thinking about the things that I do, and I hold that respect very close. It's worth a lot to me. I might not have millions and millions and millions of dollars, but I have a general respect and a place in the pantheon of music. I want to keep that; I want to nourish that because that's worth more to me than anything.

The music business has changed so much since you started your career. Do you think it's harder now to break through or maybe easier in some ways because people can distribute their music internationally without spending a lot of money?

It's definitely different. There used to be only one way to do it. There are many ways now, but with that comes many different streams of music that are constantly flowing. I think it evens itself out: It might be easier to get your music to people, but it's harder to get people to listen to your music. Still, it comes down to: Are you creating music that resonates with people? Is your music entertaining and drawing people to it? There's all kinds of music that does that. There's music that people make in their bedrooms and on computers, and there's music that people make in bars and play to millions of people. I think it's all good.

You played for years in bars and clubs before you got national acclaim. Was it fun? Was it hard?

Looking back I think it's all fun, but the four, almost five years that I played, it was every day going, Gosh when am I ever going to be signed? When am I ever going to make it? Am I going to grow old in these bars? You never know until the change happens, and you find yourself somewhere else. I look back on it now and think, Wow, those years were just so important to me, learning how to write, learning how to perform, learning how not to be afraid to put my passion and sexuality into my music. It made me the performer I am now.

That sounds like what the Beatles said about playing clubs in Hamburg. They were playing nine or ten hours a night. I'm sure you had some long shifts too.

There you go—you get pretty good at it after that.

I'm interested in enduring creativity. Some people can be creative with a song or a single album. But you've done it for decades. What's the key to staying creatively alive year after year and maintaining that spark?

I think it's about loving what I do. That's the most important thing; I think people could absolutely tell if I didn't love what I created because it wouldn't have the spark in it. That's what people relate to. The most important thing is for me to be in love and feel that the music has a place inside of myself and that I am creating something I want to share with people. That's always been the key. If I can keep doing that, then people will keep wanting to hear what I'm doing.

So it all gets back to authenticity?

Absolutely, I think people would know if I was doing something I didn't love.

I'm sure you've had people come up to you and say: "You sing what I feel." Could you talk about creating for yourself, then having an emotional impact on other people in a society where it's a virtue not to feel?

Well, that's where my music came from because I grew up in the Midwest where we didn't talk about our feelings at all even though we were burning up from them. I started putting my passions and emotions into my music. I remember thinking in the beginning: Oh wow, this is so personal. Is it going to be too personal? And the more personal I got in a song, the more universal it was, the more that people all over could relate to it. And that feeling of, wow, here I thought I was all alone burning up in this feeling, but yet there are so many who relate to it. I learned early on this is the key, to be open enough, to be able to corral your emotions and fire, and then put them in a song. That could be successful.

That is so beautifully said. What is the process of taking all that fire and emotion and putting it into a four-minute song? Could you tell me about that craft?

Craft is something I've been working on since I was 11 years old. So it's been over 40 years of working on taking those emotions, and then with economy of words, which is what the great songs are about, being able to transfer and translate that emotion, that feeling—through rhythm, through melody, through lyric, and through brevity—and put it out there. Songs like "Bring Me Some Water," that worked. Oftentimes, the craft is about editing and getting all that stuff out until there's just that beautiful nugget.

It sounds like you're sculpting, chipping away.

Exactly. It's in there, in the stone. I just gotta find it.

Are there a couple of favorite songs of yours that are not your biggest hits that you enjoy performing?

Oh yeah, that's the way I craft my setlist. We do the hits that everybody knows and loves, and I love playing them, because I love connecting with people that way. I have no problem with that. And then there are five or six other songs where I get to go deep into my catalog even though it's just me going, "I really love this song—let's do this." Oftentimes the Melissa Etheridge fan is a deep album fan, and they love that I'll go into one of my lesser-known albums like *Skin* and pull out a song that they haven't heard in a while. That's the performance I enjoy.

Having survived cancer, do you feel that you've come out with a different take on life?

My life is definitely not the same after that. And I'm grateful because it gave me an appreciation for life. Every time I open my eyes, I'm like, Yes! Here I am, another beautiful day to create. And it gave me a bit of a conquering of fear, because when you come face-to-face with fear of death and you're like, OK, I'm gonna move through that, then what's there to be afraid of? I'm just gonna rock this, and I'm gonna find my joy in every day. It set me on that path, and I will forever be grateful. I hope that others don't have to get that close to it. I don't wish chemotherapy on anyone, but it showed me what I love and appreciate in life.

The Godfather
FRANCIS FORD COPPOLA

Francis Ford Coppola was not Paramount Pictures' top choice to direct *The Godfather,* the groundbreaking 1972 film that laid the foundation for Coppola's remarkably creative career. The sprawling three-hour epic earned Coppola an Academy Award for his and Mario Puzo's adaptation of Puzo's book, was a box-office smash and won effusive praise from critics. Even more remarkable were the ways Coppola overcame obstacles to make the film he envisioned. In his early thirties when directing *The Godfather*, Coppola believed one of the world's great actors should play Don Vito Corleone. He wanted Marlon Brando—top studio executives said no way.

Despite that resistance, Coppola approached Brando and convinced the legend to try out the part, which Coppola filmed. Then Coppola took the footage to New York and showed it to Charlie Bluhdorn, the head of Gulf and Western (Paramount's parent company) who was astounded by Brando's transformation into the Godfather. Brando, of course, got the part, but Coppola said Brando earned only about $120,000 for the portrayal.

Meanwhile, Coppola met with Frank Sinatra, to assure him that the character in Puzo's book based on the singer wouldn't be overtly biographical. "I let him know that I didn't like that part of the book and that I'd minimize it in the film. Sinatra was very appreciative," Coppola told Playboy in 1975. Then Sinatra turned to Coppola and said, "I'd like to play the Godfather. Let's you and me buy this goddamned book and make it ourselves." Coppola politely declined.

The director also had to fight to set the film in the 1940s— the studio wanted to set it in the present day so it wouldn't have to pay for the vintage cars and clothes and sets. Fortunately Coppola prevailed, a savvy decision as the sequel, the hugely successful *The Godfather Part II,* could be set a decade later. "For the first time in Hollywood history, a sequel to a tremendously successful motion picture has surpassed the original in critical estimation," Playboy wrote. In hindsight that's not shocking as Coppola, then an established director, had far more creative control over the sequel.

Before taking on *The Godfather,* Coppola wrote the screenplay for the film, *Patton,* released in 1970. His script opens with George C. Scott as General George S. Patton addressing the viewer, monogrammed pistol at his side. While standing in front of an American flag three times his height, Patton says: "Men, all this stuff you've heard about America not wanting to fight, wanting to stay out of the war, is a lot of horse dung. Americans traditionally love to fight." Coppola's unconventional approach was initially rejected, but when another writer's script didn't work out, the filmmakers revisited Coppola's treatment.

"The things that you get fired for when you're young," he's fond of saying, "are the exact same things that you win lifetime achievement awards for when you're old." The *Patton* script earned Coppola his first Oscar, for Best Original Screenplay.

Coppola was born in 1939 in Detroit to a family of Italian heritage. His father played the flute for the Detroit Symphony Orchestra, and his mother's father was composer Francesco Pennino, from Naples, Italy. His sister, Talia Shire, and his nephew, Nicolas Cage (who both dropped the family name to make it on their own merits) became well-known actors, and his daughter, Sofia Coppola, is a highly lauded director (*Lost in Translation*). In the early 1940s when Francis was two years old, his father became the principal flautist for the NBC Symphony Orchestra and the family moved to Queens. Stricken with polio as a child, Francis let his imagination run wild, creating puppet shows, his first dramatic productions.

As a college student considering a career as a playwright and theatrical producer, Coppola saw Sergei Eisenstein's *October: Ten Days That Shook the World,* a silent film about the Russian revolution. "On Monday, I was in a theater," he has said, "and on Tuesday, I wanted to be a filmmaker." After studying at UCLA's film school, Coppola worked in Los Angeles for several years and directed a couple of modestly successful films. In the late 1960s, to escape what he called the "collective madness" of Hollywood, Coppola relocated to San Francisco and founded his own production company, American Zoetrope. The studio's first film, *THX 1138*, was a dystopian view of the future directed by Coppola's good friend George Lucas. Shot in the new BART train tunnels in the Bay Area, before the trains began running, it confounded viewers (now some consider it a cult classic) and nearly bankrupted American Zoetrope.

After the success of the first two Godfather films, Coppola called himself a "good gambler" and said he's "never been afraid to take a chance." Which is just what he did with another epic 1970s film, *Apocalypse Now.* When he couldn't get studio financing for the film, which examined war's toll on one's soul, he funded it himself. That bet paid off, but then Coppola sank his fortune into a film called *One from the Heart*, which wasn't successful. He was left deep in debt, and banks possessed most of his assets. In the 1980s, largely to repay his debts, Coppola made a series of less ambitious films, including *The Outsiders, Rumble Fish*, and *Peggy Sue Got Married*. Audiences saw a softer, more intimate, side of Coppola, and most people loved these movies.

Coppola also has a highly successful winery in Sonoma County, the Francis Ford Coppola Winery in Geyserville. "As an art form, wine and film are very similar," Coppola told Harvard Business Review in 2011. "They break into three phases. There's the gathering of the resources, there's the actual putting of the resources together, and then there's the finishing, which is a very important process in both film and wine." And in 1997 he founded the literary magazine Zoetrope: All-Story, whose contributors include David Lynch, Laurie Anderson, Michael Stipe, and Jeff Bridges.

In the 1975 Playboy interview, a few months after the release of *Godfather II*, Coppola is asked if he'd ever make *Godfather III*. "Nine times out of ten, people who say they're never going to do something wind up doing it," the director said. "Right now, I don't want to make another sequel. But maybe 30 years from now, when I and all the actors have gotten really old, then it might be fun to take another look." He ended up waiting 15 years—*The Godfather Part III* came out in 1990.

I spoke to Coppola in 2016, just ahead of his talk about the remake of *The Outsiders*, at an event sponsored by a Napa County group that encourages kids to read.

⚜ ⚜ ⚜

What led you to make The Outsiders?

I had this piece of paper with all these little signatures, an entire library class asking me to make the film. I had to take it seriously. So I read the book, and I was very touched because it shows that although we think of young people, young teenagers, as being concerned with boys and girls and cars, *The Outsiders* showed such emotion and love and some of the tragic incidents that take place. I was moved by the fact that young people had chosen that book as one of their favorites because of what it revealed about their ability to feel.

People who are familiar with your work may not know you made your mark as a screenwriter.

That was my first, and probably even now, my ambition: As a young person I wanted to be a writer and when I tried I was always very disappointed and despondent that as a 15-year-old, I hadn't been given that talent. Writing however is something that if you work at, you actually get better. In all arts, by practicing you get better but especially in writing.

The late Peter Matthiessen spoke about writing a lot of bad short stories when he was a young man, suggesting he had to get the bad writing out before he could produce good work.

It's true. I was always impressed that if you put your rear end on the chair every morning, you can get better. I've always had the adage or the rule to always be reading a book but not necessarily related to anything I was working on. I'm reading all sorts of fiction and history and scientific books or whatever, and it never has anything to do with what I'm actually working on. But yet in a funny way it always brings me some new perspective to what I'm working on.

You've gone back to at least a couple of your films and re-edited or expanded them. Why?

When a film comes out, it's a very frightening time because you have no idea, even though you may have previewed it, you're always operating out of fear. You don't know which way it's going to go or if the audience is going to respond to it. So it's a scary time and very often you are prevailed upon by others—oh it's too long, that's the most common criticism you get—so you start to tighten it up, make it 10 minutes shorter.

But very often that's not the right thing to do. Sometimes by shortening it you are making it longer for the audience because they're less involved in it or less absorbed by it. The right thing might be to make it longer and make certain things more clear. Very often what you do when you're under such pressure is the wrong thing. On a few occasions you might have the opportunity to correct that.

In the case of *The Outsiders,* it was the pressure of the studio wanting it to work better, and I found my solution was to constantly shorten it. I always felt very unsure of, for example, the performance of the character called Sodapop (Rob Lowe). I wasn't a hundred percent comfortable with that one brother, and I intended to take out some of the scenes. But the kids know the book, and in the earlier version of the movie, they'd always say, "What happened to the scene when Sodapop is talking to his brother?" and "What happened to the scene where they race home, the brothers?" They knew it all so well that they missed it.

I was going to show the film to my granddaughter's class; she was 9 or 10. In those days I was using Betamax tapes to save the versions. I had the version before I had removed all those scenes—so I showed that to my granddaughter's class. Watching it with them, I realized I had been wrong to cut those scenes. With that experience, I went back and made the version that I had shown to her class, and I did some other work. I had always felt that some of the music that my father had done was a little too schmaltzy. I always wanted to replace some of it with more the kind of music those kids would have been listening to rather than a score that just editorialized on their feelings.

At any rate, I made a new version and was fortunate enough to get Warner Brothers to release it in video as *The Outsiders: The Complete Novel* because essentially it was—it had every scene of the novel in it. And the kids know so this is the one that they respond to. This version is the more faithful version of the book.

So you used your granddaughter's class as your focus group?

Exactly.

When you were making this film you were working with a number of future superstars. Did you have a sense at the time that Tom Cruise, Matt Dillon, Patrick Swayze, Rob Lowe, and Diane Lane were on their way to big careers?

Well, when we auditioned it, we saw everyone. We did a whole series of auditions. I tend to do auditions in an unusual way—each time I do a picture I sometimes come up with a new way to do auditions. In the case of *The Outsiders* we would have everyone come, all the young men and women of that generation, and they would all do the auditions right in front of everybody. We were looking for those people who would emerge as the young stars of the next generation. And indeed they did. We had them all.

I look at your career in the 1970s, work such as the Godfather films and Apocalypse Now, *huge, big-canvas pictures. And as we see in the 1991 documentary* Hearts of Darkness, *about the making of* Apocalypse Now, *that film took a heavy toll on you. After that, did you want to make movies closer to home?*

The truth of the matter is I had reached a very high pinnacle with those movies, one after another, and then I had an enormous failure with *One from the Heart*. By then I was playing Russian roulette with the financing of the films. With *Apocalypse Now*, I found no one would let me make that film so I went into debt to make it. When I borrowed the money to make *Apocalypse*, interest rates were over 20 percent, so it was a very daunting period. When I survived that, I did it again with *One from the Heart*, which didn't do well. I owed the bank a lot of money, and they had all my property signed over to them. They let me keep my Napa home and the vineyards there and one particular building in San Francisco if I would [quickly] pay back a huge amount of money. And I did, by making a film every year. *The Outsiders* was the first of that series of films. I made more intimate, smaller films to be able to pay them off.

While you were writing the screenplay for Patton *or making films such as* The Godfather *and* Apocalypse Now, *it wasn't always appreciated what you were trying to do. Can you talk about trying to make the films that you envisioned, even with all the pressures?*

The style of movies and all art changes over time. Very often films start rubbing the audience the wrong way if they're doing something a little different than what is the norm. Think of the painters in France during the Belle Époque, whose names few can recall. There were, at the same time, people like Matisse and Rousseau, who are the ones we know now. We don't even know the names of the painters who were popular at the time. It's always the avant-garde that first gets rejected by the established view of what a piece of art has to be but then ultimately is accepted. The avant-garde of the past becomes the wallpaper design of the future—it's embraced by the public. So films like *Apocalypse Now* and some of what I was doing wasn't exactly heralded as "Oh wow, this is terrific," at the time. But (those films) stood the test of time, and over the years, little by little, sort of changed what movies were like.

There was a big hit movie when I was a kid that I remember all the people were wild about called *The Snake Pit* with Olivia de Havilland. When I went back and saw it, it looked so hokey and old-fashioned, yet there were films that were made then, like *The Best Years of Our Lives* or *The Grapes of Wrath* that hold up as classics or masterpieces. The joke I always make about *Patton*—the first script of *Patton* was felt to be a little too weird—I always say that the things you do when you're young that get you fired are the same things that later get you lifetime achievement awards.

Was it George C. Scott who lobbied for your original Patton *script?*

Not exactly. Burt Lancaster was supposed to play the part of Patton, and he didn't like the script. He wanted a straight-ahead script. My *Patton* script had this strange opening, which no one liked at the time. Later, when they hired George C. Scott, he didn't like the new script that they had prepared, and an executive at the studio said there was a script that a young guy did, and it was interesting. They looked at it and they decided to go with that. So it was a surprise when later the movie was made and I realized it was from my script.

I've heard you talk about Sergei Eisenstein's October: Ten Days
That Shook the World *and the power of editing. How old were
you when you first saw this film?*

I was in college—I was a theater major. I was sort of like the
character in *Rushmore*, not a good student but I sort of dominated the theater department at that age and my life totally
revolved around it. One afternoon I was on campus and
noticed a sign that said, *Ten Days That Shook the World*. I wan-
dered in there along with maybe eight or nine people, none
of whom I knew, to watch this silent Russian film. I was elec-
trified by the experience because it was silent, no music, this
was just the film. I'd never seen a film that behaved like that.
Almost in certain sequences you could hear sound just from
the illusion of the editing. I was so knocked out by this experience that when I came out of the viewing I totally changed my
mind. I decided at that moment I would go to graduate school
in film and ultimately went to UCLA.

*You've suggested film is a form of alchemy, magic, illusion. Yet
when I think of many of your films what strikes me is how realistic
they are, how true they feel.*

Oh, you tend to learn a lot about whatever subject the film
you're making is about. You do a lot of research and you begin
to want to know how this is really done. Whatever it is you're
working on, you try to find experts who have done it—there's
just a hunger for research and details. Every project has a
vision or a theme, but it's the millions of details that people
remember.

You do so many different things, from filmmaking to winemaking to literary publishing in the magazine you founded, Zoetrope: All-Story. What's a typical day like for you or is there even a typical day?

I realized some 20 years ago that one should just pursue all the things one loves and not try and make money by investing in something that seems as though it will make money. Rather, do things that you like, that ultimately other people might like too. I don't really divide it from other activities that I might be involved in.

Godfather II had many different settings and periods—it dealt with the Cuban Revolution; it had a section in Sicily; it had gangsters in the '50s; but I never in my mind divided all those parts of that film. It was all part of this bigger film. And I worked on it all as one—that's what I do now. I don't divide the wine business from whatever experiments I might be doing in film or the fact that we publish short stories—to me it's all just part of the work I do. I might be working on two of those things at the same time. I don't adapt my life to work on these things—I let those things fit into my life.

The barriers for filmmaking are lower than ever. Do you have any advice for aspiring filmmakers?

I'd say that ultimately cinema does come down to the connection between writing and acting. If you make a movie that has just the most wonderful photography and editing but the script is not interesting, the photography can't hold it on its own. I would tell people to focus on one-act plays for a while. Learn about acting; learn about writing.

Heart to Heart
JOAN RIVERS

"Can we *tawk*?"

Joan Rivers' signature line, salted with her New York accent, reveals the essence of her comedy: She's confessional, daringly open about her personal life, scathingly critical, and brutally honest. That insistent question, "Can we talk?" was Rivers' way of saying to every person in the audience: It's just you and me here; I'll reveal my pain so you can feel yours; we're in this together, it's OK to laugh, and I'll say anything.

And she means *anything*. In the stunning and critically acclaimed 2010 documentary, *Joan Rivers: A Piece of Work*, the comedian talks about her daughter, Melissa Rivers, being offered $400,000 to pose naked above the waist for Playboy. "She turned it fucking down and called me for approval," Rivers roars. "For approval!" Melissa had asked Joan in a phone call what she thought, and Rivers tells her, "What do I think, you stupid fucking cunt? What do I think? I think you should ask for $200,000 more and show 'em your pussy. That's what I think."

Rivers' comedy was too crass for some people—and she could be cruel, mocking celebrities she found unattractive or overweight—but she was revered by those at the top of her field. "Here's a woman, a real pioneer for other women looking for careers in stand-up comedy," said David Letterman. "And talk about guts. She would . . . say some things that were unbelievable, just where you would have to swallow pretty hard. But it was hilarious. The force of her comedy was overpowering."

As was the power of her will. Fueled by a bottomless desire for recognition and approval, Rivers' energy was unflagging. "All stand-ups are innately insecure," Melissa says in *Piece of Work*. "Who would stand on the stage, by themselves, and say: 'Laugh, look at me—laugh at me; laugh with me. I don't care, just laugh.'"

Into her seventies and even in her early eighties, Rivers would zip from early TV taping to late-night solo comedy shows, then get up before 5 A.M. to catch a dawn flight and do it again and again and again. She rarely turned down a job— nothing was beneath her. "I will do anything," she says in the documentary. "I will knock my teeth out and do [a commercial for] Dent-Assure or whatever it is. I will wear a diaper—I don't give a shit."

Born Joan Molinsky in 1933, Rivers grew up in Brooklyn. One of her first stage roles was in a 1959 play called *Driftwood* with a 16-year-old Barbra Streisand. "It was a man's part and they couldn't cast it," Rivers is quoted on a website called Barbra Streisand Archives, "so I said 'I'll do it! Make them lesbians!' and Barbra was really thrilled." But the playwright differed—he said the characters were not lesbians, and that Rivers made up that story years later.

Rivers gained national attention on *The Tonight Show*, appearing first with Jack Paar, then becoming a regular guest host for Johnny Carson. In the 1960s, during one of Rivers' first appearances on the show, Carson laughed mightily at her jokes and ended the segment by telling Rivers she would be a star. Carson's prophecy propelled her career. When Rivers launched her own late-night show on Fox in 1986, Carson became furious and ended their friendship, essentially black-listing her from appearing on NBC. She wasn't invited back on an NBC late-night program until Jimmy Fallon had Rivers on his inaugural show in 2014.

Fox hired Rivers' husband, Edgar Rosenberg, to produce *The Late Show Starring Joan Rivers*, but after clashes with Fox's Rupert Murdoch and Barry Diller, Fox told Rivers they planned to fire him. So she quit. A few months later, in August 1987, Rosenberg, depressed and suffering health set-backs, committed suicide. "He left us high and dry—everything just went to smithereens," Rivers said. "He left me with no career and a lot of debts, and a lot of tough times." This led to deep divisions between Joan and Melissa, who was 19 when her father killed himself.

A few years later mother and daughter did something that's perhaps unprecedented and which Joan said was "so sick." Joan and Melissa played themselves in a film about Edgar's suicide. Released in 1994, it's called *Starting Over*. "It sounds so stupid and corny, but I think by walking through it again, it absolutely mended us," Joan said. "It totally mended the relationship."

During the '90s and 2000s, Rivers hosted a daytime talk show, rolled out a line of costume jewelry for QVC that sold like gangbusters, and critiqued the sartorial choices of Hol-lywood A-listers on the red carpet before awards shows. She played herself on TV shows ranging from Larry David's *Curb Your Enthusiasm* to *Fashion Police* and *Nip/Tuck* (about cos-metic surgery). She was an advocate of cosmetic surgery; her life seemed to be a race against the clock, and any evidence of time passing had to be erased. In 2009, Joan and Melissa appeared on *Celebrity Apprentice*, the show hosted by Donald Trump. Melissa got knocked out in the first round; Joan won the contest to become that year's apprentice.

Though Rivers became a comedic phenomenon, her true love was always the theater. In 1972 she appeared in the Broadway show *Fun City,* which closed shortly after the New York Times gave it a tepid review. She wrote and starred in the 1994 play *Sally Marr and Her Escorts* about Lenny Bruce's mother, who was also a comedian. Rivers earned a Tony Award nomination for Best Actress. Her most revealing role was in her autobiographical play, *Joan Rivers: A Work in Progress by a Life in Progress*, which earned a standing ovation at Edinburgh's Fringe festival in 2008 but got mixed reviews in the British press. Rivers had hoped to bring the play home to New York and present it on Broadway, but after the uneven reviews she shelved it.

"I've never been the critics' darling," Rivers says in the documentary. "I've always been considered a comic, a Borscht Belt comic, a Vegas comic. There's always an adjective before my name, and it's never a nice adjective. Do I want to take this to New York and in six months hear this again? I don't know. I'm not going to walk into New York City and be hurt the way *Fun City* hurt me. My acting is my one sacred thing in my life, and I will not have anyone hurt me with that. You can say I'm not a good comedian—it doesn't bother me. You say you didn't like me as an actress—you've killed me. And I don't want that in New York. But I know I'm an actress. It's all about acting. My career is an actress' career, and I play a comedian. So it's over—it's over. No one will ever take me seriously as an actress. I gotta take a deep breath and start again."

In an interview with a Florida newspaper not long before her death, Rivers said, "I'll tell you how I want to go: onstage in the middle of a set. I just want to fall off the stool in the middle of a one-hour routine. I have written instructions that I am not to be resuscitated unless I am capable of doing 60 minutes of stand-up. Oh wait. I should fall off the stool after 31 minutes because they don't pay you unless you do at least 30 minutes."

But Rivers didn't expect to die anytime soon. Appearing with Don Rickles when he was in his eighties and she was in her seventies, Rivers noted Rickles was still "hilarious" and said "George Burns was amazing until he was in his late 90s, and Phyllis Diller until she was 92, she just laid it down. I'd like to beat them all, and I think I will. This is where I belong—the only time I am truly happy is on a stage."

On August 28, 2014, Rivers went to a Manhattan outpatient clinic for what she believed would be a minor throat procedure. She was given anesthesia and had serious complications. Rivers died a week later at Mt. Sinai Hospital—she was 81. The clinic was cited for negligence and settled out of court with Melissa Rivers.

I interviewed Joan Rivers by phone in midsummer of 2011, when controversy swirled about her decision to film her daughter showering, without Melissa's knowledge, for their television show *Joan & Melissa: Joan Knows Best?*. The elder Rivers was unapologetic.

I met her a month later after she performed at Napa's Uptown Theatre. Though she'd had a long day, the 78-year-old comedian greeted me after the show and thanked me for the article I wrote for a local newspaper. She was gracious and warm and interested in my family, a contrast to the persona she'd embodied onstage just moments before.

I had just one last question for her: "Can we talk?" She said, "Sure."

≈ ≈ ≈

I want to start with what you're doing right now—this Joan & Melissa *show. You got a lot of shock value with that shower scene, maybe the most infamous shower scene since* Psycho.

It's just wonderful [working] with Melissa—it's really following our lives very closely, and everyone loves the show.

What about that scene in the shower? Did she know that was coming?

No, we're trying to make it as much as possible absolute reality. There are too many reality shows that are so non-realistic these days. How many times can women have fights? I knew what I was doing, but she had no idea in hell.

Has she forgiven you for that?

Oh my god, yes. I'm your mother; you forgive your mother a lot.

And you honestly wanted her to pose nude?

Absolutely, look who's become a celebrity: Paris Hilton, which started with a sex tape. The Kardashians. It's a different world now. Melissa's got a beautiful body, and believe me it goes. She might as well do it now while she looks great.

It seems that a key to your comedy is you make fun of yourself. Is that the entree to making fun of everybody else?

Oh no, no, no, but I do make fun of myself because I think I'm an asshole. The key to my humor is I tell the truth. I've always said onstage what I say to my very good friends in private. That's the whole key. And I very often will say things that people don't say, but then they come out and say: That's right; she's right.

What's bugging you now?

My thing now is that blind people should not have apartments with views in New York; this is stupid. Everyone gets so upset, but this is just stupid. You have an apartment where you can see Central Park, and you can't see it?!

You've got a point.

You're damn right.

George Carlin said that everything we do but don't talk about is funny.

That's right. He's saying tell the truth. When you go and see a comedian, what we do is we go onstage and we talk—and we talk, and we talk, and we talk—about everything that annoys me, that bothers me, that I find insane or that I find funny.

Who are your comedic heroes?

The only comedic hero that I have is Lenny Bruce. Genius, genius, genius, and broke the whole mold of what you're allowed to talk about. He changed comedy forever for everybody.

It's amazing how many barriers he broke.

And how they ruined his life. They went after him, ostracized him. You look back, and everything he said was absolutely true.

It's hard for me to understand how strict conformity must have been in the '50s. Do you feel that part of what you want to achieve is to break barriers? You've been open about things that few people talk about: plastic surgery, your husband's suicide. Are you trying to give people the courage to talk about things they wouldn't otherwise talk about?

I think if you bring something out in the public awareness, it's not terrible if you're all talking about it. And that's exactly why I talk about Edgar's suicide. If we talk about it, we can solve anything. Just put it on the table, and tell the truth.

You seem to be one of the hardest-working people in show business, working at an age when other people might have cut down on their touring.

First of all, I love the business; let's just start with that. All I've ever wanted to do is be in this business. Of course I work hard, it's a business where you never know where your next job is coming from. So you're stupid not to accept a job that's offered to you and make it so good, because you're competing with yourself. You're truly as good as your last shot on television.

But it's not like you're in your twenties or thirties still trying to make it. You're very successful—

Oh, darling, in our business there's no such thing, and everything goes away.

What's your appeal to gays and lesbians; why do they love you so much?

I am queen of the gays, and I adore them, love them. If there are 10 gays in the audience, I know it's going to be a good show. I don't know why they love me, but I love them because they get it; they are willing to go first into places that are funny that others haven't gone. We have the same mind-set. When I look back to college, my very best friends were gay even if they didn't know it then. I've always been very attracted to them because they've always been the brightest and the smartest and the funniest, and the most daring in a way.

The Johnny Carson show was your big break, especially becoming a regular guest host, but then you had a rift with Johnny.

I dared, dared to do my own show, dared to leave the family. I think a lot of that was because I'm a woman, and he never thought I would leave. I really think he liked me better than anybody else and was really hurt that I would leave him, forgetting that it was a business.

Meaning he liked you better than any of his other guest hosts?

I think so. But everybody left him: Cosby left him, Carlin left him, David Brenner left him, Seinfeld left. They all walked off and did their own stuff. He wasn't mad at anybody but me. And he never made up with me, which tells you so much about the character of the man. I would see him in a restaurant 15 years later and he wouldn't say hello. And you go: What's your problem?

Did you ever try to talk to him?

I wrote him a letter and that was it. It made me terribly sad, still does, but move on.

Early in your career you were in a play with Barbra Streisand where you've said you played lesbians.

That was one of the first things I did. We played lesbians in a thing called *Driftwood*. I've lost the program which kills me because she was "Barbara" with all the a's in her name (not "Barbra"). And I was Joan Molinsky, not even Joan Rivers. We still see each other, and we laugh about it.

I know this must be a sensitive topic for you, but since you've been so open about your husband's suicide, I read there was a scene cut from your documentary where you say F. U. to his picture.

Melissa was very upset about that. Anyone who has gone through suicide in their family, you are filled for the rest of your life with remorse, all the normal mourning feelings, all the loss and all the unhappiness, and all the sadness is there, and also great anger. Great anger!

So that doesn't really ebb over time?

No, I'll look at a girl talking to her father, and I'll think Melissa doesn't have that, you bastard. I work very hard with an organization called Suicide Survivors because the emotions are extraordinarily complicated.

And you work with a group that delivers meals to people with AIDS, right?

I'm on the board of God's Love We Deliver. They named a kitchen after me. I hope it won't reflect on what the food tastes like. Trust me, I never thought there would be a kitchen named after me.

Now that you're in your late seventies, does the road ever get tiresome for you?

Look at last week; I had a great week. I was out in California to do *Fashion Police*. Then I worked three days filming on *Joan & Melissa*, the reality show. Then I had a major meeting this morning with QVC to present our fall line of jewelry and clothing. Then I got in a plane and now I'm driving through the most gorgeous country, and I'm going to perform live tonight. What a wonderful life, and it's never boring because it's never the same.

My mom is nearly your age, and she volunteers as a docent at San Francisco's Museum of Modern Art and travels often. When I ask her how she's doing, she likes to say, "I'm so busy!"

That's great! The happiest moment is what your mother just said: "I'm so busy!" What a wonderful thing to be able to say through your entire life. I didn't have time today to do anything, I'm so busy. How lucky and wonderful is that. Everybody should get a passion and do something.

Peaceful Troubadour
GRAHAM NASH

I t's not easy to pick a place to start when writing about Graham Nash. You could begin with his work in the 1960s Brit-pop band, The Hollies, or with his singing in the supergroup, Crosby, Stills & Nash. Or you could consider his anti-war and anti-nuclear activism. Then there's his photography. And all the awards and accolades, including a slew of Grammy nominations (and one win) and his two-time induction into the Rock & Roll Hall of Fame, with The Hollies and with CSN.

Probably the best place to start is with Nash's songwriting. He wrote or co-wrote so many songs that defined an era. Think of the pop confections of The Hollies from 1964 to '68: "Pay You Back with Interest," "Carrie Anne," and "On a Carousel." That was just the beginning. With David Crosby and Stephen Stills, and for a time with Neil Young, Nash found his voice in the late '60s and '70s. The CSN&Y and CSN songs that Nash wrote or helped write reflect the tumult and idealism of a generation that believed in making the world a better place.

"Teach Your Children," "Marrakesh Express," and "Our House" became the soundtrack of the times. While much of The Hollies' music was influenced by the Beatles, the songs of CSN&Y were original and trailblazing. They wanted to engage and inspire listeners while singing pristine three-part harmonies. Nearly every word makes an impact, and in some songs Nash and his bandmates employ alliteration, for example "Helplessly Hoping," with such lines as "Wordlessly watching, he waits by the window and wonders."

Nash's "Chicago/We Can Change the World," "Military Madness," and other protest anthems reflect the turbulence and activism of the time. Among his other masterpieces are "Immigration Man" about being detained trying to enter the U.S., and the tender "Just a Song Before I Go," which Nash says he wrote in about 20 minutes to win a bet. The story goes that friends in Hawaii challenged Nash to quickly write a song before flying out for a long tour. They bet $500; Nash wrote "Just a Song," which appeared on the 1977 CSN album and became one of the band's highest charting hits.

Music industry executive Ron Stone, who worked extensively with CSN, says in Dave Zimmer's book *Crosby, Stills & Nash: The Biography*: "Nash was always the strongest person in the group. But it took him a long time to realize that. The others made him feel he wasn't heavy, but I think Graham finally realized, 'Hey, wait a minute, I'm the one who wrote all the hits . . . I'm the one who's *feedin'* this outfit.' It's true. They were enjoying the success that he gave them. Without Nash's songs, CSN or CSN&Y would have been a big underground success, but they wouldn't have so many records. Graham has always been rapped for writing simplistic songs, but that's the very reason they're so big. Graham's got the ability to reach the largest group of people."

Born in 1942 during the depths of World War II in Blackpool, a seaside town in northwestern England, Nash grew up feeling the deprivations of rationing, which he says forged within him an attitude of not sweating the small stuff. Nash first met Crosby and Stills in 1966 when The Hollies toured the U.S. After leaving The Hollies in 1968, Nash moved to California and became romantically involved with Joni Mitchell.

Nash's activism transcended music: He co-founded the anti-nuclear Musicians United for Safe Energy after the partial meltdown of the Three Mile Island nuclear plant in Pennsylvania in March 1979. That year Nash helped organize No Nukes, a concert at New York's Madison Square Garden, with fellow activists Jackson Browne, Bonnie Raitt, James Taylor, Carly Simon, Gil Scott-Heron, Bruce Springsteen, and Tom Petty.

A talented photographer, Nash has created iconic images of Neil Young, Joni Mitchell, Dennis Hopper, and Judy Collins, catching these artists when they had no idea that they were being photographed. This adds to the poignancy of the images, presented in his photography book, *Eye to Eye*. Nash's 1969 portrait of David Crosby is housed in the National Museum of American History at the Smithsonian Institution.

Over the years Nash and his bandmates have had several falling-outs, but in the end they tend to reconcile. Nash's 1982 song, "Wasted on the Way," on CSN's album *Daylight Again*, tells of his desire to let bygones be bygones. He wrote: "And there's so much time to make up everywhere you turn, time we have wasted on the way. So much water moving underneath the bridge, let the water come and carry us away."

Crosby, Stills & Nash reunited for a tour in 2012. Nash and Crosby had recently turned 70 and Stills was approaching the milestone, which made me wonder if they'd sound as good as when I first saw the band decades before. From the moment they took the stage that September night at the Marin Civic

Center, CSN sounded as good, maybe better, than ever. The harmonies were flawless, their energy unbridled, and their musicianship unrivaled. No one will ever sound like these three voices becoming one. And they seemed genuinely happy to be back onstage together.

Before the resounding 2012 show, I'd seen Nash with CSN at San Francisco's Warfield Theatre, and Nash and Crosby were surprise guests at a 2006 David Gilmour show at London's Royal Albert Hall. Another guest was David Bowie— that turned out to be Bowie's penultimate live performance.

When I interviewed Nash in 2017, he'd recently ended a 38-year marriage, started a new relationship, and moved from Kauai to New York City. Yet his earnest desire to tap his creativity in service of making the world a better place hadn't ebbed a bit. This was shortly after the release of Nash's 2016 solo album, *This Path Tonight*. It's a strong collection, more personal than political, with his guitar evoking the haunting and insistent sound of CSN's early work. On the song, "Beneath the Waves," Nash considers his mortality, singing: "Fifty years before the mast. How long will it last, before sinking beneath the waves?"

❧   ❧   ❧

Could we start by talking about a couple of songs on the new collection? One that really struck me is "Myself at Last" and the line, "Is my future just my past?"

Well, here's what goes on when you book a studio for an album. You have to play something to see if everything is plugged in the right way before you start recording. "Myself at Last" was the first attempt at the first song we ever tried. That's when I knew it was going to be an amazing set of sessions (in 2015).

Another song on This Path Tonight *that made an impact is "Golden Days." Can you tell me about that song?*

The opening verse is about The Hollies. In a really strange way, World War II did me a lot of good. I know that sounds weird, but my point is that having survived World War II, I could deal with any problem over here, because if you can make it through World War II, the fact that your coffee is four degrees colder than you want it doesn't mean anything. Talk to me about serious stuff. Talk to me about important issues. We made it through World War II.

You were so young then. What do you remember?

I was born in 1942, and World War II didn't end until 1945. Yes, I was young, but incredibly impressionable. I remember my mother pulling the blackout curtains to block out the living room light so that the enemy bombers couldn't see the city. I remember rationing (which continued after the war ended). I remember going on railroad tracks, picking up little bits of coal for our fire. So you think this is a problem? We can deal with this whatever it is. That's just the attitude that I was brought up with.

What was it like to go from the deprivations of postwar England to the openness and freedom of California in the mid to late '60s?

It was insane. I came from the north of England where if you blink you miss summer. I came from a band, The Hollies, that I started with Allan Clarke in December 1962, but by the time '68 came along the band wouldn't go where I felt that we could go. It kind of started with "King Midas in Reverse." I just read a quote from Allan Clarke recently that said Graham's idea of a good song is "King Midas in Reverse," but our opinion of a good song is "Jennifer Eccles," which is one of the last singles that The Hollies did, and a song that I hate to this day even though I helped write it.

So have you always followed your muse? Do you feel compelled to speak out politically?

The two things are: You have to tell the truth as much as you can, and you have to reflect the times in which you live. That's the responsibility of every artist. I think that you really have to fight, with my music, with my day-to-day affirmations about what a great country this is, in spite of how crazy it does seem right now. America is one of the greatest countries on Earth. I see it very differently than you do. I am not from here. I've been here 50 years, but I'm not American, I'm English so I have a different perspective on this country. I believe that if America, God forbid, had ever been bombed like England was bombed in World War II, maybe we would be a little more cautious about going to war and doing preemptive military strikes. Yeah, it's been a strange life, and I'm loving it.

The music landscape has changed dramatically, at least from a business point of view. Do you have any words of advice for young songwriters?

If I were to offer any advice, first of all I would say: Follow your heart. You really know what's a good song, what's a good melody, what's a good set of lyrics. You know internally what it is. Talk about what's going on in your life. Talk about how the people who are running the politics of this insane country deal with things. Get involved. Research—find out as much as you can about what's really going on here. We're so dazzled by *The Voice* and *So You Think You Can Dance*, and reality TV about New Jersey housewives. We're all being deflected.

It's just bread and circuses. That's exactly what's going on. The Romans invented it; it was probably going on before the Romans, but bread and circuses. Buy another pair of sneakers, buy another cola, and shut up while we rob you. That's what's going on!

Going back in your career, with political songs like "Chicago" about that city in 1968, and later when you sang "Winchester Cathedral" (a 1977 song critical of religion), you never seemed to worry about blowback. Or did you?

No, you can't. You just can't operate out of fear. Do I think I'm being watched? Yeah, probably in my wildest imaginations, but so what. I live a good life. I live a good, legal life. I don't do anything illegal. I'm trying to be the best person I can be. It's a basic tenet with me. I'm trying to be the best friend, the best boyfriend, the best artist, the best musician. I'll never make it, but at least I'm trying for God sake.

I'm intrigued by your photography. Your work conveys a lot of feeling. Do you see photography and music as similar in some ways?

I see everything as a column of energy, from the physics of what I'm looking at as I talk to you out of my window in my apartment in New York City. And where do I want to plug into this column of energy today? If I look at a picture like *Moonrise, Hernandez, New Mexico* by Ansel Adams, I can imagine the violas in the darker clouds at the back. I can imagine the cellos and the basses playing in all the blacks in the image. I can kind of hear photographs in a way. That sounds awfully weird. And music, if I listen to the *Adagio for Strings* by Samuel Barber, my mind goes to a million places, beautiful places, that that music creates in me. And I'm incredibly pleased and thankful that I've been a musician all my life. What an incredible thing to be able to say.

I don't think what you said about the Ansel Adams photograph is weird at all. You took a photo of Neil Young in his car as he drives back to his ranch. When you said that you can hear the music in the Ansel Adams photo, I thought of that picture because in it you can kind of hear one of Neil's quieter ballads.

Absolutely. It's the gentler side of Neil. I like to be invisible as a photographer. Because I've had so many pictures taken of me throughout my life, I know when a camera is pointed at me. I always want to look like Elvis. I always want to look like James Dean and put my best side forward. But invisible: I want to take a picture of you, and you don't even know I took it.

I know you recently ended a 38-year marriage and you moved from Kauai to New York.

I'm right here in New York City.

That's a big change.

Ya, one jungle for another.

I hesitate to bring this up . . .

So bring it up.

Is there any hope that you and David Crosby will reconcile?

The truth is, Michael, you say things in anger, you react to things that happen, and sometimes you say things you don't mean. I got to tell ya, I'm a musician, and if David Crosby came to my apartment and said, "I want you to listen to four of my new songs," and he breaks my fucking heart again, I'll be in the studio with him. What's going on between me and David, and (between) David and Neil, is petty stuff that we've got to get over and grow up. We are in our seventies; we are not teenagers anymore. We have a lot of work to do. Look what's going on in this country. We need to stand up and fight what's going on. That is by far more important than our stupid arguments.

I saw you guys in 2012 and you sounded as good as ever.

You know, when we're on it, there's nobody like us. We're not the best of anything, but holy shit, you can't sound like me and David and Stephen when we sing together.

In the late 1960s and early '70s, a lot of bands wanted to sound as loud as they could or get as far out there as they could. But your sound has always been so pristine, like you just wanted it to sound beautiful.

That's absolutely right. We wanted three voices to be just one voice, one sound.

I'm sure you're often asked who your influences were, but I want to ask: Who do you think you've influenced?

You start putting more than two voices together, and you're inevitably going to be compared to whatever. Did we learn from people? Of course we did. Did we learn from Peter, Paul, and Mary? Did we learn from The Weavers? Did we learn from Bob [Dylan]? Of course we all did. Did we learn from the Beatles? Of course. So if we influenced people to make great music, God bless it. There are a lot of bands that sing great harmony now. It's great to hear.

Sweet Judy
JUDY COLLINS

The first songs that come to mind when I think of Judy Collins are her covers of Joni Mitchell's "Both Sides, Now" and Stephen Sondheim's "Send in the Clowns," both Grammy winners. What's remarkable about these songs is that Collins makes them entirely her own. With her pristine voice and delicate phrasing, Collins breathes new life into every song she sings, and has done so since her 1961 debut, *A Maid of Constant Sorrow*, featuring folk songs written by Bob Dylan and Phil Ochs.

Born in 1939, Collins grew up in Seattle until she was 10, when her father, a blind piano player, singer, and radio show host, took a job in Denver. When she was 11, Collins spent two months in a hospital recovering from polio. As a youth, she trained as a classical pianist, but it was folk music that won her heart. Collins took up the guitar and learned songs by Woody Guthrie, Pete Seeger, and other folk icons. She performed in the dingy clubs of New York City's Greenwich

Village, landed a record deal, and released her first album when she was 22. With her luminous blue eyes, flowing chestnut hair, and crystalline voice, Collins attracted legions of fans.

Her breakthrough came in 1967 with the album *Wildflowers*, which featured "Both Sides, Now," Leonard Cohen's "Hey, That's No Way to Say Goodbye," and several of Collins' own compositions. She followed that in 1968 with *Who Knows Where the Time Goes*, the title track written by Sandy Denny and originally recorded by the Celtic folk group Fairport Convention. During the 1970s, in addition to performing and recording, Collins appeared on *The Muppet Show* and *Sesame Street*. A longtime activist, in the 1980s she released a song opposing gun violence and published a memoir, *Trust Your Heart*. Collins has earned six Grammy nominations and had more than a dozen singles reach the charts. Her performance of "Amazing Grace" is in the National Recording Registry of the Library of Congress.

Yet Collins' life hasn't been all gold and platinum. She has survived substance abuse, an eating disorder, and personal tragedy. Her only son, Clark, took his own life in 1992 when he was 33. Asked in a 2004 interview with Bill Moyers how she managed to get through that period, Collins said, "Inch by inch, minute by minute, hour by hour." And with more than a little help from her friends. "Joan Rivers (whose husband committed suicide) reached out to me and said you cannot stop working," Collins told Moyers. "I'd planned to quit working—I was going to put it all aside," she said, but Rivers told her: "You can't do that—you won't heal. You have to go on with your life."

So Collins kept writing, recording, and performing. She's been open about her travails, in autobiographical books such as *Cravings*, a memoir that deals with how she transcended overeating and bulimia, and *Sweet Judy Blue Eyes: My Life in Music*. She's also turned to film as co-director of *Portrait of a Woman,* about her childhood piano teacher Antonia Brico who went on to become the first woman, Collins said, to conduct major symphonies around the world.

I had the opportunity to interview Collins as she was touring with her old flame, guitarist Stephen Stills, a half-century after they were lovers in the late '60s. I'd known that "Suite: Judy Blue Eyes" was about Collins but hadn't realized that Stills had written other songs about her as he went through the pain of losing a relationship he'd cherished. Collins and Stills remained friends and decades later hit the road together, their voices blending beautifully. My wife and I saw their show in May 2018. Collins and Stills performed together for nearly two hours, with Collins singing her songs "Houses" and "River of Gold" and of course covering "Both Sides, Now."

In 2019, the year she celebrated her 80th birthday, the everproductive Collins had dozens of her own shows across the U.S. and Canada. She was a delight during our phone interview—which focused on her tour with Stills—thoughtful, spontaneous, and quick to laugh. When our time was up, her farewell made me feel like we were old friends: "Thank you, my dear," she said. "Take care, bye-bye."

≈ ≈ ≈

What led you and Stephen to reconnect and go on the road together?

Since we've been friends for all these years, we've shared all kinds of experiences. We know each other socially and our families are friends. We talked about songs and tried to figure out what might be the ones that we would do and, by golly, we came up with a pretty good setlist and decided to give it a shot.

Can you tell me how you decided what songs to play?

We decided to give each other freedom to do whatever appeals, so I will be doing a new one of mine in my little set, and he'll probably do a new one in his set. I don't think he'd ever heard the song I wrote for him, which is called, "Houses." Finally he heard the song and said, "We have to do that." And of course at the end of the show we sing "Suite: Judy Blue Eyes" together, which is so much fun. Here I am, a girl singer and 12-string guitar player in a rock 'n' roll band with Stephen Stills, which is pretty odd.

What is it like for you to sing "Suite: Judy Blue Eyes," a song about Stephen's longing for you and sadness about your breakup?

It's hysterical (laughs). It's so much fun to do that. We don't do the whole song—we just sing the end of it, which gets everyone dancing in the aisles. It's great fun, tremendous fun.

I read that you and Stephen were at an AARP convention and that's where you hatched the idea to tour together; is that correct?

About four years ago Crosby, Stills & Nash and I, we were all at this big AARP convention [where some musicians performed]. So Stephen and I looked at each other and said: "Why aren't we doing this? Look at us. We're not chopped liver."

And with all the dissention in the Crosby, Stills & Nash, I imagine that you're a lot easier to get along with.

They've had a terrible amount of strife. He [Stills] is so happy to be out of that and on the road with me. We don't have that kind of history. Those guys have been together a long time. I don't think I ever knew a group that didn't have difficulties after working together for 10, 15, 20 years. (CSN began playing in the late 1960s, more than 50 years ago.) So I don't think it's at all unusual.

Anyway it was time for them to take a break. Kiss and make up; that's really the motto of the day. Let bygones be bygones. Let's do what we always did and have a good time, even a better time. Of course, they'll get back together. How could they not? So in the meantime we have this refresher course, kind of a new approach, something different for both me and for him. And I think it's good for both of us. He and I are such good friends, and it's also good for our careers. It's like we're saying (to the world), guess what, we can do this too.

You and Stephen have said your late-in-life collaboration is "a triumph of art and friendship over time."

When we started doing this, he said, "We should have done this from the beginning and skipped the romance." And I said, "Yes, but then you wouldn't have written 'Suite: Judy Blue Eyes' and there may not have been any careers." Who knows, that was their [CSN's] first big song, and it made all the airwaves. I get in the car in Los Angeles with my granddaughter, and of course "Suite: Judy Blue Eyes" comes on. It's hysterical.

Does she know who it's about?

Oh sure, she knows everything. My granddaughter is 30.

Oh, I thought you were talking about a kid.

I have a great-grandson, and he knows who his great-grandmother is too. And they know Stephen—he got absolutely locked into my family right away in 1966. He came out to Denver where we all lived and took pictures of my family home, and we went skiing in the mountains. He was practically a family member and still is.

Do you feel that the audience is there to see both of you together, or do some come for Stephen and the old CSN songs, and others for you and your songs?

We have a band in which my musical director takes the lead on keyboards and piano. He and Stephen get along beautifully, and [Stills'] bass player is on bass, and we have a drummer that both of us have worked with over the years. So we are very simpatico, all of us. I think the audience has the capacity to appreciate both of us separately, and they also like us together. I think it's a big deal for them to see us together. They've heard us apart for so many years, so this is refreshing. It's different; it's fun. Not that it wasn't fun before, but this is a new experience, which is exciting for everybody.

What's interesting is that no matter how close you are to somebody, you can't guarantee that your voices will work well together, but your voice and Stephen's voice seem to be made for each other.

Yes, they do. We think along the same lines musically, and I think we have a lot of resonance together as singers and musicians. Then I get to be on the stage and listen to this brilliant guitarist. He's one of the greatest in the world. He's magical; when he starts playing, you just go nuts.

I'd like to ask about your voice. Do you do anything special to take care of it?

I just watch it. I'm careful. I eat right; I sleep a lot. I don't scream or yell. I don't smoke, don't drink. I don't do drugs. I live like an athlete; I exercise. You have to.

Do you and Stephen take your spouses or families along when you tour?

No, it's too expensive to take our spouses and families on the road, and they would never want to do it anyway.

The song, "So Begins the Task," about starting over after a breakup, is that Stephen writing about the end of his romance with you?

I think it's Stephen writing to me. He has confessed to me now that he wrote all kinds of songs for me, not just "Suite: Judy Blue Eyes" but things like "Helplessly Hoping" and the song "Judy," which nobody ever heard until this tour. I know that emotions are what drive our songwriting, and it's very flattering to be the subject of "Suite: Judy Blue Eyes." He has said, "I would do everything in my power to get you back," and I said, "Well, you finally did. Let's look at it that way."

The title of your 2017 album with Stills, Everybody Knows, *comes from a 1988 Leonard Cohen song. I know you helped Leonard gain recognition in the 1960s. Could you tell me about why you chose that song and made it the title of your album?*

I was discovered by Leonard even more than he was discovered by me. He found me in 1966 and told his friends that he wanted to come to New York and sing his songs for me. He chose me out of all the other people he might have chosen, primarily because he knew I didn't write songs [at that time]. By 1966 I had already recorded Dylan and Pete [Seeger] and Woody [Guthrie] and Tom Paxton. So he knew that I was a person who would listen. It was just magical. He came to my apartment and sang me "Suzanne" and "Dress Rehearsal Rag" and "The Stranger Song." I recorded two out of three, which is sort of the average for the songs that he would send me in the coming 20, 30 years. When he died it was a great loss to everybody. But I also thought he was the smartest man I ever knew because he died the day before the [2016 U.S. presidential] election.

The morning after Election Day, I started singing, "Everybody Knows," which I had never done. I thought, Oh my God, this is the story of where we are. "Everybody knows that the dice are loaded. Everybody knows that the good guys lost. Everybody knows the fight was fixed; the poor stay poor, the rich get rich. That's how it goes; everybody knows." Then Stephen and I cherry-picked other great songs [for the album] that we know and love.

Could you talk about coming of age in the 1960s and if that time was a moment of peak creativity?

Neil Young carries that tradition. I saw him (perform) two nights ago, and I got that flash of what it was like in the old days, what it was like to go into a venue of any kind and see one artist on the stage doing songs that one could understand. It evoked storytelling around a campfire, something that speaks to all of us always. I think you can go to some of these festivals and have the same experience. It's very intimate, very creative and expressive, and it's very inspiring to all the people who are listening, in case they had in their minds, you know

I might be able to do that. I've got a guitar; I've got a few thoughts; let me see where this can go.

It has the feeling of the village in a way, not to mention Greenwich Village, those dark smoky nights when one artist or two artists might be doing something . . . this wasn't firecrackers and fireworks and light shows. This was about intimate stories that move you. And that's what Neil has always been about too. Of course there's magic going on all the time, all around us. It was maybe condensed in the '60s in a way that was a little bit different, but it's still around. It's still burnin' (laughs).

Field of Dreams
MIKE KRUKOW

The seeds of Mike Krukow's future as a baseball announcer may have been sown on October 10, 1987, the best day of the San Francisco Giants pitcher's playing career. When he took the mound that day, the Giants were down two games to one in a taut playoff series against the St. Louis Cardinals. Krukow pitched a complete game to lead San Francisco to victory and afterwards was interviewed on network TV.

On camera he took a wad of gum out of his mouth and stuck it on the button atop his cap. After the field reporter congratulated him, Krukow said: "Joe Garagiola (who broadcast the game with Vin Scully) is an ex-catcher, and he's not gonna let me forget that 0-2 pitch I threw to [opposing pitcher Danny] Cox. It was a fastball right down the, the cock. I thought I could sneak my 85-mile-an-hour heater by him, but that was real costly. Fortunately my troops picked me up; it was fun to get back in this son of a gun. We needed this game."

When the broadcast went to break, as revealed by an off-air recording, Scully said: "Right down the . . . see what happened, did you hear that great line? You know what he said? He said, 'I threw the fastball right down the cock.' Ohhhh lord."

That was a line that had probably never been uttered on network TV, yet every true fan knew exactly what he meant. It was descriptive, colorful, inventive, perhaps a bit on the edge. In the two-minute interview, the good-natured and irreverent Krukow was self-deprecating (an 85-mph fastball isn't that fast) and appreciative of his teammates, qualities he has brought into the broadcast booth.

Ultimately, Krukow, a married father of five, is simply a great guy to hang out with night after night. After listening to him for decades, countless Giants fans in the San Francisco Bay Area and beyond consider him a friend. Even in down years, he and broadcast partner Duane Kuiper make the telecasts worth watching. Krukow's baseball knowledge, especially about pitching, is extraordinary, and he communicates his insights with precision, enthusiasm, and humor. Former Giants coach Tim Flannery says Krukow is "everyman" and understands how difficult the game of baseball is. He's "very humble," Flannery said. "We love to bring him into our house every night."

A former pitcher for San Francisco, Philadelphia, and the Chicago Cubs, Krukow has been a Giants color commentator since 1990, working alongside former teammate Kuiper, who handles play by play. The two were best friends when they played for the Giants in the 1980s, and that camaraderie is abundantly evident in the booth. Kuiper is Midwest low-key; Krukow is California exuberant, known for expressions like "Grab some pine, meat" after an opposing player strikes out. Kruk and Kuip (pronounced "kipe"), as they're known, complement one another perfectly. And they're consummate pros.

Two examples: during a Giants game against the San Diego Padres in April 2019, Krukow described infielder Manny Machado's easy grace by saying: "If he were any more relaxed, he'd be asleep." During the summer of 2018, when a Florida Marlins runner inexplicably left first base after a Giants outfielder caught a routine fly ball for the inning's first out, Krukow said, "I can't tell you what he could have possibly thought. Based on what he possibly did, it was impossible."

The highlights of Krukow's broadcasting career were the Giants' title runs in 2010, 2012, and 2014, he said. During the postseason, national networks handle telecasts, so all four Giants announcers worked together in the radio booth. At the World Series victory celebrations at San Francisco's Civic Center, fans cheered Krukow and Kuiper as enthusiastically as they applauded the players.

Yet even before the 2010 season, Krukow had noticed his muscle strength declining. Initially he attributed that to aging, but when he had difficulty descending stairs and started tripping over curbs, he saw a neurologist. He feared that he had ALS, a fatal disease, so was relieved in 2011 to learn he had a rare condition called inclusion body myositis (IBM), an inflammatory disease that's not curable but not fatal. He didn't mention IBM on the air; it wasn't until a 2014 magazine profile that his condition became widely known.

As players, Kruk and Kuip did mock broadcasts from the end of the bench, Kuiper told me, but he and Krukow have "never, ever had more fun than right now." Krukow, he says, is like many old ballplayers in the way he approaches life. "They're stubborn; they don't like to ask for help; they think they can accomplish anything even though their body is not allowing them to do that. He's like that, as tough as anybody. He never, ever complains. I probably bitch more about life than he does. His glass is never half empty. And I probably know him almost as good as his wife."

Kuiper carries Krukow's luggage off planes and helps in other ways. "If we are going to a restaurant, he needs to have a chair that has arms. Otherwise he can't get up. How tough is finding him a chair?" Kuiper said. "You make sure that when you're with him, you look down to see if there are any obstacles that he could trip over. He might need to put his arm on your shoulder when he's walking. Rarely does he even ask for it. You just do it." Ever the loyal friend, Kuiper said he didn't want his assistance "to be overblown," emphasizing that Krukow "does a lot of stuff on his own."

Though Krukow can no longer call every game of the season, a marathon that lasts more than six months with few days off, he works almost all home games and goes on some road trips. When I interviewed him in April 2019, he said he planned to work 110 of the 162 games that season. In a 2019 Sports Illustrated story, Kuiper said: "The fact he's doing 110 games, to me, is a bonus. I'll get to be with him 110 times." During the Postgame Wrap, when the announcers appear on screen to discuss the game's highlights, Krukow doesn't hide his wooden walking stick. But if you didn't see that, you might never know he was having physical difficulties.

Krukow is "meeting the challenge and staying at the top of his game," said Marty Lurie, who hosts Giants pre- and postgame radio shows. "He's just as personable and generous with his time as ever. Baseball is all about a new story every day, and Krukow lives it. For me, he's baseball. Nobody does it better." Lurie believes baseball mirrors life and says Krukow's optimistic outlook is emblematic of that. "Life is tough but you never give up, and he's never going to give up. He's an inspiration to everyone. Mike Krukow is a good man."

I met Krukow on an April afternoon at Oracle Park, the Giants home field in San Francisco, three hours before first pitch. When we met, the 67-year-old broadcaster put his hands on a table in the broadcast booth and pushed himself to a standing position. Then he gingerly put one foot in front of the other to move to the booth next door. "This is warp speed," he joked. We sat in Willie McCovey's suite (McCovey, a legendary Giants slugger, had died the previous October). As we spoke, Krukow occasionally glanced at the field below to watch batting practice, part of his game preparation. Yet he remained fully engaged, answering questions thoughtfully and astutely, offering perspective on the creativity he taps to bring the game of baseball to life.

❧ ❧ ❧

In a year like this when the Giants may not be great, do you feel it's your role to carry the broadcast, or do you do your job the same way as when the team may be playoff bound?

There's a responsibility to tell the story of the team. You have to make these players come to life to the listening audience. What are their personalities like? What has he done in the past? You watch that athlete every day and you get a sense as to when he's putting it together; you can anticipate that this guy is about ready to go on a run. Or this guy's struggling. It's your responsibility to tell the story of the team to the listener every day. It's a volatile, ever-changing story. When somebody's red-hot, there are two guys who are stone cold. When somebody is just coming into his prime, there are two guys who are just hanging on by their fingernails.

When you tell the story, you gain a trust from those who follow the team. Once you have the trust of your audience, you have to be very careful that you don't abuse that trust. You have to be honest—it may be painful. When Barry Bonds was retiring, and he was physically not capable of doing the things he was renowned for, you had to describe what was going on. You have a responsibility because of the trust these folks have in you. But it's also the lure of the job, the beauty of the job. Because when a fan base loves this team as hard as fans in Northern California and all around the world love this team, and the team can justify that love and give them back a championship, a flag, like they've done three times, it is the most beautiful thing to witness and be part of. It is a privilege to be the person who tells that story.

Of all the things that we've ever done in our broadcasting careers, Jon Miller, Dave Flemming, Duane Kuiper, and I, we all felt that the work we did postseason was the most special because we were able to convey the feeling and the wonderful story that we were watching. Then we got to watch the players give back the ultimate gift to the listening audience. We don't take one day for granted, not any of us, especially now. We're all getting older. I'm not able to do 162; I can do 110 [games] now. We love our time here, and we really take it seriously.

And it shows in the preparation you guys do and the rapport you have. How special is it for you to work with a guy like Duane?

We played together in 1983 through '85. I retired in '89; he started broadcasting right after he stopped playing in 1985. We hooked up in 1990; that was only for 15 or 16 games, but it was our start. We've been doing it since then, with the exception of 1993 when he [Kuiper] went to Colorado. The team was being sold—he wasn't guaranteed a job—he had to go find a job elsewhere. Then the Giants brought him back the next year.

I get to go to work every day with my best friend. He was my best friend when I was playing: great teammate, fun, funny. We had the same relationship as players that we have now. We've been lucky enough to stay healthy and do all this. And you know what, we've had young families together and our kids are close; our wives are close. We've shared life together beyond the baseball field. It's pretty special to be able to go to work with your best friend.

When you started out, what was challenging for you as a broadcaster? What did you find hard your first year or two?

Oh my gosh, thank god for [longtime Giants broadcaster] Hank Greenwald. I really had some gifted broadcasters that I had a chance to work with, Ted Robinson Joe Angel, Lon Simmons. When I started, I was just a wild animal. I was talking the language of baseball; nobody knew what I was talking about, just vernacular from the bench. I was talking so fast. Hank would always tease me: "I need to pour a little water on you. Go drink some milk. Calm down." I could see the game, and I knew that there was a story within the game that was situational baseball. You try to convey what's going on in the minds of the hitter, the pitcher, the manager, everybody on the field. It was just a matter of being able to calm it all down and find a rhythm. It took years (laughs).

We did a little show as players (on KNBR, the radio station that broadcasts Giants games) so the Bay Area kind of got used to my voice. And they were patient with me. I was blessed with pretty good teachers. They covered for me when I would stick my foot my mouth, which I did on a number of occasions. We all do. You had to learn it.

It's sensual, broadcasting a baseball game, as is playing a game. You're smelling the cut grass, you're walking out there every day identifying how that field is going to play. Is it cold? Is it hot? Which way is the wind blowing? At Candlestick, you had to be able to identify that from inning to inning because it would change within the game. So you're relying on your senses; you're relying on sounds and smells and eyesight.

It's like a golfer or a fisherman. The weather has everything to do with how you're going to prepare that day. That's what you learn as a player, you learn how to do that. As a broadcaster you learn to be able to do that and to verbalize it, all of the sensuality going on with that game, and how important that is to that particular day. It such a great game, and we get to do it every day. No other sport does that every day. It's very cool because it's always different.

Would you say no other sport has the spaces and cadence of baseball, which offers the chance to set up the action?

Football allows you time to prepare a situation, what their options are, who the good matchups are. Hockey and basketball to a lesser degree, but baseball certainly. You have a chance to talk about what the situation is, what the pitcher type is, what the hitter type is, but you also have a track record. When you play every day, you know how hot a guy is. When you play once a week in football, you don't know if this guy is going to be in the same rhythm he was in last week. When you get a hot streak here, you can tell when a guy is hot. You see them every day. So that helps our ability to create anticipation. I think that is really what separates the men from the boys, when you can create anticipation of something that could happen and then have it happen. Baseball allows you to do that.

I can't count the number of times I've listened to you when you've predicted what was going to be thrown and where it's going to be hit. I've seen you call homers, which is kind of amazing considering how infrequently they're hit (about once every 33 plate appearances in 2018, according to Baseball Reference).

You get the smell for it. Like last night, San Diego's Franmil Reyes, we really like this kid. He's 6-5, 285 pounds, 23 years old. He hits the ball inside out; he's a good breaking ball hitter. We were watching his batting practice in the cage, and [in the game] he gets a hanging slider, middle in. Bang! Game over.

They took the lead. We never got it back. We had a feeling. Just two old ballplayers going, I'm feeling bad things here.

You seem to have found a balance between clearly being on the home team's side and still maintaining the utmost professionalism.

Well, I think you owe it to the game to be able to tell the stories of both teams because that's what makes it interesting. If a guy makes an error, you mention the error and move on. There's always a negative and positive side to a play. If a guy just hit a rocket to right field, well, the pitcher is pretty bummed out about that. If you don't exalt the opposition, then it minimizes the achievement of the home team. If you're talking about how great Manny Machado is, which he is, how exciting this Franmil Reyes is, and he is, if you don't mention that on the days that the Giants win, then it just doesn't seem like it's that much of an accomplishment. But when you've created a relationship with your listening audience of all the personalities involved, then they have an anticipation of fear when Machado's on deck.

I was raised in Los Angeles, and [renowned Dodger broadcaster] Vin Scully, that's how he did it. I always loved that about him, and I loved it when I was a player. I'd come in with the Cubs or the Phillies or the Giants, and he told your story, just like he told his own players' story. We all knew who Vin rooted for, but he also allowed you to know the opponent, to familiarize yourself with the greatness of who's out there on that field. It elevates the entire game of baseball, and it really adds to the achievement when your team wins. People are going, man did you see what he did to Machado? He struck him out three times. That's an accomplishment. If you don't know who Machado is, he's just another player.

That gets back to storytelling right? You're building suspense and creating drama; that's what keeps listeners riveted.

And we'd rather talk about a guy's at-bat, a hit to the opposite field, a one-hop topspin bullet to the second baseman that handcuffed him. He made an error but that was a hell of an at-bat.

After your playing career did you consider becoming a pitching coach? When you see something a player could do better, do you ever say anything to a coach or player?

When I got out of the game in 1990, Roger Craig offered me the job to be his pitching coach. And he said to Bob Brenly: "You be my bullpen coach, and I'll teach you how to be managers because I think you guys can do it." (Brenly became manager of the Arizona Diamondbacks in 2001 and led them to a championship that season.) It was such a compliment because we just adored Roger. I had five kids [including] a brand-new baby in December 1989; I couldn't leave. It hurt me to say no to Roger, and I've always had some regret about that.

As to whether or not I talk to (Giants pitching coaches) Curt Young or Matt Herges, I don't, out of respect for them because they're both really good. We talk baseball, and we talk pitching and whatnot over a beer on occasion, but I don't run to them and say: "Hey, I think this guy is opening up too soon," because they'll see it; they're that good. Same thing with hitting, you can't have a player listening to five or six or eight different voices. He's going to trust one voice. That's his teacher, his coach. I'm respectful of that so I just stay away from it. If they ask me a question on a plane or something like that, I'm more than happy to answer it, but I don't seek to share my experiences because I think it's the responsibility of the coaches.

You mentioned broadcasting the World Series runs of 2010, 2012, and 2014. How was it for all four of you to be in the radio booth together?

Well, it's rare because usually you have a radio team and a television team. When you get to the postseason, network TV picks up the playoffs. So all those television teams basically are done. They may do a pre- and post- [a show before or after a game] or some sideline stuff, but in most instances the radio team takes the helm and that's it; they don't share. Our situation is incredibly unique because Jon Miller and Dave Flemming do most of the radio, but when we get to the playoffs, we all share time. Dave, instead of doing three or four innings, he gets down to two, and Duane who was calling six innings (on TV), gets down to two. Everybody shares, and there's no greed. It's just the joy of telling that story. It's one of the things I'm most proud of about our team.

When I recall your playing career I think of your complete-game victory over St. Louis in the 1987 playoffs. When you look back, was that the moment?

No question, that was the pinnacle right there. I had won 20 (games) the year before. I was having arm troubles in '87; I won five games, and I had to pitch my ass off in September to make the postseason roster. Roger came to me before Game 4 and said, "Just give me three or four [innings], whatever you can. That night at Candlestick . . . as beautiful as this place is, as spectacular as Oracle Park is, it's nowhere near the volume of Candlestick. Candlestick was loud! It just reverberated; the noise spun around you. It wrapped around you. It was awesome—it invigorated you. You could go two days without sleep, walk in there, and if you were in the middle of that cheer, you'd walk out of there like you just had 10 cups of coffee. It was exhilarating.

That night in '87, we were down two games to one, everybody came in and the anticipation was so cool because every pitch in that game, there was a reaction from the crowd. As the moment built, and we got to the end of the game—it ended on a double play—the way that it erupted, I'm getting chills right now.

I am too.

It was the most incredible feeling that I've ever experienced. And it's the moment that I'm most proud of.

Thank you for that moment because we fans remember that.

That was a good one.

One thing you do on the air quite often is highlight teachable moments for Little Leaguers. Is that your way of teaching us all about the game?

We just had a Little League day on Sunday and there were about 1,500 or 2,000 Little Leaguers there with their moms and dads. A lot of these kids are five, six, seven, eight years old. You have all the moms and dads, boys and girls sitting there. They're all psyched up and they have their uniforms on. This is early in the year so the hats are new, the gloves are new; they're stiff.

It's such a cool moment in the lives of kids when their mom and dad support them in an event, whether it be dancing or football, soccer, baseball, whatever. That little one is looking to their parents for guidance and instruction. To be able as a baseball broadcaster to say something that might be passed on from the parent to the kid, thus establishing credibility in the eyes of the child because mom or dad has something to tell me about this, it works. That's the whole goal behind it.

We talk about things that are pretty basic: throwing skills, your eyes should pick up a target on the person's chest, and you should never take your eyes off the chest. Most people throw the ball and they watch it. Their eyes roll up because they're watching the ball. But when you throw it, your eyes never come off the target. And when you're throwing to the target, you don't throw to it; you throw through it.

When you talk about it on air, the parents are going to remember it. And when their eight-year-old little girl who is pitching that day is kind of lost because she can't throw strikes, mom is going to go out there and say: "Hey listen, keep your eyes on the target." There are moments in every game when you can pull out something pretty basic and describe it with the hope that it's going to get passed on. And a lot of times it does. We've had parents come up to us and say: "Hey thanks. That was a great tip. I didn't know that, but it really works."

I know you really enjoy playing music. Do you see any similarities between what you do in the broadcast booth and being creative or improvising while you're playing music?

Totally, because the story is always different. We don't know what we're going to talk about that night. We're going to talk about the game and something is going to remind us of something we did as a player. We don't know where the story is going to go. Inevitably something will happen that reminds us of something we haven't talked about in 20 years, but it's relevant to that moment in the game. So there is a lot of ad-lib; but the game brings that out of you.

It's the coolest part about why we love doing this game. It's never the same. Not only that but you're going to learn something new. I've been in professional baseball since 1973, what haven't I seen? There will be something tonight that happens that I haven't seen. You gotta roll with it. It's like the other day, [Giants second baseman] Joe Panik dives to his backhand side, spears a one-hop pea rod, and while he's lying on his stomach he does this hook shot. It's a perfect feed to [shortstop Brandon] Crawford who gets the out. I look at Kuip and he goes: "They don't practice that," and as broadcasters we don't either.

Hank Greenwald was so great because he would go through the periodicals every day: newspapers, magazines, whatever. He'd cut these little things out and have them in his mind; then he'd set them aside. All the stuff that he wrote down and prepared for that day, he may not use any of it [in the game]. But a week down the road something will happen and all of a sudden, it triggers the memory in his mind that he has something to enhance that moment. Sure enough there's a five-paragraph story that completely makes the broadcast, and he was ready for it. He set himself up to succeed. I think a lot of young broadcasters make the mistake of doing the homework and then feeling like they have to force-feed something into a game that doesn't fit. It's irrelevant. So we try to be relevant to the game with what we bring.

Could you talk a bit about your preparation process?

A lot of it is right here, watching BP [batting practice]. When I was a pitcher, I would watch batting practice of my opponent. Hitters will give themselves up; if they're pissed off, if they're goin' bad, if they're up there grinding. If they don't have a good session, or if they're pulling off the ball, they're walking out of the cage, shaking their head. If they're top-spinnin' the ball to the pull side, they're not backspinning the ball to the other side.

Then there's the other guy who's out there telling jokes; he's got no helmet on that day, and he's a freaking peacock getting into the batting cage. You watch him, he's backspinning the ball; he's hitting the ball behind the runner; he's launching balls halfway up the bleachers; he's doing any damn thing he wants. That's the guy you stay clear of. From up here it's easy to watch and see this guy's got it going right now, he's had a good batting practice today, so we watch that. We also watch how the ball is carrying, how the ballpark is playing.

You've been honored with Emmy awards, an All-Star selection, and the Willie Mac Award twice, given by players to their most inspirational teammate. What do these honors mean to you?

I was 10 years in the big leagues before I finally made an All-Star team. I made one All-Star team in 13 years.

That's one more than most players.

But I got to watch teammates go. I got to hear their stories when they came back. You wanted to hear about the other guys in the league—was so-and-so a good guy? Was this guy a dick? My idea of Keith Hernandez when he was playing with the Cardinals and the Mets, he was just a hard-ass competitor, smart, and a great player. But when I saw him in the clubhouse in Houston [at the All-Star game], he was a character with a great sense of humor. And we've been friends ever since.

So I really wanted to go, and I got a chance in 1986. I took my son who was seven years old, Jarek, my oldest. We were like two little seven-year-old kids. We got to the hotel, layin' in bed that night watching an All-Star channel. I came up and we were watching me on TV. He said: "Dad, that's the coolest thing ever." I go, "That is the coolest thing ever!" It was just such a great experience.

But the Willie Mac Award, that was different because you were elected by your teammates, and that means more than anything. Now it's evolved to where managers, trainers, coaches, former Willie Mac Award winners, and fans have a pretty strong voice in it. We watched it last year when Will

Smith won it. He was completely overwhelmed by it. He got to shake hands and look into the eyes of Willie Mac, and Willie Mac said to him: "You're who I voted for." That was the last one [while Willie McCovey was still alive; he died on October 31, 2018].

Do you have any sort of plan, like: I want to work five more years. Or do you just want to ride it as long as you can?

Stay on the horse. Just keep going, keep showing up. It's too much fun. I need this game now more than I ever did. C'mon, how lucky are we?

To the Ends of the Earth
DERVLA MURPHY

"Come over for lunch. You can help me get a few things done 'round the house. Ever since I hurt my shoulder, I haven't been able to do any hoovering," said Dervla Murphy, Ireland's most intrepid travel writer, when I let her know I was coming to the southern Ireland town of Lismore. I'd met the sturdy and informal author when we were panelists at the Key West Literary Seminar in 2006. That was a long way from Ireland: powder-blue skies, pink taxis, and abundant sunshine—Dervla had just returned from a reporting trip to Cuba for a book titled, *The Island that Dared*.

A few years after I met her in Key West, I had the chance to visit Dervla—she's far too informal to be called Ms. Murphy—at her Lismore home in County Waterford. On the banks of the River Blackwater, Lismore dates to the year 636 and is best known for its commanding castle, which now hosts a farmers market on weekend mornings. Lismore is a place almost removed from time, a town no longer served by trains, a village that didn't get mauled by the Celtic Tiger. "The streams of history run very deep through Lismore," said then-Mayor Bernard Leddy.

Born in 1931, Dervla remains feisty and unapologetically liberal, a true populist who sides with the world's underdogs because her travels have shown her how the deck is stacked. Her father was the county librarian, so she grew up in a family that treasured books.

In 1963, Dervla rode her Armstrong Cadet bicycle through Europe during one of the coldest winters of the 20th century, then continued pedaling solo across Iran and Afghanistan, all the way to India. *Full Tilt*, her book about this journey, was enthusiastically received and put her on the literary map. At the time, solo cycling to remote regions was something women just didn't do, and Dervla served as an inspiration to many. Perhaps the most harrowing moment of that trip was when she was pursued by wolves in the country then known as Yugoslavia.

Until she reached her eighties, Dervla traveled the hard way: in Ethiopia with a mule, across Tibet on foot, through 1,300 miles of the Andes on horseback. Her titles just hint at her adventurous spirit: *Muddling Through Madagascar, Eight Feet in the Andes* (a reference to her and her daughter's two feet, and the horse's four hooves), *One Foot in Laos* (she'd injured her leg and hobbled through that country), *Through Siberia by Accident* (she'd intended to cycle but a leg injury changed her plans), and *South from the Limpopo* (a journey through South Africa after the fall of apartheid). She's long emphasized the importance of taking meticulous notes daily, before memories are colored by subsequent events. During her travels, she slept with her arms around her journal and said the loss of any other item wouldn't concern her, but that her journal was "the one thing I would defend with my life."

Though she dismisses the health issues she's faced during more than a half century of rigorous travel, there has been "amoebic dysentery in Pakistan, brucellosis in India, gout and hepatitis in Madagascar, and tick bite fever in South Africa," according to The Guardian, a British newspaper. "She fractured her coccyx and broke her foot in Romania, badly injured her knee and ankle in Siberia, and required a new hip after a fall in Palestine." But "the triple tooth abscess in Cameroon was the most painful of all," she said. "I thought I was going mad." Yet her most frightening encounter may have been when she was cornered by armed bandits in Ethiopia during her 1966-67 journey there. "That was nasty, and I knew it was very much in the balance," she told The Guardian. "I was lucky then. Extremely lucky."

Approaching Lismore in spring, I marveled at the broad River Blackwater (which some have called Ireland's Rhine), the blooming rhododendrons, and lush emerald hills that surround the town. In the pubs, locals welcome you into their circle, and Irish music spontaneously takes flight, as people drop in to play together. In a pub called The Classroom, I met Joe the postman who takes his tools on his route, in case any of the older women need something fixed. Most people have lived here for several generations—I overheard a conversation about a man whose parents had moved to Lismore in the 1950s. The comment, suggesting the native was a newcomer, "Oh he just blew in, did he?"

When it was time to visit Dervla, I arrived at The Old Market's towering iron gates. She greeted me with a powerful bear hug and thrust a can of beer into my hand. I hesitated—it wasn't yet noon and I'd only been awake a couple of hours. Dervla laughed and raised a toast to debauchery, saying in ebullient southern Irish tones: "I love debauching people." We spoke first in Dervla's untamed garden, the music of birdsong and the bleats of sheep complementing the conversation, then moved inside.

When she was 10 years old, Dervla told me, she sat on Round Hill, about a mile from The Old Market, and vowed to pedal her bike to India. In her twenties, she became her mother's primary caregiver, and it wasn't until her mother passed that she was able to fulfill her promise of completing that arduous ride. During our conversation, Dervla laughed about how she took her tea from a mug at a time when ladies used a cup and saucer, her penchant for blue jeans when women wore skirts or dresses, and her decision to have a baby out of wedlock because she wanted a child but not a husband. Into her eighties, with her short gray hair, powerful build, ruddy complexion, and exuberant spirit, Dervla appeared ready to embark on her next adventure.

When I asked her if there's any place she didn't visit but wished she had, she said: "I do wish I'd sailed down the Yangtze before they put in the three dams." She asked me where I'd been recently and I told her that a magazine had sent me to Patagonia where I stayed in an upscale ecolodge. "I'd run a mile from that!" she said, shuddering at the luxury. "I really would."

Later we talked in her dining area, which like the home's other rooms has bookshelves covering most of the wall space. A Tibetan flag, a gift from the Dalai Lama whom she'd met decades earlier, covers her typewriter. Her terrier Wurzel rested comfortably on her lap. In Ireland many people name their houses; Dervla's home is called The Old Market. But this isn't just a name—for several centuries this was Lismore's center of commerce. Artifacts, such as a rusted wagon wheel, remain strewn throughout her overgrown yard.

"So how did your *event* go yesterday," Dervla asked, laughing at the word I'd used to describe an appearance in Lismore the night before to promote my book, *A Sense of Place*.

"Is 'event' too grand a word?" I responded.

"No, it's just that the word amuses me," Dervla said. "To me, event suggests something really momentous, really important. So when I'm told I'm having an event in Edinburgh or wherever, it's as though I'm coming along and creating an earthquake," she said with her hearty laugh. "It's ridiculous."

With our pints drained it was time to get to work. Dervla, tilting a bit and hunched due to her shoulder injury, retreated to the kitchen, affirming our arrangement: "A little hoovering, then a little lunch." She showed me to an old vacuum with a long hose and metal cylindrical attachment. I started in the dining area, which is also where she writes on her computer. The place looked as though the dust had piled up for months; the suction pulled up clumps of matted dog hair. I pushed the hose under the counter when suddenly the vacuum started to wheeze. A thermos top lodged at the front of the hose. I handed it to Dervla and she exclaimed, "I haven't seen that in years!"

Dervla brought out a salad of boiled potatoes, hard-boiled eggs, and peas with abundant mayonnaise, accompanied by tomato salad and a loaf of home-baked brown bread. Then she went back to the kitchen and emerged with an armload of cold beers. "The drunken orgy's underway!" she hollered. "I'm a wreck."

Another pint drained, I asked where the bathroom was and Dervla laughed, thrust her arm toward her neglected garden and bellowed, "Go kill a weed!" After a dessert of rhubarb with ginger and custard, Dervla poured coffee and lit a slender cigar. We talked about Lismore's annual travel writers festival, called Immrama. Dervla planned to leave Lismore because she didn't want people "fizzing" about her.

She invited me to spend the night in The Old Market's "piggery," which had been converted into a simple bedroom—it's where Michael Palin slept when he visited. Though I wished the conversation could roll on forever, I had to leave for a meeting in Dublin.

As I moved toward the heavy wrought iron gates, I looked up at a spire rising in the distance. "That's the Catholic church," Dervla growled. "The other one (Protestant) is over there. As far as I'm concerned you can have them all."

She gave me a farewell hug, asked if I had another "event" tonight, then howled with laughter as the gates of The Old Market clanged shut.

≈ ≈ ≈

Let's start by talking about this place and what it means to you, this home, Lismore, County Waterford. You were born here, right?

I wouldn't want to live anywhere else. I do think it's one of the most beautiful places in the world. It's very quiet, really. Obviously I am biased because I've seen so many really magnificent landscapes in so many different countries, but I suppose I just feel I belong here. I think I'm very lucky because there have been so many changes in Ireland for the worse during the past 15 or 20 years. But this little corner of West Waterford is unchanged from the time I first remember it 75 years ago and I was learning to swim with my grandfather.

This collection of buildings that you call home, what's the history here?

I bought this place, The Old Market, years ago (1978 or '79). It literally was the old market of the town and had been for centuries. But then it had been unused since the market was closed in 1909. My study, that building there, was a dwelling in the late 17th and early 18th centuries; then it was converted into a forge, and now it's been converted into my study. When I bought this place it was a complete ruin, no roof and rubble piled up inside, earth and weeds and all the rest. So I bought it from a friend, an artist and Englishwoman, and she had hoped to do a certain amount of restoring work that I've since done, but her personal circumstances didn't allow her to do all she planned to do.

I remember in your book, Full Tilt, *when you were about 10 years old you were given a secondhand atlas—*

And a secondhand bicycle.

And you went up to a hill here in Lismore and vowed that you would ride to India. Is that hill near here?

Yes! I can remember the exact spot, about a mile away, a mile and a half maybe. That was by the Round Hill, which historically was the first site of Lismore.

Beyond your roots and beyond the beauty of the place, what connects you here?

Well, that's enough. It's a feeling for the landscape, really. I can't imagine living anywhere else.

But you always felt eager to travel, to see new places?

Oh yes! Having said that, neither can I imagine living here permanently. Definitely not! It's a place to which I always have to come back, but then when I finish a book, I always have to get away from it. I can't imagine being here not working. Though, no, correction, people often say to me, where do you spend your holidays? Well, I spend them here, because at the end of the book, my holiday is to invite my friends to stay. While I'm working, I don't have any social life. So then maybe for a month or two, I just relax with friends and drink lots of beer, while planning the next journey.

When you're working, you work very intensely. What is your process? Is it that you come back from a trip, transcribe notes, and then just write?

I come back with lots and lots of notes, far more than I ever use, because every day I have to make notes as I go along or I forget the details. Then I lock the gates and just settle down to work. Some people think that I'm just being neurotic because most writers can lead normal social lives—they don't have to lock themselves away. But I find that distractions, say going out for an evening with friends, it just breaks my concentration. It's not just a question of going out for an evening—it would take me two or three days to get back to where I was before I went out. The other thing is that when I'm writing about somewhere like Cuba or Siberia, mentally I stay where I'm writing about. And that's much more difficult to do if you have intervals of normal social life.

Do you curtail other distractions as well? I find it easy to get side-tracked by television or the internet.

Well, I don't have television, and I just got the computer so it doesn't form any sort of temptation.

Typically how long do you work to produce a book after a trip?

It really is so different, depending on the amount of reading you have to do. I would say much, much longer now than with my earlier books because they were more straightforward accounts of journeys, and latterly the books have been much more political in a sense, or dealing with the social problems of the country I'm traveling through. And that needs much more research. That's too pretentious a word really, but more reading up.

That makes sense because the nature of travel writing has changed. When you rode your bike in 1963 to places like Afghanistan, it was so exotic that I think all you had to do was write about the place.

Yes, it's completely different. But also I think travel writers as they get older, they're no longer satisfied to write about the excitement of traveling. They're looking more below the surface.

I think that's what readers want today. They want more than travelogue. They want a human connection or sense of the social/political condition.

Yes, because they can go and travel for themselves now in a way I suppose you could say the majority of people didn't do in the 1950s and '60s.

And even if they don't go there's so much more media saturation.

Yes, they can see it everywhere on television, documentaries. No landscape is strange now to anybody.

So what do you do in your later books that you didn't do earlier?

Definitely deal with the political in the wider sense, the frightful mess that we're making of the world. And it's getting grimmer by the minute.

I've read about some of the great women travel writers that you consider influences: Freya Stark, Isabella Bird. Can you tell me why they appeal to you so much?

I wasn't able to travel outside of Europe until I was 31.

You were taking care of your mother.

That's right, yes. Those travelers—Freya, Isabella Bird, Mary Kingsley, they all had done the things I longed to do, so I suppose they were my way of escape. Of all of them, I suppose Isabella Bird was the real kindred spirit, just the way she did things. She just sort of went along and took things as they came, no fussing. She didn't regard her journeys as any big deal, even though they were.

I remember within the first quarter of Full Tilt, *you were riding through rain up to your knees, snow that was maybe higher—*

That was the coldest winter of the 20th century.

I wondered as I read that, why did she choose to travel in winter?

I was so impatient after 16 years (of caring for) my invalid mother. I just couldn't wait. It's as simple as that. I love traveling by bicycle, but I don't think I've ever chosen to ride in those conditions. Obviously, when I planned the journey I didn't know that the coldest winter of the century was about to start. I might have thought twice if I'd known that. It was really, really quite an extraordinary winter.

Now that you've done it, are you glad that you did it?

I never think about it at all actually unless somebody brings it up in an interview. That's half a century ago.

Tell me about what has attracted you to Africa. You wrote a book In Ethiopia with a Mule—

That was one of the best.

What made it so special?

Well, the extraordinary landscape, being able to escape completely from the 20th century. There was a period of six weeks when I was in an area where people just didn't use money and when I didn't see any object that had been made outside of the area. Everything was made of wood and corn and stone. I don't think that could happen anywhere in the world now.

I've been to some remote places, but there's always a Michael Jordan T-shirt or—

A tin of Coca-Cola. After that, Rachel and I went to Madagascar when she was 14, and then Cameroon. Cameroon came about because I wrote to friends who had recently retired after living there for a very long time. They said you should go to the highlands of Cameroon with a packhorse so that's what Rachel and I did. That was our last journey together until Cuba when the granddaughters were with me too. It was a fabulous journey but rather stressful because our horse was scared away one night by a leopard when we were camping. We were left there with all our camping gear, probably about 150 miles from the nearest motor road, but anyway we overcame that; we borrowed a donkey that somehow got us out.

Could you tell me how your travels differed when you began traveling with your daughter and if that changed the reaction of the local people to you?

Yes, well of course she was only five when we first traveled together in Coorg (for the book, *On a Shoestring to Coorg: An Experience of Southern India*). The Coorg journey was very mild. That was tailored for a five-year-old to break her in to travel outside of Europe. There is a special sort of quality about traveling with a small child. And she was nine when we trekked through the Andes. People receive you more readily in very remote places if you're accompanied by a small child.

Later on, in Cameroon, when Rachel was 18, I realized that it would be our last journey together for some time because at 18 she was her own person and wanted to make her own journeys. Now it was two adults in the eyes of the people we met. That definitely put up a barrier—I don't mean anything unpleasant—it was just that much more difficult to get on easy terms with the local people.

And then you had another chance when Rachel had kids and you went to Cuba with the grandchildren.

That was wonderful. That was for a month with Rachel and the three grandchildren. Then I went back for three months and then I went back for another month. Three trips. As you well know, it's quite a complicated country. When did you go?

In 2001, I spent a couple of weeks biking around the eastern part of the country.

It wasn't a country I would have wanted to cycle in. It would have been far too hot. I have no heat resistance. I don't mind spending three months in Siberia in the middle of winter, but Cuba, the heat. And it wasn't their hot season. Anyway, how were you treated?

Overall, I found that most people were willing to accept me and could distinguish between American individuals and their government. I was there when George W. Bush was inaugurated (January 2001) and I was probably more upset than most Cubans. So tell me more about your impressions of Cuba.

I think we have so much to learn from Cuba that we better get on with it pretty fast. I personally would not want to live in a country where I couldn't travel, where I would be confined to my own country, and where I couldn't write exactly what I felt

like writing, where I would to some extent be censored. That
said, thinking of the majority of the population, and compar-
ing it with the huge areas of the so-called Third World that
I've seen, I think the Cubans are damn lucky. Compare them
to the Haitians or almost anybody in Latin America. And
the other thing is from the point of view of the environment,
remember when you went to get your fruit juice, you didn't
get it in some polystyrene thing by the side of the road. You
got it in a glass or a mug that was washed and reused. That's
what we need to get back to, and fast!

What I found so wonderfully relaxing was the absence of
the consumer society with its incessant advertising and press-
ing people to buy what they don't need, the completely arti-
ficial wants that are created now. You can't have a growth
society on a planet that has its natural limitations.

*What we are doing now is not sustainable. We came across organic
farms in Cuba that were organic out of necessity because people
could not afford pesticides and herbicides.*

That's right. And the way they collected all the dung. Did you
notice the horses wearing their nappies (diapers), every ounce
of dung collected?

*You seem to have a different vision of success than most people. It's
not about material gain. What is success to you, and do you feel
like you've achieved it?*

Just to be free to travel and to write. As long as you have
enough money to protect you from having to worry about
money, you don't need any more than that. I can't see why
people want millions. And once they've got millions, then of
course they want billions. I can't understand it (laughs). But
then it takes all sorts.

Do you think that becoming more political has caused you to lose some readers?

Oh, I think definitely. To some extent, I think I've acquired a different sort of reader. I know that from the letters I get from readers. Some of them say, "Why have you gone so political— why can't you just keep on telling us about your journeys?" And then others say, "I'm glad you've begun to take an interest in the problems of the countries you travel through."

You've become an ambassador for bicycle touring.

Which is ridiculous, really. If you think of it: *Full Tilt*, cycling, yes, but Ethiopia walking; Madagascar walking, Peru walking. So most of my major journeys have been on foot rather than on bicycle. But then back on the bicycle for Africa, from Kenya down to Cape Town. More than half the really significant journeys have been on foot rather than on two wheels. But because *Full Tilt* somehow caught the public imagination, I've ever since been trademarked "cyclist."

I can't conclude this interview without asking about the numerous ways you've injured yourself during your travels.

Well, really very little when you think about it. Some of the worst things have happened right here at home. I seriously shattered my left arm. I have seven pins and a plate in it.

That was when you tripped over your cat?

That's right, Sebastian, there in the doorway. The bullock (castrated bull) fracturing my spine, that was down by the river. I'd come out after a swim, and this herd were in the field where I swam every day. I was drying my hair with a big towel flapping, and a salmon jumped, a huge salmon. This is one of Europe's most famous salmon rivers. I moved over to the very edge of the bank to watch and see if it would jump again as they often do. One of the bullocks rushed up behind me and tossed me back into the river and fractured my spine, though I didn't discover that for 10 days. It was all very painful and unpleasant.

I was one of the leading figures in the Campaign for Nuclear Disarmament. I appeared on the platform [at a Dublin anti-nuclear event] absolutely covered in plaster from armpits to groin, but I still spoke against Reagan. It was a good time out. I think the public has lost heart now.

Do you feel like there's apathy?

Ya. Militaries have taken over the world. They really have.

I won't ask 'What's your favorite place?' but are there places you've fallen in love with?

Several places. You can begin with Afghanistan. And I think that's why I'm so desperately upset by what goes on there now. Ethiopia, the fact that you were completely escaping from our 20th-century world. It could have been any century, and wonderful people. And well of course the Andes, but you can't say favorite place.

What would you say you are most proud of?

My daughter, and my three granddaughters.

More than your books?

Of course.

You were able to do so much traveling before the age of connectivity. I had one trip on my own just after college when I really got away. That was to Central America in 1989-90. A decade later I was in Laos and most travelers were hunkered over computers in net cafes writing emails home.

Well I often think about the grandchildren, that it is no longer possible to travel the way Rachel and I traveled in times past. I don't think there are any really remote, genuinely isolated parts of the world now that you could get there on your own, without any outside help. That's the difference I think.

Any final thoughts?

It's quite important for the young as they think about and plan their travels not to try to do too much, not to go too quickly. This sort of round the world, collecting passport stamps and visas, that's not travel. So many of the youngsters now are so lucky that they actually can afford to travel, but I think they should be so much more selective. Choose one country or if the country is big enough, one area of the country, and spend three or six months there, instead of whoosssh-hhh around the globe.

Less is more.

Absolutely. They don't know whether they're coming or going.

❧ ❧ ❧

Postscript: I returned to Ireland in the spring of 2017 for a quick trip that was to end with a couple of days of touring the western and northern parts of the country. But it felt wrong to visit Ireland and not see Dervla, who was then 85. I emailed her to let her know

*I was in Ireland and would come down to Lismore if she were
available. I quickly got the following response:*

Hurrah!!! Will be delighted to see you next Thurs. The past
4 years have taken their toll on me but still able to down the
beers! Longing for your news from Trumpdom . . .

Love, Dervla

Songs from the Heartland
GREG BROWN

Greg Brown was humming when we met, his deep baritone a perfect counterpoint to the chirpy croaking of countless frogs in the marsh behind the cookie-cutter hotel in Sebastopol, about 50 miles north of San Francisco. It wasn't as though Brown was humming a catchy tune he'd just heard. Rather, the music was coming from deep within him, welling up like an overflowing spring. Tall and brawny with a mop of unruly dark brown hair, the Iowa folk singer met me on a rainy March afternoon in the west Sonoma County town of Sebastopol, about an hour's drive north of San Francisco. The town, where Brown would play that night, suited him just fine: progressive, down-to-earth, with lots of mom-and-pop stores on Main Street.

Brown was born in 1949 in the Hacklebarney region of Iowa; his mother played electric guitar and his father was a traveling preacher. Brown grew up in the 1950s listening to church songs, Irish ballads, Ozark hollers, bluegrass, gospel, rock, and unvarnished country music. When he was 18, he rounded up fellow folkies for hootenannies at Gerdes Folk City in New York's Greenwich Village and knocked around L.A. and Las Vegas before returning to the Midwest, getting married, and having a baby. Brown played bars and clubs, but he was barely eking out a living. To supplement his income he'd taken odd jobs including working at a meatpacking plant where in an accident his left thumb was severed just above the knuckle. As his 30th birthday approached, he decided to go back to school to pursue a career in forestry.

That's when Garrison Keillor called. Brown's appearances on *A Prairie Home Companion* didn't make him an American idol—he wouldn't have wanted that anyway—but it built his following and enabled him to support his family by working as a musician. The New York Times has described Brown as an "itinerant Iowa Zen beatnik folkie, with a voice so deep, rutted and dark it seems as if it's slithered up out of some primordial ooze, singing about the poet Kenneth Rexroth, slant-six engines, and the wind-swept corners of Iowa and Kansas."

Brown may not be a household name, but devoted fans and fellow songwriters revere him. His songs have been covered by Carlos Santana, Joan Baez, Ani DiFranco, Shawn Colvin, and Willie Nelson. As evocative as Brown's lyrics are, you have to hear his music to fully appreciate it. His songs have a poetic quality, and his guitar playing and resonant voice can make the most stoic among us weep. Unimpressed with the music business, in the late 1970s Brown founded his own label, Red House Records, which published his work as well as albums by fellow folkies including John Gorka, Ramblin' Jack Elliott, and Lucy Kaplansky. Brown has garnered Grammy nominations, and Rolling Stone said he's "a wickedly sharp observer of the human condition." On a tribute CD called *Going Driftless*, female artists, including Gillian Welch, Lucinda Williams, and Victoria Williams interpret his songs.

During our interview, conducted before Donald Trump became president, Brown said he rarely writes overtly political songs. "I don't really think that politics and music make a very good combination," he said. "The songs tend to be finger-pointing; they tend to be divisive." But the 2016 election changed that. Shortly after Trump became president, Brown released "Trump Can't have That," a song about people coming together and taking care of what they love. It has a melancholic tone but ends on a hopeful note. "Let's keep talking and walking too, let's stay together the whole way through," Brown sings. "Let's keep holding on to what is right. Let's keep protecting every little light."

Brown has three children from his first marriage, including Pieta Brown, a musician who began touring in the early 2000s. In 2002, Brown married folk singer Iris DeMent. The couple moved to Brown's farmhouse in southern Iowa, not far from where he grew up. Late in our interview, I asked Brown what type of music he likes. "I really like listening to my wife," he says, laughing at the double entendre. Do he and Iris sing together? "She says she can't sing with me because I don't ever sing anything the same way twice, which is true. For her I would try to but . . ." His voice trails off. As in his songwriting, not everything is said, but you know exactly what he means.

⁊ ⁊ ⁊

Did having a musician and a preacher in the family lead you into music and a creative life?

It might have, but some people have the same influences and experiences as I did and end up being a lawyer. I think it's something that's kind of inborn. The church music was good—my dad was a good singer, my mother sang and played guitar. My grandma and grandpa both played and sang, uncles . . . There are a lot of storytellers on the Ozark side of the family. I was exposed to all that stuff really early. I sang in the car, sang in church, and eventually ended up singing onstage. You have to have an inclination that way, and then if you have a lot of music before you when you're little, that has an effect too. It's kind of a two-way street.

When you were a kid, did you think playing music was something you might do, or did you think you might want to be a fireman or a baseball player?

You know, I really liked singing and playing, but I didn't really care a lot for show business. I started playing when I was 18 or 19; I went to New York, then ended up in Los Angeles and Las Vegas. I knocked around for a while and I met people in the music business, and I thought, hmmm, I don't really think that's for me [laughs].

I came back to the Midwest and got married, and we had a little baby. I never stopped playing and writing, but in terms of doing it professionally, I stopped for about five years.

Then I just gradually eased back into it when I was about 30. But I didn't really see it going anywhere so I was going to go back to school and study forestry. Then I got a call from *Prairie Home Companion*, and people started recording my songs. After I did the *Prairie Home* show I could go a lot of places I hadn't been, and I could get some kind of a crowd because they'd heard me on the show. A lot of stuff just kind of fell in my lap so I stayed with music; otherwise I'm sure I'd be doing something different now.

You might be in a forest somewhere.

I might be.

I think you're one of our finest songwriters in terms of the way the lyrics work with the music. How do you write?

When I get to writing, it comes in fits and starts. I do keep a notebook where I write various things down that occur to me, a little bit of words, little bit of melody, but when I really get to writing the biggest change for me is that I feel like some part of me kind of wakes up. Things I would not ordinarily notice, I do notice, rhythms, words, all the things that go into a song. I get kind of hypersensitive for a while. And it's done usually in a few months. Then I just go back to poking around. Writing to me, it feels like a gift. I try to get good at my craft; I try to be a better singer, it's important to work at that. But the whole deal of writing songs is fairly mysterious to me in that I don't know exactly where it comes from. In another way it seems very common. I think it's a very human activity. And I think we've been walking along and beating on a stick and singing some kind of little chant or song for about as long as we've been here. Writing is just a very natural human thing to do.

In Australia the aboriginals trace their path through life, literally, through song.

There's that great scene in Bruce Chatwin's book (*The Song-lines*) where several of them are riding in a Jeep and it's going fast and they're just singing for all they're worth. I feel kind of like that (laughs).

Are you saying you feel life is going faster and faster and you're trying to keep up?

Not really. Society is definitely cranked up, but you've got to live your own life. Everyone is affected by things going on, but I never did get in the fast lane.

I recall you saying that after you wrote the 1994 album The Poet Game, *you were trying to write another* Poet Game *and then you realized that you wrote* The Poet Game *already, and it was time to do something new.*

Yeah, but I've never thought too much in terms of albums. I never write for an album. I just write when I write; eventually if I feel like making an album I'll dig through and see what I got. I did really enjoy writing the songs that went on *The Poet Game.* A lot of them are fairly long, involved and wordy. I wanted to keep doing it, and I tried to do that for while and realized, well, that's not really what's in there. And so once again I just had to stop and listen and wait, and let what was wanting to come out, come out.

You've set William Blake's poetry to music.

In terms of the things I've loved in my life, if someone said choose between poetry and music, I'd be screwed because I don't differentiate between the two. I heard Blake poems when I was a little child. I just think he's a remarkable poet. He himself *sang* the "Songs of Innocence and Experience." Michael Doucet, from BeauSoleil [a Cajun band], who's a Blake scholar, told me that William Blake played guitar. I still love those poems. I'll take a poem I love and put some music with it.

Poems, good poems, are music really. And when you hear a good poet reading, they're really singing their poems. Poetry without the musical element to me, it's not poetry, it's something else. If the music isn't there, if the rhythm and the sound are not there . . . poetry is not a position paper or anything, it's a song. So people like Allen Ginsberg, Gary Snyder, Lawrence Ferlinghetti, William Carlos Williams, Walt Whitman, these all have been very important singers to me.

One thing that distinguishes your art: you'll often pause in the middle of a song and tell a tale, like that story you tell in the middle of "Canned Goods." How do storytelling and song work together?

They work together very well. I remember way back hearing Lead Belly (Huddie William Ledbetter), it might have been "Rock Island Line." As he played, he told the story about the train that was coming through. I loved the whole thing—it's really fairly common in country blues where a story and a song will go right along with each other. Old sermons too, the old singing style of Pentecostal sermon—the preacher would preach a while and then he would often burst into song. The preaching itself often had a very songlike quality. It's all kind of one deal—I don't see any reason to chop it up if it feels natural. When I started singing that song "Canned Goods," I wanted to tell people a little bit about where the song came from, so a story just seemed to fit right in.

But it does sound as though your stories are carefully crafted.

The stories start out spontaneously, and then they'll change over time. I approach performing more like a jazz player would where you just kind of start and know the basic structure of the song and then you play with it and improvise. I might improvise new words. I might go to a different tune, or a different rhythm. I don't really have a plan—I try to work on the inside so that whatever comes out will have some push behind it.

In "Spring Wind" on the album Dream Cafe, *you sing: "We're a cross between our parents and hippies in a tent." Are you still a cross between your parents and hippies in a tent?*

I'm still definitely a mix. A lot of stuff from the hippie days was really good stuff. A lot of it has had a profound effect over the years on American culture, paying attention to food, what we eat and how it's grown, that comes up out of those days. The whole idea of living in a more communal way instead of everything being based on competition, the whole anti-materialistic approach, I think was a very good way to live in this world. I think hyper-capitalism has led us to the brink of the abyss. Whether or not we'll go, I have no idea. But I know that unbridled greed and a life based solely on accumulating possessions and selling stuff is a recipe for doom. So a lot of the old hippie stuff made really good sense, but of course the powers that be try to turn it into a joke, and you can see where that's brought us.

I certainly feel very much a part of my parents. Most people have that experience of doing something that you didn't know you're going to do. Then you think, why did I do that? I went out and bought a cheap sleeping bag somewhere and put it on my bed. I thought, why am I doing this? The next day I remembered, oh, my dad, when he was about this age for some reason he had a sleeping bag on his bed. But I just went and got the bag—we all do things like that. That's who we are.

You seem very connected to your Iowa roots, and I sense you're spending more time at home and less on the road.

I feel like I'm easing out of touring. I might do a few gigs around the Midwest, but I'm definitely heading out of it.

Is it the rigors of the road or do you just like being home?

Well, both of those: The road gets less interesting after a while, but also traveling now, when you fly you feel like you're a criminal. And the whole landscape now is just so corporate. It's just not very interesting anymore. That plus just having done it for a long time, it's time to stay home more. It just feels right.

You live on a farm in Iowa?

I got about 190 acres of land around there. The land there is very cheap—you can't really farm on it or anything—it's pretty rough land. I'm in the very southern county, Van Buren County. That area is old coal mining country and in general the soil is not good—it's clay. Up along the Mississippi River, there's some very pretty country particularly up in northeast Iowa called the Driftless Area.

When I listen to somebody like Bruce Cockburn, I hear more of a political bent. Do you ever think about getting more political?

I became more political in my songs during the (George W.) Bush administration. A lot of political songs I don't really like. I don't really think that political speaking and music often make for a very good combination. The songs tend to be finger-pointing; they tend to be divisive, and I haven't written very many of them. In my songs mostly the political elements are a background for the story. A song like "The Worrisome Years" talks about a couple having trouble. The background is the political situation that has led them there. I find that those kinds of things work much better in the background.

Let's get back to songwriting. The show that really hooked me on your music was when I was living out in Mendocino County. You played at the grange hall in the Anderson Valley when you were touring The Poet Game. *It seemed like you had this fountain of words come out, and now your music seems more ruminative and meditative.*

That's really hard for me to answer because I'm inside of it. I think what you're saying is probably true, but the whole process is not something I can step back from and analyze too much. Writing and singing since I was little has just been part of who I am, part of what I do. It came very naturally to me.

The one thing I can tell you is that around the time of *The Poet Game* there was a big batch of songs; I really liked them, and I wanted to write more songs like that. I tried, and it just wasn't happening. And as soon as I gave up on that and kind of let the songs come in as they wanted to, they turned out to be a lot simpler, different songs than what I wanted to write. Those songs became *Further In*.

I feel like my job is to listen and to be open. I don't have a way of directing it very much. In terms of being critically aware of what I do, you have to be your own critic. If I write a song I hope I know if it's got life in it, if it's got juice, if it's a song. I usually know that, but not always. I'm sure there are a number of clinkers along the way.

I once heard Carlos Santana say that for him it's about clearing the channel.

Yeah, that's very much how I feel. When I start writing I feel very awake. It's like all your senses are much more alert—you hear things you wouldn't hear—you just pick up on a lot of things. Several times I've had an idea that I wanted to write a certain kind of song—maybe a ballad or a soul tune, I had a definite thing in mind that I wanted to go for. But I find if I try too hard to write a certain kind of song, that's about the best way to guarantee that nothing will happen. You have to be prepared: Just waiting for inspiration to come is not going to get you very far, and when it does come you gotta be ready. A lot of it is just listening, listening to what's going on.

But you just have to keep working—Santana would probably say the same thing—you gotta keep playing your guitar and listening to things, but that's because you love it. You do those things naturally if you're into it. I never feel like I'm forcing myself to do something for some outcome. It's really a beautiful thing to be a part of. I feel grateful to have gotten to be a part of the whole communal effort. Music is so many people of all different styles and cultures. You really are all in it together somehow. You learn from each other. I feel links back to a time that not even much is known about. Songs, poetry, whatever you want to call it, that urge, it just goes way, way, way back there. And that's a good connection to feel to life. It's hard for me to imagine life without that.

It sounds like you're connected not just with songwriters but with this poetic tradition.

I do have this feeling that there are such deep connections between theater and music and dance and I would say religion. All these things, the connections go back so far. Poetry has gotten pretty far from its origins. It's not oral anymore—it's something written more for the page. When you hear poets read, a lot of them don't seem to be aware of the poem being anything like a song with rhythm and melody. A lot of the poetry I love does have that urge to it—it has music. I have tapes of Pablo Neruda reading which make me weep; he's singing. I've heard old tapes of Ezra Pound and Gary Snyder, the poet from right around here. Gary is a little more formal, but his reading is like little Zen movements—it's very musical.

Didn't you read a Gary Snyder poem at the Kate Wolf Festival years ago?

I did—it ended up on the collection, *In the Hills of California*. It's called "For All." It starts off, he's outside, he's running down the slope, he's down by a river, and then he pledges allegiance not to the flag but to our world, to Turtle Island, the old Indian name. It's a beautiful poem; I feel very connected to that kind of poetry that has not lost the old chant factor.

I was in Ireland and when I told this bearded man that I'm a writer he said, "Oh, a failed talker, are ya?" because in the Celtic world, if you can't tell a story, you write it. I was there for Blooms-day [June 16] when they dress as characters from James Joyce's Ulysses. *They read the book aloud in the town square, and act it out down at Sandy Cove. I finally got it. I tried to read that damn book in college and couldn't get through it, but when people started reading aloud it came to life.*

Very musical book, as is *Finnegan's Wake* [also written by Joyce]. *Finnegan's Wake* is so intellectually complex, but I love reading it just for the sound—I love the music in there. I don't know what else is in there with all the poems from 12 languages, but I love the sound of it.

Wasn't it invented language?

You could call it invented language, there are a lot of different languages mixed in there, words he invents, but the rhythm of it is just great, the sound of it. It's almost like an Irish person speaking in tongues.

Your father was an itinerant Pentecostal preacher—do you see your life as a performer as following in your father's footsteps?

Friends of mine have told me that. In a way I see myself as continuing my father's work, just trying to spread that message or whatever you want to call it, that feeling. Get people together and get that good thing going in the room, that's a beautiful thing.

*That's one of those rare moments where that spirit of community
is rekindled in our culture.*

I think so too—music has a very strong role to play there.

*When I was driving here I saw a bumper sticker that said, "Music
really does make the world a better place."*

Mmm-hmm. It really does. You know, a lot of music I really
love, like Ali Farka Touré, he sings in French and he sings in
some African languages: I don't understand his lyrics but yet
I do. Music can communicate across all those barriers. Sometimes when people talk about song lyrics, I think: That's not
really it; it's the whole of a song that really reaches out to people. When I first hear a song, I'm listening to the whole thing,
and I won't really pay much attention to the lyrics specifically.
That's part of it.

So what's the rest of it?

You could call it the groove, the feeling. It's a physical reaction to it. I don't even remember the first time I heard Mavis
Staples sing, but today we were driving up here, and Mavis
came on the radio singing along with Jerry Lee Lewis of all
people. When Mavis starts singing, it just grabs you—you just
feel. And that's the stuff I love. It can be any style or anything,
if it's got what I would call the Holy Spirit, that big connection that's really past your thoughts or anything—it just goes
somewhere in there, and that's what I respond to.

Who else are you listening to these days?

I really like listening to my wife [laughs]—she [folk singer Iris
DeMent] won't let me listen to the records around the house.
Something about what Iris does just really stirs me.

Does she sing to you?

Oh, we sing around the house a little bit, and in the car and stuff. And we joke around with it a lot. She says she can't sing with me because I don't ever sing anything the same way twice, which is true. For her I would try to but . . . I go back and listen to Jimmie Rodgers sometimes. I got a friend who's been dead for a while named Rainer Ptacek. His music is very moving to me. I got a friend named Joe Price who lives in northeast Iowa. Joe is a blues guy—however you're feeling he will lift your heart. You have to smile when you hear Joe—he's just got the spirit too. I like listening to Merle Haggard—he kept on writing really good songs. He's not on country radio like he used to be, but who is on country radio?

What do you want people to come away with, or experience, at your shows?

When I walk out of a good show that I've enjoyed, I feel lifted up, I feel awake, I feel kind of light. I remember one time many years ago I was playing in New York City and I was really shot—it had been a long tour. I probably had a gig down in the Village—it was late—and I walked into a little club, might have been the Blue Note. A guy named Abdullah Ibrahim, a piano player from South Africa, an exile in New York for many years, influenced by the township music of course and by Duke Ellington and Thelonious Monk, and by old church hymns which the missionaries had brought down there, so just unbelievably beautiful music. I was so tired I could barely keep my eyes open. I leaned on a pillar with my eyes closed and listened. When I walked out I just felt revived, filled up but light. When people leave my shows, I hope they have that kind of good feeling.

Do you feel that even though you have this really loyal following, you're making a living and people really appreciate you, do you feel any sort of frustration that the kind of music you play doesn't get aired more?

No, I have to say I don't (laughs heartily). That just never mattered to me. I've just been really surprised that I did find an audience and I could make a living. I still can't really believe it when I step back and look at it 'cause, as objective as I can get, what I do seems kind of quirky—I know it's not mainstream. I've written a very few songs that somebody could maybe sing on the radio, just a handful [laughs]. And that was accidental. I just feel really fortunate. I think the kind of career I've had suited me. I never liked record company people, I still don't— they have a funny look in their eye. I've met a lot of those birds along the way, and that's why I started my own label.

That's when you started Red House Records, around 1980?

Actually, a couple of years before that.

So what's that funny little look in their eyes, dollar signs?

Well, I think it's the dollar sign, they're kind of sizing you up. Years ago I was doing a gig in Nashville, and I was making a living by then. I had done the *Prairie Home* show and I think I had a couple of records out. One of those Nashville A&R [Artists and Repertoire] guys, or whatever they call them, came up to me after my little gig and said, "Well, I like that one song of yours, would you have any trouble if we changed the chorus and did this or that to the verse?" I just said, "Get out of my face buddy, don't say anything else, just get out of here." I just can't take that approach.

Is it a protective feeling for your art?

Not that so much because my songs are on their own. Once I write them and get them out there, I wish 'em good luck, but I feel like they gotta walk on their own feet. I just wanted to do what was natural for me to do. I didn't want to shape it to be some other way.

I hesitate to put music into a category, but the type of music you do is being grouped with people like Lucinda Williams. Do you feel a kinship with Lucinda and other Americana artists?

Sure, but I also feel that with Howlin' Wolf, Cecilia Bartoli, and I feel it with a lot of different people. Americana, or folk, is just to give people some idea what they're going to hear—you gotta have some kind of label. So I don't mind labels—I just don't take them seriously.

So you don't bristle...

No, Hank Williams was a folk singer.

You often play with Bo Ramsey and sometimes with a band. Can you discuss the difference between playing solo and playing with other musicians?

Playing with Bo is great—we've played together for such a long time. We have a really good groove together. Playing solo you have total freedom to play any song that pops into your head. I can do even some song that I've never sung before— and I do that when I'm playing solo.

Do you ever write poetry?

I write a lot of stuff that I don't know what I would call it. I just call them "scraps" because I didn't know what else to call 'em. Some you could call a poem, or a prose poem, short stories. I do write other things that are not specifically a song that I would sing.

When you're developing songs, do you key off the audience much and see what people respond to and what they like?

I think that's dangerous. On the other hand, I've had songs that I was unsure of myself; then I go out and play them. If I play 'em half a dozen times and I feel nothing from the crowd, I'll look at that song a little bit harder 'cause I want the song to communicate. But I don't think I've ever thought, well, what could I write that's going to go over good.

How do you see your spiritual life these days?

My general attitude toward being alive is one of gratitude. I feel fortunate to have been born, and I feel thankful. If I could have invented my own church, it would probably have been some kind of Pentecostal Buddhism where it's mostly quiet and reflecting, but then there's some shaking your butt and singing. I don't have any traditional feelings for an afterlife—I think what we are is made up of a lot of things that have always been here and will always be here. But I don't see any need for or have any desire for any sort of personal immortality. Heaven, the way it's pictured, sounds like hell to me. To be as this in some glorious place singing for endless time, that's very frightening to me. Being this now and having been other things before and gonna be dirt and other things coming up, that feels natural to me. What I see happening in the natural world is a big compost pile, a lot of things go in and different things come out. The process is beautiful and worthy of respect.

So when the time comes, you want to be put back in the earth?

Oh yeah, definitely, if I had my druthers I'd do it the way they do it in India with the big bonfire. Iris was telling me this little story about her dad and her uncle. They were both old men and one of them said to the other, "Ain't you glad that this doesn't all end with us." Meaning, we're going to be gone soon but look at the little kids . . . and that's a very powerful, very good feeling to have that. I've been working on a song, "Now That I'm My Grandpa." I do have that feeling that now that I'm an old one—it makes life so much less lonely if you don't see your life as being just this little isolated desperate bit.

Was your song "Driftless" autobiographical—did your parents put pressure on you?

No, not much at all. My dad thought I should get a degree so I'd have something to fall back on in case music didn't work out. I respected that, but I didn't do it—I went to college for a year I think. My father worried about me, I know he did, when I was young and struggling. It wasn't until around the time I did the *Prairie Home* show . . . I remember him coming to one of my shows, and he put his arm on my shoulder and said, "Son, I think you're going to be all right." My mother was just supportive; she didn't put any pressure on me.

So was that song more universal?

I think it was. I was thinking of those first two lines, that's what you say to your father: "Have I done enough father?" And with your mother you often say, "Have I learned enough, can we really talk now?" I don't really understand that song too much, but I like it.

Why do you think music moves people like it does?

For me, it's a physical, whole-self response to it. I don't think that can really be explained. It's a mystery. My wife's got a great song called "Let the Mystery Be." I think that's generally a good idea.

Walking on a Wire
RICHARD THOMPSON

Richard Thompson writes songs with the authority and brilliance of Pete Townsend, plays guitar with the dexterity and precision of Mark Knopfler, and sings with the ferocity of a wrongly convicted prisoner. So why isn't he better known? That's hard to say. It could be the sophistication of his songs or that his music is so hard to categorize; on his albums a ballad is often followed by a searing electric rock crescendo. And record company executives didn't seem to know how to market his music.

Here's what you should know about Richard Thompson: He was born in 1949, to a father who was a Scotland Yard detective and an amateur guitar player. Ever witty, Thompson described his father as "a bad amateur player . . . with three chords, though, unfortunately, not C, F, and G," according to The Observer, a British newspaper. Thompson was voted one of Rolling Stone magazine's Top 20 guitarists of all-time; he grew up listening to traditional Scottish tunes and mid-century jazz, and, as a teenager, joined the Celtic folk-rock outfit Fairport Convention.

Fairport started in the '60s by performing cover songs. Yet even when he was 18, the impatiently inventive Thompson was dissatisfied with performing others' work. So he learned to write songs. He left Fairport in the early '70s and released a solo album to mixed reviews. Then he married the singer Linda Peters. Their first album as Richard and Linda Thompson, *I Want to See the Bright Lights Tonight,* has been an enduring critical success. The couple embraced Sufism, a mystic branch of Islam, a faith that Thompson has pursued quietly for decades.

Revered by musicians and fans in the Celtic world, Thompson became better known worldwide in 1982 when he and Linda released *Shoot Out the Lights.* With heart-breaking lyrics about a couple in crisis—on such songs as "Don't Renege on Our Love" and "Wall of Death"—the album sounds like a husband and wife fighting to the bitter end of their relationship. "Even in the best days of our marriage, Richard and I didn't communicate with each other fabulously well," Linda Thompson told Rolling Stone. "I think that the reason the music was good was that we tended to save it for work."

Rolling Stone listed *Shoot Out the Lights* as the ninth-best album of the 1980s, saying: "On *Shoot Out the Lights,* Richard reclaimed what he calls his 'license to rip' and came up with his most inspired and unrestrained guitar playing since the glory days of Fairport Convention. Nowhere is Richard's renaissance more apparent than on the masterful second solo of 'Shoot Out the Lights': alternately soaring and twitching, Thompson's guitar echoes a psychopath's flitting emotions, ending on a tantalizingly unresolved note."

After he and Linda divorced, Thompson rebuilt his career as a solo artist, hitting new heights on his 1988 album, *Amnesia,* with its riveting song "Can't Win" about the emotional wounds parents inflict on their kids. *Amnesia* and Thompson's next album, *Rumor and Sigh*, demonstrate the range of Thompson's work, from personal songs—"the names were changed to protect the guilty," he says—to fictional narratives.

Released in 1991, *Rumor and Sigh* received a Grammy nomination and gave Thompson some radio airtime with the song "I Feel So Good" about a convict just granted his release from prison. The album shows the panoramic range of Thompson's subjects, from the adolescent who thinks he can be a good lover because he "Read About Love" to the disheartened husband who has to beg for his wife's touch in "Why Must I Plead." Yet it was his cinematic ballad, "1952 Vincent Black Lightning," about a James Dean-like bad boy and his motorcycle, that became the album's most beloved song and made Time magazine's list of top 100 songs.

Thompson has become one of the best storytellers in music. On his 1994 song, "Beeswing," about a wanderer for whom "even a Gypsy caravan was too much settling down," he sings: "She was a rare thing / Fine as a beeswing / So fine a breath of wind might blow her away." Combine lyrics like these with Thompson's guitar virtuosity, and you have a performer who deserves a place among rock's royalty.

In the liner notes to the Thompson collection *Watching the Dark*, Greil Marcus writes, "In Thompson's music, at its heart, is the specter of trouble that can come at anytime, whole and undiminished." That's leavened by Thompson's distinctively British wit. During our 2009 phone interview in advance of his show at Petaluma's Mystic Theatre, I asked why he split his time between Los Angeles and London. He said: "London for the weather, L.A. for the culture."

Thompson's best albums improve with age, revealing ever deeper layers of emotion and musical subtlety. Like Jethro Tull's Ian Anderson, Thompson has a knack for empathizing with the fringe and downcast characters who live on the margins of society. In the chorus of "God Loves a Drunk" he sings: "But a drunk's only trying to get free of his body / And soar like an eagle high up there in heaven / His shouts and his curses are just hymns and praises / To kick-start his mind now and then / O God loves a drunk, come raise up your glasses, amen."

In 2018, Thompson released his 19th solo album, *13 Rivers,* which Amazon called a "very stripped down, bare-bones" recording. "There are 13 songs on the record, and each one is like a river," Thompson says on his website. "Some flow faster than others. Some follow a slow and winding current." Though his songs are scrupulously crafted, he says, "I never really think about what songs mean. I just write them. Some of them reflect on what happened a few months ago or even a year ago. It's a process of surveying my life."

During his Capitol Records days in the late '80s and early '90s, Thompson's work was authentic and distinctive, but since he began producing his own records, they sound more personal. "Sometimes I am speaking directly about events, at other times songs are an imaginative spin on what life throws at you," Thompson says. "The music is just a mirror to life, but we try to polish that mirror as brightly as possible."

Still, he's not sure about the source of the music. "I don't know how the creative process works," he says. "I suppose it is some kind of bizarre parallel existence to my own life. I often look at a finished song and wonder what the hell is going on inside me." Suggesting that songs can take on a life of their own, Thompson says his work can astonish even him. The songs on *13 Rivers* "came to me as a surprise in a dark time," he says. "They reflected my emotions in an oblique manner that I'll never truly understand. It's as if they'd been channeled from somewhere else. You find deeper meaning in the best records as time goes on. The reward comes later."

≈ ≈ ≈

*Your songs sound so personal. Do they come from your life experi-
ence or your imagination?*

That's one style of writing, when the inspiration comes from
your own circumstances. Other things are just from the imagination, but having said that, there is always a bit of you in
there, a bit of your life experience and a bit of your morality
and general makeup that goes into a more fictional song. Fiction reflects on reality, reflects on the human condition, so yes
I do write both kinds of songs.

   People have described fiction in various ways. Some people
say fiction is a lie in order to tell the truth. Sometimes I think
fiction is an exaggeration of reality in order to highlight reality. You have to compress and condense. You tend to write
about people who are going through extreme circumstances;
everyday life doesn't necessarily show you human attributes.
It doesn't show how people reveal their humanity. You have
to have shipwrecks, you know, and mining disasters to show
things like heroism more clearly.

Especially if you have four or six minutes for a song.

And most of them are shorter than that. In a song, you have
three verses to tell a story. Traditional ballads can be longer,
but in a modern song you can use more of a cinematic technique to tell a story. You can jump into the middle of the
action and use the first-person narrative to have a point of
view that tells the middle of the story, and through suggestion
it tells you what happened before and what's going to happen
afterwards.

One thing that impresses me about your technique is it almost sounds like you're playing two guitars at the same time. Can you say how you do that?

As a kid listening to a lot of piano players, I was frustrated that the guitar couldn't do the thing that piano players could do. They could do separate things with the left hand and the right hand. Some guitarists started to break that down, country players like Chet Atkins were able to develop a style of playing a bass line and a melody line at the same time. And I just adapted those approaches to something more suited to the times. Through a style of fingerpicking, I'm able to cover more ground. It also came from being an electric guitarist and playing in a band and then going out to solo shows and trying to fill in the gaps. I was very aware of the spaces in trying to perform the same songs. I'm thinking, where's the bass line and where's the rhythm? So it was through necessity, trying to fill it out, to orchestrate the songs with just an acoustic guitar.

For me the true test of a song is: Does it make you feel something? Are you trying to evoke feeling in the listener or just express yourself?

It's a combination of things. I think as a writer, you are trying to please yourself to some extent, and you're trying to enjoy yourself. Writing should be an enjoyable process. At the same time, I think you're aware that for a song to have any kind of legs, it has to communicate, and as a musician you're an entertainer. You have to get something across to people. One of the things you're trying to get across is the emotion of the song. I think sometimes that's the thing that people get before they get the lyrics or before they really understand what the tune is. The emotion is an important thing, and as a songwriter you try to get emotions across.

Does a song like "Now That I Am Dead," about artists gaining fame after their demise, express your feelings about how creative people are often overlooked during their lifetimes?

I didn't actually write that song, but I think a lot of musicians would be happy to sing that because it's an area of common experience. So many musicians are frustrated by the music business. I think every musician gets frustrated when they see people that they consider to have no talent being very successful. We won't mention names. I'm fairly happy to be where I am. I sell out concerts all over the world. Even in a dying market, I sell a lot of records. I've earned a living as a musician, so I shouldn't really complain, though what I do is definitely below the radar for a lot of people.

I'd rather be underrated than overrated. There's a different kind of frustration that goes with being a successful but bland musician. I remember that the band Queen, they were always frustrated at their lack of artistic recognition. They were a huge pop band but always felt they should be treated as art. So I would rather have it this way around.

How is it to watch your son Teddy Thompson gain a good measure of musical success?

It's fantastic, I'm so happy. It's totally on merit. He's a great singer and a fine writer. I have other kids who are musical who are coming up. It's great to see them succeed, not in a shallow commercial way but actually to develop a real following.

How does Sufism affect your life and does it inform your art?

Whatever your belief system is, it affects everything you do. I don't proselytize about the things I believe in, but it affects the morality of what you write, without question. I'm glad if people are unaware of what I believe in and come to the music first without prejudice.

One of my favorite John Martyn songs has you playing mandolin on it; is that something you do much?

I play mandolin on a regular basis. I'm always happy to do it—it's just another string to the bow.

Perhaps your best-known album is Shoot Out the Lights, *with your ex-wife, Linda Thompson. It sounds on the album as though you're splitting up, but I've read that those songs were written before you planned to separate.*

The songs were written a year to two years before we split. I suppose if they were presaging something, it was unconscious or subconscious. We weren't consciously charting our demise, I don't think. Sometimes we would switch who would sing a song depending on keys and vocal ranges. I'd sing the song that Linda had been singing and vice versa. It's really after the fact that you can look at it and say: Oh it's a divorce album; look what these people were going through. I think that's in there, but it's not something we were really conscious of.

Years ago, you left your label and started putting out your own music. How has that worked for you?

I wasn't alone in doing this because major labels couldn't really do anything for musicians. The old traditional music contract would be illegal in almost any other business. There was a frustration with the traditional music business structure. It's much nicer to be in control of the production of one's own records and not have to answer to anybody else. In a cottage industry it just seems to be more the way the world is going.

It's a bit more local, a bit more down-home. I really enjoy that aspect of it and hope I can continue to do it that way.

Could you tell me about the soundtrack that you recorded for Werner Herzog's 2005 film, Grizzly Man?

As they were editing the film, they used as a temporary track some old things of mine. As often happens with temporary tracking, it stays with you, the image becomes associated with the music. So they asked me to do the rest. We decided to improvise the whole score. We got together a half-dozen interesting musicians, including Henry Kaiser and other people from the Bay Area. We basically recorded the whole thing in just two days; it was extremely efficient. It worked for this but probably wouldn't have worked for 99 percent of other film projects. We were fortunate to have the right people.

How long would you like to keep playing?

I'd love to still be playing in 10 or 20 years. It would probably be nice to tour a bit less, but I can't think of anything that I would rather do than keep touring and just die onstage. That would be fine.

How Sweet It Is
MELVIN SEALS

When keyboardist Melvin Seals walked into the Grateful Dead's Marin County studios in 1980 to audition for the Jerry Garcia Band, he had no idea he was about to fall into a rabbit hole that would change his life. Not because he'd get caught up in psychedelics or any other peripherals of the scene; he had no interest in that. For Seals, who came up playing gospel music in churches, it was all about the love.

Remarkably, though Seals had heard of the Grateful Dead, he had no idea who Jerry Garcia was and didn't recognize him during the audition. After the first session, Seals said to Garcia, one of the world's preeminent musicians: "Man, you play some pretty good guitar," sparking peals of laughter among the band members. Despite his lack of familiarity with the Garcia band members, Seals was conversant with much of the music they played, especially the Motown covers. Seals' virtuosity on the Hammond B3 organ made a strong impression, and he would play with the Jerry Garcia Band for 15 years, until Garcia's death in 1995.

With his Cheshire Cat smile and easygoing demeanor, the larger-than-life Seals was an instant fan favorite. His spiritually uplifting approach to the organ brought Garcia's fans to their feet on songs such as "Tangled Up in Blue," "The Harder They Come," and "Run for the Roses." (The band played both covers of other artists' songs and originals in a jam-band format with plenty of space for guitar solos and keyboard explorations.)

Seals was born in 1953, grew up in San Francisco, and started playing piano when he was eight years old at his local church. Before joining the Garcia band, he played keyboards with bluesman Elvin Bishop. Seals also produces gospel songs for other artists.

Today Seals carries the torch with a number of Garcia-influenced bands, including Melvin Seals and JGB, attracting new fans to the music while longtime enthusiasts remain forever grateful. I spoke with Seals in 2018, in advance of the Petaluma Music Festival, a fundraiser for music programs in Sonoma County schools. Teaching and training young musicians is "one of the greatest things on Earth—they are your future musicians," Seals told me during our phone interview. "If we can leave our legacies behind, the music carries on."

☙ ☙ ☙

Could you tell me about some of your early music experiences growing up in San Francisco?

I was kind of a church boy—my parents were very involved with the church. My father was a choir director and a musician at the church. That's where I first started paying attention to the piano and organ. Then I started hearing other organists outside the church; jazz was very popular. You had Jimmy Smith and Johnny Hammond [Smith]; the list goes on. Then you had rock 'n' roll organs, guys like Billy Preston; he came out of the church too. He showed me how a church musician could evolve to play rock 'n' roll, R&B, and blues.

Was there any sentiment in your family or church or community that you should stay with gospel?

There was a whole lot of that. But as you wise up and understand where it's coming from, it gets broader than that. Pastors would want to keep you in their circle to help build what they're trying to build. When you realize the talent that has been given to you is much bigger than these four walls, then you understand it's not meant for me to do this all my life. God didn't give me this to sit here and direct a choir every Sunday morning.

How did you get involved with the Jerry Garcia Band?

It was really different for me because I didn't know who they were. I was not a Deadhead. I knew very little about the Grateful Dead. I knew the name because being in the San Francisco Bay Area you would hear about the Grateful Dead. I knew they were a rock band, but I didn't know anything about who they were. So to fall into that door and not have any knowledge was really overwhelming for me. I'd done some secular things, music other than gospel, but that was a 180-degree turn right there, the psychedelic Grateful Dead music. Even the name, the Grateful Dead, when you're a church boy fresh out of church . . .

And the imagery, the dancing skeletons.

I didn't know what was going on. I really didn't. I was a little concerned because of my lack of knowledge. It wasn't too long after Jim Jones had the massacre of the cult (in 1978 at the People's Temple in Guyana). Here I am, a church boy walking into a world of all these skeletons and all these funny people. It was a serious moment: What am I getting myself into? It was overwhelming to see all that. I quickly found out that these are some of the most loving people on the face of the planet.

When I think of gospel and soul music, I think of well-rehearsed musicians, very tight, hitting every note together. And though the Dead and Jerry Garcia were amazing musicians, they had a different approach. What was the first rehearsal or first gig like with the Jerry Garcia Band?

I got the call from John Kahn, the bass player of the Jerry Garcia Band and Jerry's lifelong friend. I was doing some work with [singer] Maria Muldaur, and John Kahn was her boyfriend at the time. He asked me one time: Would I be interested in playing in another band, sitting in? I said, sure I'd love to. So I got a call from him one day asking if we could have a little rehearsal and see how it sounded. They all came in—I didn't know who Jerry or any of these people were—I met them all at one time.

You got to remember five or six people walk into a room, and they introduce themselves. Ten minutes later I couldn't tell you their names again. I got there before all of them. I was there on time, trying to make a good impression. We went over three Motown songs, just to see if the charisma and the vibe were right. I think it was "I Second That Emotion," "The Harder They Come," and "How Sweet It Is." Then we took a break and went back in the lobby. Jerry said, "Yep, yep, that's pretty good—that's what I'm looking for."

So after the first three songs I did say to the guitar player, "Man, you play some pretty good guitar," and everyone is just laughing because I don't have a clue [that Garcia was considered one of the most talented guitarists in rock]. So the guitar player said, "Likewise, you play some pretty good organ." It was a joke but I didn't know it was a joke at the time.

They were having a good time with me because they knew I didn't know anything about what I was involved with. They liked it because I didn't abuse the situation in any kind of way. I just played and got the hell out of there because I wasn't sure what was going on. And I didn't want to know. After we did those three songs everybody disappeared for about 20 minutes. They had a lot of rooms in the Front Street warehouse [in San Rafael, just north of San Francisco, where the band rehearsed]. I didn't know where they went; and then they all came out, yeah, that's really good. There was some funny stuff that went on there. But it worked out just fine.

It was not your average garage house band. There were gigs at the Keystones [nightclubs in San Francisco, Berkeley, and Palo Alto, now defunct]. Lots of people were there, and they were boogeying and they loved it. I know they didn't know me, but they were acting like they knew me.

What else were you doing then and how did it differ from the Garcia band?

Before Jerry, I played with Elvin Bishop for six years and had done Broadway plays for seven or eight years. I was developing a gospel record company. I had been producing gospel from a young age. I worked that into my own label. That's where my strength was, R&B and gospel.

In R&B and gospel, you dot your i's and you cross your t's. If you are coming up for a musical accent or turnaround or some sort of special bridge, you work on nailing it and making it strong and tight. So when I got with Jerry, that was the first lesson, I didn't know it was a lesson at the time, I just thought: Man, these guys are too good to be playing this stuff so sloppy. Everybody hit it all offbeat; I couldn't believe it. It used to frustrate me; everybody just kind of hit it their own way. It didn't matter.

I had to learn that this style of music had nothing to do with how tight and how badass a musician you are; it comes from the heart. What leaves the heart reaches the heart. This was heartfelt music, and the fans were just having the greatest time out there. It took a while for me to understand it. Sometimes we made a mistake and they knew we made a mistake. Jerry would forget some words or do something wrong, and the biggest applause was for that. How do you do this? But it was all in the realm of what was going on, and I was in school.

Soon you were one of the foundations of that band and brought a new element to it, the soulful sound of your Hammond B3 organ. Did you realize after a while that you were becoming an important piece of this band?

I don't know if I did. I knew that whenever I soloed I got a great response, but I was so different I thought it was maybe because of that. I never saw them with Merl [Saunders, who played keyboards for the Garcia band during the 1970s]. Merl and I were very good friends. We used to talk when I was with Elvin and he was with Jerry. We would talk on the phone about our experiences playing with these guys.

I never thought that one day I would be with Jerry. I never heard Merl with Jerry, and when I got with them they would not let me listen to anything that Merl had done with them because if they had I would have grabbed what he was doing. I would have thought: That's the comfort zone of what they're used to so let me give them what he was doing. Not one song did I ever hear. The rehearsals were at Front Street in San Rafael, and their tapes and vault were there. They could've played me anything.

I figured out later that Jerry wanted me to play what I felt was right. There was no guidance, no direction, not play this or try that; they left me alone. It was difficult for me because I didn't play that style of music. I didn't know how it was supposed to go, what I was supposed to do. I had no idea. I was really green at playing that. As the years went on, I got a better handle on it; or they just never told me I wasn't playing it right, one or the other.

I don't think many people who saw you play would say you weren't playing it right. You played with the Garcia band throughout the 1980s, and in 1990, when Brent Mydland died, the Grateful Dead lost their keyboardist. Were you approached for that gig or interested in it?

There were a lot of fans who thought I should be the next keyboard player. I never got asked by Jerry or any Grateful Dead members, but there was a lot of dialogue that I should be the guy. I don't know if I wanted it. I would have loved to have done it until they found somebody. But that was a hot seat, and I didn't want to be in a hot seat.

Meaning the history of who'd sat in that seat and what happened to them? [The Grateful Dead had a number of keyboard players who died prematurely including founding member Ron "Pigpen" McKernan, Keith Godchaux, and Mydland.]

I looked at that and said, Whoa, I don't know what the mystical thing was about that, but I didn't want it. I had a gospel record company, and I was putting out records and working it. The Garcia band didn't work as much as the Grateful Dead and played a lot of local gigs, Warfield dates. So it gave me all the time in the world to work on other things. The Grateful Dead was this mass band; I didn't know if I was ready for that, not that I was even offered it, a whole lot more songs and stuff went on there. And I didn't do a lot of things that I heard they did. I barely drink wine. I didn't do drugs, nothing. So to be out with a group of people that you're not like would have been hard for me.

You played with Jerry for 15 years. How well did you get to know him personally?

Oh, I've been to his house, and he invited me to his Christmas parties. Sometimes he would ask me over just to sit while he played his guitar or was doing his artwork. I rode with him in limousines, Lear jets; I knew him very well.

Did you have a sense near the end that he was backsliding into addiction?

I didn't watch that. I didn't pay attention, and I didn't see death. There were others that saw it, and now when I think of some things that went on just before then I should have thought something was going on because things were shutting down even when he was still alive—things were changing. One of the last times I saw him alive, we did a Warfield date and he was walking kind of sideways, his neck bent to the side. He was telling me his body hurt all over. He was in a lot of pain, but I didn't see death coming.

After Jerry died, how did you decide to continue playing the music of the Garcia band? Was there discussion about whether you should keep doing this?

There was an interview with Jerry. They asked him: "What would you like to see happen with the music when you're no longer here?" He said, "I would like to believe that the music is bigger than me and that the music will live on." I remember hearing that, and to my knowledge, when he passed, the Grateful Dead said, It's done; it's over. We are no longer working as the Grateful Dead. They shut it down. (Members of the Grateful Dead played in other configurations under band names such as Furthur and reunited as the Grateful Dead for a set of 50th anniversary farewell shows in 2015.)

I got a call from John Kahn maybe five or six months after Jerry died asking if I wanted to do some gigs. He had one gig lined up in Santa Cruz at a place called Palookaville, and he asked me if I wanted to work. So we got all the surviving members of the Jerry Garcia Band and added a couple of other musicians to form the John Kahn Band. The first gig sold out so fast they added a second night. The fans were weeping and crying but wanted to hear the music. Even in the sorrow of it all, they still want to hear these songs. John didn't do too many songs that we did with the Jerry Garcia Band. He did a few, but what he did do were songs that Jerry would have done because it was his style, like "Stop That Train."

At the end of the night there were people who called to me as I walked out: "Hey Melvin, you guys gonna do any Jerry Garcia songs tomorrow night?" And I was saying, "Hey, this is not my band; it's John's band," but I paid attention. These folks still wanted to hear this music. We were getting ready to go out [on tour] as the John Kahn Band, but a couple of months before the tour, John passed.

So now I am the longest [surviving] member in this band. I got approached by the agency that was going to work with John Kahn: Are you interested? And I thought about it and thought, well why not? I wanted to call the band Tribute, as a tribute to Jerry, but the agency said it would be too much work trying to get all the folks to know who you are. They said, "Why don't we just call it JGB?" I was scared to death to call it JGB because Bill Graham used JGB to refer to the Jerry Garcia Band. There was a lot of resistance. Some folks just didn't like the idea that we were calling this band JGB now that Jerry's not there.

Who was your guitar player at that time?

When I first did it, I got some of the baddest guys I knew who could mesmerize anybody. But I hadn't finished learning my lesson. It wasn't about how bad these guys were—it was did they fit the scene? They had neither the look nor the spirit; they were great musicians, but they didn't fit. John Kadlecik was the first guy I played with after Jerry died who had a great deal of Jerry's style. Even some of the mistakes that Jerry made, John did some of that same stuff. It was scary. I rate John as number one. But there are a whole lot of others out there who can sit in the seat pretty well.

Could you say a few words about why this music continues to inspire audiences?

I don't know if I have the answer to that. It's heartfelt music; it goes back to the '60s and the love of the Haight-Ashbury scene. But why young folks—the Deadheads' kids and their kids—have taken on this music and are living and breathing it just like their parents did, it's a mystery to me. I'm not shocked, but I really don't know. Some young fans that come and see me today were not around when Jerry was alive. And I'm watching them sing in the front row. For every song, they know every lyric. How does this happen? People have met at gigs and got married to "How Sweet It Is" or said that our music kept them from committing suicide. I've heard it all. That's why it must continue. That's why I think that what's going on here is a wonderful thing.

So where does your creativity come from?

Mine is God-given. I could not give that credit anywhere else. It is truly highlighted by the heavenly father above. Without what was given to me, I could do nothing. I work hard to bring it, but there's a lot more going on than I realize. I don't get it. I see tears in their eyes. What just happened? There's something that goes through me, and it's being treated on the other side a different way. It can mean so much more to them than what I think I'm giving out. I didn't write the songs—I am trying to re-create them—I might add a little sparkle or something because of who I am, but this is the music I learned from Jerry.

Is there anything I didn't cover that you wanted to talk about today?

No, I think you got it all. You got a lot more than I've ever, ever given out.

Deep Down
AMY TAN

Amy Tan, author of the bestselling novel *The Joy Luck Club*, swims with sharks. This is not a metaphor for navigating the literary world; while visiting Isla Mujeres off Mexico's east coast with a conservation group called WildAid, Tan swam with whale sharks, at 30 feet long and 20,000 pounds, the world's largest fish. "We were in waters where there were quite a number of them. It was like a traffic jam," Tan told me. "Somebody would call out, 'There's one coming up behind you.' You'd turn around, and there would be a huge mouth, five feet wide, coming towards you."

Swimming with whale sharks was "inspiring, life-changing," Tan said, but not because it's perilous. "I think the most dangerous thing is the possibility of falling out of the boat and getting hit on the head," she said. What so moved Tan was that she was able to get eye to eye with these gentle giants, and that she felt a sense of communion.

"I had a number of them that stayed with me—when I slowed down they slowed down and just looked at me the whole time—they're very curious." It's no wonder that Tan appreciates curiosity: Her books, from her landmark debut, *The Joy Luck Club*, to her recent novel, *The Valley of Amazement*, are creative explorations into her roots and the places that have shaped her ancestors and ultimately herself.

Born in Oakland, California, to Chinese immigrants, Tan lives in Marin County just north of San Francisco. She was co-producer and co-screenwriter for the film adaptation of *The Joy Luck Club* and played herself in an episode of *The Simpsons*. She's appeared on NPR's news quiz, *Wait Wait . . . Don't Tell Me*, and was a guest on the PBS kids show, *Sesame Street*.

After visiting San Francisco's Asian Art Museum for a Shanghai exhibit a few years ago, Tan saw a book in the gift shop about Chinese courtesans in the early 20th century. While leafing through its pages, she came across a photo of ten women, "which stunned me," she said. The caption read: "The Ten Beauties of Shanghai." They were courtesans who had won a contest in 1910. Five of the young women were dressed in the same clothes her grandmother wore in one of Tan's favorite photographs of her. This is how Tan learned that her beloved grandmother, the woman she calls her muse, probably worked as a courtesan. That led Tan to completely change the course of the novel she'd been working on.

The result is *The Valley of Amazement*, set at the dawn of the 20th century. Like *The Joy Luck Club*, it's the story of a tense and painful relationship between a mother and daughter, and of the clash between East and West. The novel became a New York Times bestseller.

Tan recently published a nonfiction book, *Where the Past Begins* (Ecco, HarperCollins, 2017) "about the mind of the writer, which is basically my mind, and about what's gone on in my life," she told me, including "the deaths of my father and brother in the same year" when Tan was a girl. In the book, Tan reveals how the events of her life have driven her to create the books she has written. "The process of writing is the painful recovery of things that are lost," she writes. "This is why writing is so deeply satisfying to me."

In *Where the Past Begins*, Tan says: "And yet much of my writing, I realize, is about uncertainty—the heartbreaking moments when something is not clear, when the situation is changing, when a truth turns into a half-truth and then into a lie. My childhood with its topsy-turvy emotions has, in fact, been a reason to write. I can lay it squarely on the page and see what it was. I can understand it and see the patterns. My characters are witness to what I went through. In each story, we are untangling a knot in a huge matted mess. The work of undoing them one at a time is the most gratifying part of writing, but the mess will always be there."

Though she doesn't fear sharks, Tan faces another type of fear, "a kind of existential terror . . . that I'm going to fail according to my own standards and have that become public and . . . humiliating. Every writer has that. I'm sure I'm not the only one, and in fact I think I suffer less from that fear than most."

In a 2019 interview with Center for Asian American Media (CAAM) in celebration of the 30th anniversary of *The Joy Luck Club*, Tan said, "I was just starting out writing fiction, and with my earliest stories, I picked characters that were very far from my own reality. . . . The stories absolutely failed because they were inauthentic. I didn't have any genuine emotions attached to them. So one day, I decided, Well, what the hell? I'll just write something that's a little closer to my life. No one has to read it. The very first story I wrote was about a chess player—a champion little girl who had a very fierce mother."

That's when Tan realized that fiction could be a portal for understanding oneself. "There's an aspect of writing fiction that is hard to explain because it has to be felt. It happens when you are writing and then suddenly, something clicks into place. It just aligns itself with a deeper understanding. . . . It really is a feeling of recognition, almost like having a double; somebody who understands you completely," she says in the CAAM interview. Tan added that since she was a little girl she has loved words and read the thesaurus for fun. And that love hasn't dimmed. "I love the craft of it. I know a lot of people may hate revision. I love revision. I love playing with the sentences."

As inventive as Tan is with words, writing is not her only creative outlet. Tan serves as lead rhythm "dominatrix," backup singer, and second tambourine with the literary garage band, Rock Bottom Remainders. The group—which formed in the early 1990s and includes Stephen King, Mitch Albom, and Dave Barry—"retired" some years ago, Tan said. But like many rock bands, they occasionally re-group for "reunion" performances, donating ticket proceeds to literacy charities.

Throughout her life Tan has sought a deeper understanding of herself, but unlike many Northern Californians, she has not done so through prolonged psychotherapy. Tan says she sees some overlap between writing and therapy in that you're seeking to understand the present by recalling the past. But she only saw a therapist briefly and quit when he seemed to have trouble staying awake during their sessions. I spoke to Tan in 2014 during her book tour for *The Valley of Amazement*. At the time she was working on her memoir, *Where the Past Begins*.

≈ ≈ ≈

How does your writing help you learn more about yourself?

Everything I'm writing about has to do with identity, self-identity. It has to do with the meaning of my life, with who I am and what I'm looking for. My predominant influence would be my mother, and that accounts for why a mother figure appears so often in my books. I cannot seem to get away from it.

Were you concerned about revealing a part of your grandmother's life that some might see as not virtuous?

It was difficult—not simply because of what the family would think. It was hard because my grandmother is my muse and I often feel her in the room with me. By even considering she might have been a courtesan, I feared I might offend her, especially if it had not been true. And if she had been, I feared that she wouldn't want people to know. I also feared that mother—she died in 1999—wouldn't want people to know. Yet I think that my mother and grandmother were strong believers in truth and that they'd think it is a good thing. I decided to write about courtesans because I could not stop thinking about that world. It is not a story, however, about my grandmother.

Violet, the central character in The Valley of Amazement, *is half white and half Asian.*

You have a girl who thinks she's American and looks down upon the courtesans even though they're like her sisters. Then she's flipped into the other world. And she's become that other half: Chinese. She's become actually less than that other half—if you're Eurasian (especially in early 20th-century Shanghai) you don't belong to either world. So she has really taken a tumble, and she has to remake herself. She has to understand and figure out who she is.

You pursue truth through fiction.

I realized that if I described what I felt—the complexity of it, the history of it—in a fabricated story, paradoxically, I'd find truth through creating fiction. I found something I'd written when I was 25 that reminded me of things I've thought about since I was very young, that was no one would ever understand who I really was and the thoughts that I had. I was trying to make sense of who I was in this world. I had to capture it for myself, and the best way I could do that was in a story without going through my whole life and saying this is what happened. I was struck by the fact that I thought this at a very young age, and these are exactly the thoughts that I have now. It has to do with memory. Every single moment I've had is not a lost past; it is completely a continuum of who I am. All of these moments are who I am. Writing fiction is finding the meaning of my life, what I think, what I feel I have to remember, what I know about myself.

So it's more than identity?

Identity is certainly part of it, but it goes far beyond that. And the thing about writing to me also is not the finished book. That's the end of the journey. The most important, the most satisfying part, is the writing. It doesn't matter if I have to throw pages away. It comes from the frustration when I was young of not having enough words to say what I felt. I realized later I could describe better what I felt, the whole complexity of it, the mystery of it, in a fabricated story of all things, which seems paradoxical. You can find truth through creating fiction—that's how it works.

Do you enjoy the process of writing?

I don't like the word "process"—it sounds mechanical as if there's a process that's coherent and organized, but there isn't. In the same way, our lives are often not coherent or organized; we have to make sense of things afterwards. We find the connections and the associations later; that's what fiction does. A lot of it is finding patterns in life, those larger associations that grow as one becomes older.

Let's talk about sex. The Valley of Amazement *isn't* 50 Shades of Tan*, but are you concerned that because of the sex scenes, some people might take this book less seriously than your other work?*

So many of my readers want that mother-daughter story, and while this is a mother-daughter story, I don't think they would expect the mother to be running a courtesan house and the daughter to be a courtesan. I don't think I've had a sex scene in another book. There are people who do object to the sex. Some reader reviews say, "Sex, this is horrible."

Was it difficult to write about sex?

I was afraid to write corny love scenes. I was also afraid that people would think they were peering into my bedroom, that this was my sex life, especially if they've seen photos of me dressed as a dominatrix.

You have said writing fiction is better than going to therapy.

I suppose that fiction overlaps with therapy in that you are seeking understanding and working things out by remembering moments from the past. The way that you're remembering it is very distorted, now that you're looking at it through hindsight. In fiction you would want to go back and feel the pain. I've only been to a psychiatrist once for about four months, and during that period he fell asleep three times. I really didn't get anything out of it except the motivation to quit therapy.

You talk about secrets in your family—can secrets be a gift?

I love the secrets. I thought, I'm done—I've found out as much as I can about my family—my mother has died. But after learning about my grandmother, I'm encouraged by knowing I probably will never be done finding out secrets in the family.

In your nonfiction, you write very specifically about your life, but are you also seeking to convey something universal?

When I'm writing, I'm not trying to say, "Oh that's universal. We all go through that." If I did, it truly would be manipulative. I'm more surprised when I write something that's very specific to me, very personal, and then somebody says, "Oh, that's true for me as well." That's nice. At the same time, there are a lot of people who say, "I never would have done that." And that's fine too. This [*Where the Past Begins*] is completely me, how I work, and if you find resonance with it, that's great. I just have to say what it is for me.

Say Anything
DAVID SEDARIS

It's Wednesday, May 8, 2019, in the San Francisco Bay Area, a night when *Hamilton* is playing at the Orpheum, the Golden State Warriors have a pivotal postseason game against the Houston Rockets, the San Francisco Ballet is performing *Shostakovich Trilogy,* the San Jose Sharks are playing a decisive seventh game in their hockey playoff series, and *The Avengers: Endgame* has just come out. Yet, at the Marin Center, about 12 miles north of the Golden Gate Bridge, the 1,900-seat theater is packed with people who've paid $50 or more to see an author read his work. It's reminiscent of the crowds who came out more than a century ago to hear humorist Mark Twain speak—only back then there was a lot less competition, and they didn't have HBO or Netflix.

Author, playwright, and humorist David Sedaris has become an international phenomenon. It all started with him taking a job as one of Santa's elves during Christmastime at Macy's department store. National Public Radio's Ira Glass heard Sedaris read an early version of "The Santaland Diaries," his story based on that experience, in a Chicago performance space. That led to Sedaris reading the story on NPR in 1992. Sedaris recalled, "I went from an audience of 400 to an audience of 10 million overnight."

Sedaris has become a regular contributor to The New Yorker and to *This American Life*, the radio show hosted by Glass that is broadcast on NPR. As enjoyable as Sedaris' stories are in print, they're even better when read aloud by the author. His comic timing is impeccable, his tone intimately personal. Readers and listeners not only like him; they feel they know him. They may not want to be him, but they'd sure like to be his best friend.

Often wincingly confessional, Sedaris will talk about things few others would consider sharing. Who else could write the following sentences, in The New Yorker of all places, in a story about the satisfactions and losses of late middle age? "Yes, my hair is gray and thinning. Yes, the washer on my penis has worn out, leaving me to dribble urine long after I've zipped my trousers back up. But I have two guest rooms."

Sedaris was born in 1956 and grew up in North Carolina, after his father, an IBM engineer, moved the family south. A key to Sedaris' eventual success was that he kept a diary, enabling him to recall specific details from events that occurred years or decades ago. His first book was *Barrel Fever*, a collection of essays and stories. He then published *Naked, Holidays on Ice,* and, in 2000, the bestselling *Me Talk Pretty One Day*, which begins with a tale of how he frustrated a speech therapist who was trying to get him to stop lisping. He did this by avoiding any word that had the letter "s" in it, (note the book title has no "s," but his family name starts and ends with that bedeviling letter).

Self-effacing, politically incorrect and disarmingly honest, Sedaris' success continued with *Dress Your Family in Corduroy and Denim*, which reached the top spot on the New York Times bestseller list. A longtime smoker who quit when he was in his fifties, Sedaris used to allow cigarette addicts to go to the front of his book-signing lines because, to paraphrase, they have less time than the rest of us. He also likes to give small gifts to teenagers who come to his events, and for a time, he'd give some of them condoms.

Sedaris and his sister, Amy Sedaris, have written several plays, and he's been nominated for Grammy awards for his spoken-word albums. At press time his most recent books were 2018's *Calypso*, which includes recollections of his family gatherings during holidays and *Theft by Finding, Diaries 1977-2002*, a selection from his personal jottings published in 2017. And in 2013, he titled one of his collections *Let's Explore Diabetes with Owls*.

I interviewed Sedaris as he was promoting his book, *Squirrel Seeks Chipmunk*, a collection of short stories in which the characters are animals. "It's bedtime stories for people who drink," Sedaris quipped. A friend of his called it, "Aesop with no morals." When Sedaris appeared at the Marin Center in 2019, he spent much of the evening reading stories he hadn't yet published, which is typical. He likes to gauge audiences' reactions to his essays; then he refines them before sending his work to his editors. What some writers receive from critique groups, he gets from live audiences. In other words, people pay to see Sedaris' theatrical events and he gets feedback to refine his stories. That would make Mark Twain's fictional Tom Sawyer, who got kids to pay to paint a fence, proud.

His fans are amazed and grateful that Sedaris will spend hours before and after his events signing books and talking to them. But this isn't entirely selfless; some of his best material has come from readers who share stories or jokes with him. He clearly relishes meeting people and appears genuinely curious about their lives. One fascinating aspect of Sedaris is that the wellspring of his creativity seems to be his connection with people while on tour; that stimulation fuels his writing when he gets back to the solitude of his quiet office.

When I spoke to Sedaris the first time, in 2010, he and his boyfriend, Hugh, were house-shopping south of London. One home they saw had the address, "Faggots Stacks, Titty Hill, West Sussex," Sedaris told me. He swears he's not making this up. Sedaris was tempted to buy the house just for its address, he said, but unfortunately, the house wasn't right for them.

❧ ❧ ❧

There's a lot of darkness in Squirrel Meets Chipmunk, *in terms of what your animal characters do to one another. Could you talk about the dark side of that book?*

I think people have it in their mind that fables are just little lighthearted stories with animals in them, but if they actually went back and read them, like La Fountaine's, and Aesop's Fables, it's a bloodbath. I think if the characters had been humans, then people could have said: Oh, this violence is over the top. Animals are pretty horrible to each other. But I don't really think of these as fables. I hesitated to call it a book of fables because fables have morals, and some of these have morals and some of them don't. I think being dark is one of the requirements for the genre, plus it's just where I go if I'm writing fiction, the more violent and horrible the better.

Does having the characters be animals lessen this sting?

If the character is a cat or something, perhaps you'll read it and get to the very end and say, "Fuck, this cat is mean." Also, if the characters are animals, you can just get into the story quicker. If you say, "A cat went to a baboon to get herself groomed for the party," everyone knows what a cat and a baboon look like; you could spend time saying what color the cat is, but you don't really need to do that. You can just sort of go, and there's something about that that I liked. The animals give it a little distance too, and it's nice to have that distance sometimes.

You came under fire for your story on China in which you talk about a toddler defecating in a grocery store. Do you ever ask yourself, "Am I being too hard here, and am I being unfair?" Or is it all about the writing?

I wrote two stories about China, and that's one of them. When I got back from China, I went to everyone I knew who had been to China, and I said to them all: "How could you not have led with the human shit?" I led with that. When I got there, nothing was more inspiring (laughs) and eye-popping than that to me. But that's what I have an eye for. Some people might say, "Well why don't you write about Chinese medicine?" Well, *you* write about Chinese medicine. That's not really my topic. But if I go somewhere and people are spitting in elevators and they're shitting in stores, that's exactly my topic. So that's what I'm going to focus on.

I think what you did so well in that story is that you talked about the things that everybody sees and notices—but no one writes about these things in glossy travel magazines. Stories like, hey you wouldn't believe it, but there was a kid dropping a turd in the produce aisle.

And that does not keep me from going. I would've gone sooner (laughs), if I'd known that I could see that. It's not that I didn't have a good time. You're right, in a travel magazine, they're going to have your story next to an ad for a nice hotel. They just want you to write things that would encourage you to go. To my mind, that story said: Go, but bring your own food. I would never have felt self-conscious reading that story in front of the Chinese person.

The guy [Jeff Yang, who wrote a piece condemning Sedaris' story on the website SFgate.com] said they eat crazy things in North Carolina too. Fine, go ahead and write about it; it wouldn't offend me in the least bit. Again, that's sort of what I have an eye for. You can go to China, and your story would be different, and his story would be different. This just happens to be mine.

You would have gone sooner for the experience or because you knew you would get a great story out of it?

Nothing charges my imagination like seeing a human turd on the ground. Nothing gets my wheels spinning like that. I went to the Philippines a couple of years ago; it's a bit different because China is a powerful country. It's not a dirt-poor powerless country. So I didn't think of it as picking on anybody.

Do you workshop your stories on your tours and then edit them based on audience response?

Yeah, I like to learn as much as I can on my own before I turn the story in. There was a story that I had in The New Yorker, maybe a year ago; the story begins with a lot of information I've gotten from flight attendants and pilots. So I had a bit of information that a pilot had given me and I just thought it was fascinating. I had it in the story and when I read it out loud, I felt people stopping. I still think it's completely fascinating. And I think the audience wanted me to judge it. But I wasn't judging it; I was just presenting it. And they stopped. So I cut it out of the story because it was like a speed bump preventing people from moving on.

It sounds like you're saying that people want you to be their ally, that they want you to feel the way they do so they can say, "David Sedaris, who I admire as a writer, supports my view."

I don't know if it's that. It was a pilot, and he flies from Palm Beach to Newark. He was flying two days before Christmas. The flight attendant got on the PA system, and she said, "Ladies and gentlemen, please fasten your seatbelts in preparation for landing, and make sure the overhead compartment is securely closed." So then they land in Newark, and the flight attendant gets on the intercom and says, "Happy holidays, and to those of you already standing, Happy Hanukkah." Then the story just goes on.

I don't judge it; I just present that and then I go on with the next part of the story. And people got hung up on that; it's a lot to think about. It's a really telling story on several levels, and I think it's a horrible story, and I think it's an amazing story. But it just acted as a speed bump. I needed them to come with me into the rest of the story, and they couldn't. They were like: "I have to think about this for a while." On the page it might have been different, but it wasn't working out loud, so I cut it out. When I say I test things out in front of an audience, that's what I want to learn.

And sometimes I think everyone's like me. Like we're all alike and everyone's had this experience. Then I realize no, no. It's just me.

But I think what contributes to your success is that it isn't just you. There's a lot of common human experience you write about, and you have a knack for doing it in a way that's engaging. People relate.

I often find that it's generational as well. I have a story in The New Yorker ("Company Man," May 27, 2013), and there's a scene that takes place in a station wagon. My sisters and I are in what we called the "way-back." And then I hear in the audience, "Way-back, way-back," from people who haven't heard the term way-back in years, who are my age, whose family had a station wagon, and they used to ride in the way-back of the station wagon. Sometimes you can hear the audience murmuring because you've touched something that they've forgotten about.

Many of your readers don't actually read your work; they listen to audiobooks or hear you on This American Life. *People like the way you read. Is there a connection you engender by reading your stories rather than just putting them on a page?*

I think that comes from being on the radio because when you're on the radio people feel as though you are speaking directly to them. There's a sort of intimacy to it. They feel betrayed at a big event when they hear everyone else laughing too. They'll tell me: "They [others in the audience] laughed at all the wrong parts."

Your typical tour is 40 cities in 40 days. Do you enjoy that?

To me, that's my reward for the solitude of writing—you get to be in front of that audience and you get to read it out loud. As I am writing, I think: How am I going to read this? You tend to think rhythmically when you think about reading things out loud. Anyone who writes things on paper thinks rhythmically, but especially if you're going to be reading it, you sit at your desk reading out loud what it is that you're writing and just kind of hear how the sentences tumble into one another. I really look forward to it.

You have kept a diary since you were a young man, but now that you've started reading parts of it at your events, has it changed the way you write in your journal?

No, most days nothing really happens. I carry a notebook around and I make notes all day. I get up in the morning and I write my diary, and I write in my notebook. Sometimes you just get in the mood to make something out of nothing. Every now and then, things happen, and I get a pretty good idea that this might work in front of an audience. Sometimes it's just direct from my diary.

You're known for being incredibly patient in signing books and talking to everybody who wants to meet you after your events, rather than rushing through the line.

The longest I've ever signed books is ten and a half hours. That was in a bookstore, I think it was in Louisville, Kentucky. But in a big theater you'd never sign that long. And I get there early [to sign before each event. For those in line] it's hard because they're standing up, but I'm fine. I have a chair.

I try to have different themes for every tour. Last fall I started asking people for jokes and I got a whole lot of jokes. I thought about having a book printed, a chapbook with some of the best jokes. Instead I had 9,000 postcards printed out. I'm going to give away 150 per night. I've never done anything like this before.

A woman asked me to sign her book and write, "Explore your inner possibilities." I said, "You know, this is not something I would really say, but I will write something with the word 'explore' in it." So I wrote "Let's explore 'diabetes' with owls." That's what I wanted to name *Squirrel Seeks Chipmunk*. The publisher said, "Please don't put the word 'diabetes' in your book title." So I got this designer to make it (the postcard) look like an old book cover; it looks like it's a book from the late 1940s, and there are these owls on one branch and the book is beat up like it's been really loved. It's one of those things that you would look at and you'd be taken aback because you'd think it's a real book. Then you'd think, "What do owls know about diabetes?" (Sedaris cackles.)

A couple of years ago I was in Denver and I'd been signing books for a long time. I guess I was just getting silly and I started drawing signs in people's books, rustic signs, a board with rough edges with words burned into it, so I wrote in this woman's book: "Abortions $3.00" because I just thought that's such a good price for an abortion. Even if you'd been trying for years to get pregnant and you finally got pregnant, if you saw that sign, you'd think: "Well, that's such a good price, how can we not have an abortion?" This woman got back in line and waited like another three hours and she said, "I'm sorry, I'm a very liberal person, but I just don't want this in my book. I didn't know what I could do, so I changed it (he pauses) to "Abortions $13.00."

What are you most proud of?

Probably writing for The New Yorker—that does wonders for a person's self-esteem. I just got the galleys for a story that's coming out next week. You just see it [your essay] in that type-face and all of a sudden it seems legitimate, just by nature of the typeface. When a book comes out now, I tend to think: How bad can it be if 90 percent of the stories were in The New Yorker? I'm very hard on myself, but The New Yorker has allowed me to think more highly . . . that sounds bad too. Well, it's something; when you're feeling bad, you can say, "Well, at least The New Yorker likes me."

I did a series on the BBC, and this woman wrote me a card. The card said, "Congratulations." On the inside of the card she had written: "Dear Mr Sedaris, Congratulations, I just crossed you off my book list so fast it would make your head spin. I heard you on the radio, and I laughed. Then I got your book from the public library, and it was awful." And I thought, OK, you got my book from the library; it didn't cost you anything. And the stories in the book are the exact same stories I did on the radio. But even a thing like that, it kind of hurt. So then you think, at least The New Yorker likes me.

After a book tour, do you miss the attention? When you get home, do you sit at a table and ask Hugh to walk up with a book so you can sign it?

At the end of the tour, I think, oh no, my tour's going to be over. I really enjoy going on tour, and it is really hard for Hugh when the tours are over because I'm so used to getting the attention, and I so enjoy it. There's no way that he can give me all the attention that I need. So I must be really horrible to live with.

Honest Outlaw
MERLE HAGGARD

In 1963, Merle Haggard saw Johnny Cash before a TV tap-ing when Cash mentioned playing at San Quentin prison. "I said, 'I was there,'" Haggard said, "and he said, 'I don't recall you being on the bill'. I wasn't," Haggard told Cash, "I was in the audience." In an interview not long before he died, Haggard said he spent two years and nine months in San Quentin—he was sent to the prison because he'd been locked up at reform schools and lower security detention facilities and kept escaping—17 times, he told Vanity Fair.

The harsh conditions at San Quentin may have forged Haggard's creative spark. He saw hardened career criminals, many of them lifers, and vowed to focus on playing guitar and writing songs as his ticket out of a life of crime. "They locked me up with just a bible and a blanket," the laconic Haggard, told me in 2010. "That sounds like a song title, don't it, 'A Bible and a Blanket.'"

Born in 1937, Haggard grew up in Bakersfield, California, where his family sought work after Oklahoma became a dust bowl. The family lived in an old train boxcar, and Merle's life got harder when his father died; Merle was just nine. After a string of crimes caused him to be jailed often during his teens, Haggard turned to music. Starting in 1966, he cranked out a series of chart-topping hits including "Sing Me Back Home," "I Wonder If They Ever Think of Me," "That's the Way Love Goes," and "Mama Tried," later covered by the Grateful Dead. He helped define what became known as the Bakersfield sound, a spare and unadorned brand of outlaw country some saw as a reaction to the slick Nashville songs of that era. Haggard received Kennedy Center Honors in 2010, won four Grammys, and was inducted into the Country Music Hall of Fame.

Because Haggard's family had moved from Oklahoma during the Depression, Haggard understood the sensibility of the middle of the country. While in a tour bus near Muscogee in 1969, Haggard and his drummer, Roy Edward Burris, started joking about all the things you just don't do in Oklahoma. They wrote "Okie from Muscogee" in 15 minutes, Haggard said. The 1969 song became an anthem for heartland conservatives who felt their patriotism attacked by Vietnam War opponents. At concerts, fans would sing along with The Hag, as he was affectionately known, at the top of their lungs: "I'm proud to be an Okie from Muscogee, a place where even squares can have a ball. We still wave Old Glory down at the courthouse, and white lightnin's still the biggest thrill of all."

Soon the song was an anthem for the "silent majority" as President Nixon called his supporters, who were far from quiet whenever Haggard and his band played the song. In a review of a 1969 concert in Dayton, Ohio, the Atlantic Monthly said of Haggard's fans: "Suddenly they are on their feet, berserk, waving flags and stomping and whistling and cheering . . . and for those brief moments the majority isn't silent anymore."

Despite all the success it brought him—Haggard's fee went way up and his audience grew—he suggested at times that he had misgivings. In 1990 he told The New Yorker: "Sometimes I wish I hadn't written 'Okie.' Not that I'm ashamed of it. I'm not sure, but what bothers me most is the people that identify with it. There is the extremity out there. I don't know. It made people forget that I might be a much more musical artist than they give me credit for. I was indelibly stamped with this political image. I had to play that song every night for 18 years. And sometimes, out of a little bit of rebellious meanness, you know, I say I'm not going to do it. But very seldom. Your own songs become like living creatures. They are like children. They are individuals. You forgive them. God dang, you fall back in love with 'em, you know?"

Later in life, Haggard, always enigmatic and willing to change his mind, appeared to embrace his most popular song. "The main message is about pride," he said. "My father was an 'Okie from Muskogee' when Okie was considered a four-letter word. I think it became an anthem for people who were not being noticed or recognized in any way—the silent majority. It brought them pride." He told the Village Voice: "Listen to that line: 'I'm proud to be an Okie from Muskogee.' Nobody had ever said that before in a song."

In 1983, Haggard and Willie Nelson covered the Townes Van Zandt song "Pancho and Lefty," playing the two characters in a video. Just days after Haggard died, Willie Nelson told Rolling Stone: "Merle and I were buddies from way back. I first met him at a poker game at my house in Nashville in the early Sixties, before he went back to Bakersfield and I went back to Texas. We always had a lot in common. We both hopped trains as kids. We both got our starts playing bass in other bands before stepping out on our own. We'd both been married for the last 20 years. We both had our sons playing guitar with us.

"Over the years, we played a lot of dates, a lot of poker. He was a great audience for my jokes. I told him recently, 'You know what you call a guitar player without a girlfriend? Homeless,' and he laughed. In the early Eighties, he came to stay with me in Texas to record. We were living pretty hard back then, but we'd also try to be a little healthy. We used to go jogging a lot. We'd burn one down and run two miles in cowboy boots. In Texas, we went on a 10-day cayenne-pepper juice cleanse. It was horrible. One day after we'd been up all night, Merle went to the condo to get some rest. Around 4 a.m., we woke him up to sing his part on 'Pancho and Lefty.' He sang it half in his sleep, but Hag sings pretty good in his sleep."

Years after I'd interviewed Haggard by phone, I saw him perform on his final tour, at the Luther Burbank Center in Santa Rosa, about 50 miles north of San Francisco. Haggard had recently been released from a hospital's ICU, where he'd fought off double pneumonia. At one point he'd canceled his February 2016 show in Santa Rosa, then un-canceled it. Though attached to a breathing tube, Haggard performed with intensity and grit, and his inimitable voice sounded just like it should: well-worn, reassuring, and familiar, burnished with decades of hard work and countless miles of bus travel.

At the show, Haggard told the audience he'd received a call that day from Donald Trump's campaign asking if they could use his song, "Are the Good Times Really Over?" Haggard said he always gets suspicious when someone says the word "use" and wasn't inclined to let a politician use anything of his. But then he slyly said, "Well Trump does have a lot of money . . ." During his show-closing performance of "Okie from Muscogee," Haggard flung aside his breathing tube, put down his electric guitar, waved his black hat in acknowledgment and exited stage left. Okies and hippies, rednecks and activists, and everyone in between stood and cheered.

Three days later in Oakland he would play his final show. Haggard died less than two months later, on April 6, 2016, his 79th birthday. "When my last song is sung and my life's work is done," he sings in a 1977 song, "and my old faithful guitar loses tone, you won't find me troubled then, wishing I could sing again. When my last song is sung I'll be gone." Haggard probably didn't know he was playing one of his final shows that night in Santa Rosa, but when he left the stage and strode into the night, he had the quiet confidence of a man who had led an honorable life and said everything he needed to say.

≈ ≈ ≈

You've been on the road so many years. Why do you keep playing?

Well, it's what I do. If I quit doing it, the next big event will be my funeral. It's an exercise for somebody who has used my lungs like I have all my life; if I don't use them, well I will get pneumonia (this interview was in 2010, before he became severely ill in 2015). I need to sing, I need to perform, I enjoy it; I make a good living at it, and the people seem to like it as much as ever if not more. As long as I'm able to walk out there and people still enjoy it, I'm gonna do it because if I don't it will be over for me.

You had a rough time during your teens and landed in San Quentin, one of California's most notorious prisons.

I didn't like being confined—I got into trouble when I was young for not going to school. I wound up running from the law; I was playing a game with them. I escaped 17 times from different institutions in California. It became a challenge. They finally put me away in the Big House when I was like 19 years old in San Quentin. All of a sudden I realized I was close to the end of the rope. I started reading the Bible when I was about 19; it kind of turned my life around, and I've been going in a different direction ever since. I've never looked back.

Tell me about the time you told Johnny Cash about seeing him at San Quentin.

Cash and I were friends, we'd been friends for some time, when I told him that. He said something about playing San Quentin (in 1958) and I said, "Yeah I was there." And he said, "I don't remember you being on the bill." And I said, "No, I was in the audience." It blew him backwards. Another time he said, "Hag, you are everything people think I am." I said, "Yeah, but Cash, we don't choose our destinies. I didn't choose this." People thought Cash had done a lot of time and had been in prison and all that, but he was in the Navy; he was a radio operator; he probably spent four hours in jail one time for picking flowers at the wrong time a day. Johnny Cash was a big lovable paranoid person that was one of my closest friends. I loved him to death. He helped me a lot in my life, and I might have helped him a couple of times.

Can you tell me about your new album, I Am What I Am?

It stands for itself; it is what it is. I could be recording with the philharmonic if I wanted to, but this is me, just an up-to-date report on my life. It's my feeling that if you intend to perform for people the rest of your life, be careful what you record because you will have to sing it for the rest of your life. I get more real about what I record and more choosy, and I find myself doing a bigger part of the album onstage than I used to. A lot of times I did songs that weren't really me, and I would never do them again. I only did them for records, but as I grow older I seem to be more selective.

Do you play similar sets nightly or mix it up?

We do a different show every night; we let the chips fall where they may. We walk onstage with a good career to choose from—we've had over 100 songs in the top 10—we usually start off at the same song for four or five nights and go from there. We have a basic idea of what we're headed for, but it's an ad-lib show. It's my job to walk in there and set the condition and give it to you according to what I think you'll enjoy the most. That's what I try to do.

Who has influenced you, either within music or beyond?

There were people who influenced me throughout my life, everybody from Bing Crosby to Muhammad Ali, that I've known and admired and learned something from.

Tell me about your family.

I'm married to a younger woman (Theresa Haggard, formerly Theresa Ann Lane). She's young and beautiful and still in the prime of her life. She keeps me young. I have a son graduating from high school today. I have a daughter on her second year of college—she's 20. We have a cabin on Lake Shasta, and we do a lot of fishing and boating. We have a studio here. We're in business to make a living and to stay healthy and to give people what they seem to want.

What are you most proud of?

Well, I think songs, individual songs, my best songs, you know, they're like children, and as time goes by they seem to grow and become more popular. I've written about 16 songs that have been played over one million times: "Mama Tried,"

"Workin' Man Blues," "Big City," "Sing Me Back Home," "Okie from Muskogee," "Silver Wings."

You've said you have lots of friends outside the realm of country music.

Yeah, the Grateful Dead: I've become friends with all those guys now. As a bonus track on this new album, there's a song called "It's Gonna Be Me" with Keith Richards playing guitar on it. I opened the show for the Stones in Little Rock, Arkansas, and they all came out on my stage and watched me perform for an hour and a half. Mick Jagger and Keith Richards standin' out there watchin' me (laughs). So that's about as good as it gets.

Is there anything you still want to do?

I got a yearnin' to cut a hit album with my wife. I think we can record a hit record, that's what I got on my mind right now. She sings and has worked the stage with me the last several years. She's a student of mine—she wasn't a singer when she came aboard, but she is now. (Note: Theresa sang background vocals on 2010's *I Am What I Am* and 2011's *Working in Tennessee*.) I'm writing songs. I'm trying to write what we need to record—I believe we can have a hit record. She's laughing. The Lord has blessed me late in my life with a young woman—that's another reason why I have to stay active. I mean, I have to light a fire under this young lady.

The People's Chef
JUAN JOSÉ CUEVAS

The soft amber lighting and smooth Latin jazz playing in the background at 1919, the flagship restaurant of Puerto Rico's Condado Vanderbilt Hotel, belied the turmoil the island faced during the previous year. I was on a magazine assignment in San Juan to write about how some Puerto Rican farmers have shifted from growing food for export to cultivating produce for local consumption. I found that one of the drivers of this transition is Juan José Cuevas, the executive chef at 1919.

A native Puerto Rican who was born in 1972, Cuevas made a name for himself by working internationally at restaurants that have earned Michelin stars, such as Akelarre in Spain and New York's Blue Hill. In 2012, Cuevas returned home to Puerto Rico to bring his vision of local, light, and fresh food that's true to itself to San Juan's most luxurious district.

I sometimes shy away from tasting menus, but Cuevas' food was a revelation: yellowtail with tobiko and ponzu; slow-cooked king salmon with a local white bean fricassee; ricotta ravioli; grilled short rib with organic polenta, local onion and blistered shishito peppers; and a dessert of banana sorbet with meringue, glittering with gold leaf. Cuevas' originality and precision were peerless; I wondered how 1919 hadn't earned a Michelin star and learned that Michelin stars aren't awarded in Puerto Rico. The guidebook spawned by the tire company hadn't gotten to the island yet; maybe because you can't drive there from the mainland.

I met Cuevas in September 2018, a year after Hurricane Maria devastated Puerto Rico. More than 3,000 people were killed and countless homes destroyed as power outages lasted for months on much of the island. At least 100,000 people had left Puerto Rico and hadn't returned a year later. But Cuevas chose to stay and help. Working with Bacardi, the rum company that provided trucks and other support, Cuevas organized food caravans that fed thousands of people. He didn't just toss sandwiches and paper towels at hungry Puerto Ricans; he cooked comfort food and served it during communal gatherings in town plazas.

It's often said that you learn more about a person in tough times than when things are easy. During difficult times, it's natural to retreat and take care of oneself and one's family, but Cuevas' response was to expand the creativity he'd cultivated as a chef to help those most in need. It never occurred to him to do otherwise.

I spoke with Cuevas on my first day in Puerto Rico, in the Condado Vanderbilt lounge, which has floor-to-ceiling views of the adjacent Atlantic Ocean. Cuevas expressed a deep love for his home, its beaches and mountains, and its hardworking farmers. He was relaxed yet energetic, enthusiastic about how hard Puerto Rico's people had worked to recover after the hurricane, and hopeful about the next chapter in the island's future.

≈ ≈ ≈

How would you describe the cuisine at your restaurant, 1919?

I use local produce as much as possible, what people call farm to table. I can help my country by offering stuff that is grown here in Puerto Rico. My cooking style is organic, very simple. We respect the ingredients and don't try to mask them with cream or butter.

If somebody comes to your restaurant and only has one opportunity to dine with you, what would you recommend?

I would have a slow-cooked fresh fish, cooked at a very low temperature, nice and soft with the full flavor of the fish, with a light fricassee of vegetables in season, combined with basil, parsley, and chives.

Could you say how you developed your sensibility as a cook?

I was lucky enough to work with some amazing chefs. Working at Blue Hill, I pushed myself to use nearly 100 percent locally grown ingredients, and to respect the seasonality of these items. So you can have great tomatoes in July, August, September, but not before and not after. In Puerto Rico I can get eggplants year-round, but there are other items I cannot get all year, so I figure out which ones are seasonal.

What inspires your creativity as a chef?

Being a chef gives you freedom and makes your heart beat. Doing the same thing over and over is great because you become better, but that's sometimes very boring. We have to have consistency, but sometimes you want to improvise. When you respect the produce, then a recipe is nothing except a sentence on a piece of paper. When you let your emotions feel it, then you are creating something. A recipe doesn't have a heart.

Cooking is a living thing. You have to feel the food. All your senses are engaged. How does it [an ingredient] smell? How does it look? How does it feel when you touch it? That's your biggest guide, your senses. You have to be free—you can't constrain yourself to one particular recipe. Maybe today the eggplants didn't feel the same way, or the parsley didn't smell right. You need the freedom to do things.

After I had dinner at your restaurant, I didn't feel heavy, but I was totally satisfied. I felt energized.

I don't like to call my food "healthy" because people have this perception about food that's called healthy; they think that it lacks flavor, but it doesn't. Healthy is the way that we approach food. Yes we use fat, but we don't use a lot. Our seasonings are very simple because the ingredients are so great; there's no need to mask the food with other flavors. We have a local beet salad with watermelon and shishito peppers. What we do to enhance the flavor is we juice some beets, and that juice is what we use for the vinaigrette. So basically we are just increasing the flavor of the beets.

What was your experience during the hurricane? What happened to farmers here?

Of course Maria swiped the island. Some farmers harvested just before Maria so they had some stuff for that week. And that was it. After that we had a period of two months when there was nothing available locally. By early December we began to see some of the fast-growing items like kale that grew in a greenhouse, and then in February/March we began to see a lot more. What I am getting now is ten times better than what I was getting before Maria, better in quality, diversity.

When I moved back to the island six years ago, most of the farmers were growing the staple diet of Puerto Rico: yuca, cassava, plantains, and green bananas, the diet of our ancestors. It began with the Indians and the Africans, they had to do very physical labor; you eat a plantain and you get full very fast. There is nothing light in there. But of course all that was swiped, so the generation after me is younger—they're in their early thirties—they see an opportunity to grow something else, more diverse, more modern. They're still growing yuca and malanga but they will not take the whole field for that, so they do carrots and beets and eggplants, more diverse, a lot more greens, kale, collard greens, different kinds of herbs, purslane. It's a lot better than before when farmers grew the same thing.

You mean what they were used to, what their parents grew?

Exactly. I'm 100 percent Puerto Rican, but I lived so many years outside (the island). My food is quite different from that of most of the people in Puerto Rico. My concept of food here is not the same as I had in the States. And the vision I have for my food is quite different than that of most of the people here, so I was looking for different ingredients the whole time. You have to change your concept of food to fit the ingredients where you live. I still love the lighter side of my food. It's difficult for me to go to more hearty, heavy food.

I still use many of the traditional ingredients, but it's not the base of my dishes. There's a lot of meat in our traditional diet. My restaurant is mostly vegetables and fish. Maria gave (Puerto Rican farmers) the opportunity to grow something else besides the traditional. They can see that there is the potential for that. We understand that there is still demand for our traditional ingredients, but there's a demand for something else.

So crisis offers opportunity?

One hundred percent. I hate to say that, but every bad thing that happens in your life, I believe that perhaps now I can do something else. Everything good or bad gives you another opportunity. In this case, it gave us an opportunity to re-grow and also to see that we cannot depend so much on importing stuff. We can grow the item ourselves so we can be sustainable if another disaster happens. It's a reality.

Do you feel there's a sense on the island that farmers need to shift what they grow so that Puerto Ricans can take care of themselves the next time disaster strikes?

That is the feeling among farmers. I was visiting a few people throughout the island last week; most of them feel that Maria was the tipping point for them to realize they have to diversify more and to be ready if something else happens. Not only for them as a business, but there's a strong thinking that it's not only about the person who grows but everyone else. We have to be able to depend more on ourselves.

Can you speak to the chef's role and how restaurants can help farmers make the transition to growing more for local consumption than for export?

Chefs can have a huge impact on the economy of the country, in Puerto Rico more now than ever. We have the power to support farmers so they can continue growing. When I moved back to the island six years ago, most of the farmers were a little bit resistant to work with a hotel because in the past the chef might change the menu and not buy what they said they'd buy. So they didn't want to do business with hotels. I would tell them, "I'm sorry for your bad experience, but I can promise you that won't be the case. I am a man of my word—if I look into your eyes and tell you I am going to do something, trust me, and if you deliver, I'll pay you the same day.

Say we want eggplants. If I don't buy them for my restaurant, I buy for the hotel, so I have some power that most other people don't have. I wish more hotels would do that. If we joined, all the hotels, we have the power to help farmers—the biggest thing is they need cash to continue growing—but most hotels don't do this. I use a lot of tomatoes. I have two growers doing tomatoes consistently for me, but it took six years for them to believe that I need a certain amount. I use them for salad, but most of the tomatoes I use are for tomato sauce. I hate canned tomatoes; I cannot stand the flavor or the texture. So every tomato sauce in the hotel is made with fresh tomatoes, whether for a pizza or a more complex dish.

Since the hurricane, you and a number of other chefs came together to help Puerto Ricans; in the media you hear mostly about José Andrés (World Central Kitchen, Chefs for Puerto Rico) and Jose Enrique.

They are friends so when José Andrés came to Puerto Rico after Hurricane Maria, he called on Jose Enrique because of their friendship. The first couple of days they did it from Jose Enrique's kitchen, but then they went to the Coliseum (stadium) and went to other places and made kitchens. This is not food for the few—it's food for a lot of people, things as simple as mac and cheese, ham and cheese sandwiches, *sancocho* (traditional Puerto Rican soup). I was not part of that group, but we did something else with Bacardi (the rum distiller based in Puerto Rico). We would go to towns, and they would bring water to drink in trucks with water to wash. They would bring in doctors, music, DJs, speakers. My job was to bring the food.

Really, I heard about food and medicine, but why music?

I asked somebody about the music, and they said: "What do you mean? You are Puerto Rican. We are a very happy country—we love to celebrate—we like parties. Everything cannot be just crying about what happened; we need to celebrate that we are alive. Of course we need music." They were bringing happiness.

They asked me to help. I said I know how to cook; I just need a truck. Of course they have trucks; they're Bacardi. They would pick me up around eight in the morning and we would drive to a town (that had been devastated by the hurricane). We made simple homey food, but hot food, something that people were not tasting perhaps for a long period of time. This was about a month after the hurricane hit, and it lasted close to two months.

I read about José Andrés and his famous ham and cheese sandwiches—what were you serving to people?

We wanted to serve hot food—people were missing hot food. People were eating cold food or canned food, and they couldn't even warm it because they didn't have the stove. These people must have been craving really good hot food. That's what we did. And we would bring fresh fruit, not canned, and salad, and a rice dish with everything so one day was a fish rice and another chicken rice. With the hotel, I have equipment and can transport hot food and keep it hot for a long period of time. With Bacardi we would go to the countryside and set up in a plaza in the center of town.

And I'm sure once you were there everybody would tell their family and friends.

The first one I did with Bacardi was around 200 people. The last one was close to a thousand. To see the happiness of the people, even during a difficult time, it was fantastic. The hotel stayed open all the way through the hurricane. We were feeding people at the hotel, visitors, staff, and local people.

How did you take your skill set and ramp up to feeding a lot of people so quickly?

We can do banquets for a thousand people, so this was not a problem. The dishes were more simple, more homey, more Puerto Rican, so it speaks to my heart completely. I know what my family will eat when it's raining outside. I would think about my family, how I grew up and who I am now.

That speaks to you being a native Puerto Rican. Perhaps people who came from the outside, though they helped tremendously, wouldn't have the same idea of what the local people crave.

There is the connection you have with the people plus your feeling. It's not like my family was having a party every day. My sister in Utuado, in the center of the island, needed food, water, electricity. When Bacardi asked me to help, I said: "I have only one request. At some point, I want to go to Utuado because I spent my childhood there." That town got pretty devastated. It's a community connected by a bridge. The whole bridge just broke so they were completely isolated. There was no electricity, no communication, so nobody knew about them. Somehow they took a supermarket cart, like a basket, and put stuff there and pulled it over [on a cable]. They did that with everything: food, water, gas, diesel, you name it, but they were without communication for at least a week.

In the continental U.S., many people weren't aware that Puerto Rico is part of our country. What would you want people to know about what happened here after Hurricane Maria?

This was the strongest hurricane in at least 50 years in Puerto Rico. Nobody was prepared for that. That included our own people, our government. In a war they can transport thousands of soldiers; they bring food. Why then to help a human being you cannot do that? I cannot understand how you can move so much to go to war when you cannot do it for your sister country. In San Juan, we had no water, no electricity, but life goes on. My life was not bad, but in the center of the island, people were suffering terribly.

You had chefs and volunteers helping people more efficiently and more effectively than governments. Is that because local people can do things more easily? What was the reason the chefs were so effective?

I think that we realized that we were on our own, and something had to be done. I did what I can do. I can cook. I wish I had more knowledge about electricity, but I don't. So my power is cooking; I can feed people. Once we realize how bad was the situation, we had to leave our comfort and go and help.

What would you say is the best way that people in the States can help their fellow Americans here in Puerto Rico?

Visit them. Puerto Rico is more than ready to receive people. This island is beautiful. I wouldn't change what I did with my life, living so many years outside the island; it helped me to grow. But coming back, this island is gorgeous; the weather is amazing; people are great. You just need to drive a little bit, and you'll go from oceanfront to a river to the mountains. The music is unbelievable. People are happy here. It's a very good place to relax. The food is very good on the island. So for me, it's simply visit. We love and we need the tourists.

Hope Dies Last
STUDS TERKEL

Growing up as a high school student in the late 1970s, I stumbled upon a paperback that introduced me to people I'd never have met. That paperback, whose title *Working* was diagonally inscribed in bold black letters across its scarlet cover, became my little red book. Its pages contained interviews with a hundred hard-working people, from the footsore waitress to the gas-meter reader who dodges canine pursuers. Its compassionate interviewer somehow led gruff garbage-truck drivers and bristly strip miners to reveal their deepest feelings about what they do and engendered empathy for those who, day in and day out, put their shoulders to the wheel.

The interviewer, Studs Terkel, then in his sixties, seemed impossibly old, a relic from the bygone age of Wobblies, Depression grit, and union battles. Louis "Studs" Terkel—he's nicknamed after the fictional character Studs Lonigan from the novels of James T. Farrell—was born in New York

City in 1912, lived in Chicago most of his life, and died at age 96 at his home near the shores of Lake Michigan on Oct. 31, 2008, just four days before Barack Obama won the presidency.

In 2005, Terkel published *And They All Sang: Adventures of an Eclectic Disc Jockey*, a compelling collection of archival interviews with more than 40 of the 20th century's greatest musicians. Among those interviewed are gospel singer Mahalia Jackson, classical guitar maestro Andrés Segovia, and jazz legends Louis Armstrong, Betty Carter, and Dizzy Gillespie. Terkel worked as a disc jockey in Chicago, including 45 years at WFMT, creatively mixing jazz, opera, folk, blues, and gospel, along with interviews of musicians and the leading thinkers of the day. His first radio show, which began in 1945 just after World War II ended, was called *The Wax Museum* because the 78-rpm records were made of wax—Terkel laments that he kept breaking the fragile discs. The eclectic shows ranged from Delta blues to Terkel's recitations of short stories by Flannery O'Connor, Ring Lardner, and Anton Chekhov.

Terkel first became enamored with African American music during the Depression, when, on his way home from law school classes, he listened to the blues at record stores in the predominantly black Bronzeville neighborhood. That's where he first heard Big Bill Broonzy—the son of a former slave—Tampa Red, Memphis Minnie, and other artists who brought the music of the Deep South to the cities of America's heartland. Terkel favored Big Bill's definition of the blues: "Ain't nuthin' but a good man feelin' bad."

In the mid-1950s, a few years after Terkel was one of the first deejays to expose white audiences to Mahalia Jackson, she returned the favor, insisting that he host her national radio show. A CBS executive told Terkel to sign a loyalty oath—it seems Terkel's left-leaning politics had attracted the attention of Senator Joe McCarthy and his minions—but Terkel refused. Mahalia backed up her old friend saying: "If you fire Studs, find another Mahalia Jackson." Which she knew was impossible. Terkel kept his job.

Calling himself "a guerrilla journalist with a tape recorder," Terkel's first book of interviews with ordinary people, 1967's *Division Street: America*, was a groundbreaking look at the lives of Chicagoans, rich and poor, black and white. Rather than interview celebrities or scholars, Terkel conducted hundreds of interviews with people he met all over the city and chose the best conversations for the book.

Whether Terkel is talking with a prostitute in *Working* or interviewing jazz great Earl "Fatha" Hines on the radio, he was driven by compassion and curiosity. Perhaps most important, he never judged his subjects, one reason why people were so comfortable opening up to him. Terkel won the Pulitzer Prize (for *The Good War,* about those involved in World War II). He's most proud of helping readers understand the lives of everyday people, such as waitress Dolores Dante. "I'm never going to speak to a waitress again the way I did before," a reader once told Terkel, who said, "I affected that guy. Dolores affected that guy. It was her moment of immortality."

In many of his published conversations, Terkel deletes his questions, letting the interviewee do the talking. But his presence illuminates his interviews, and sometimes, as in his 2001 book about death and dying, *Will the Circle Be Unbroken?*, he reveals his inner feelings. During the research for that book, Terkel's wife and companion for 60 years, Ida, died at the age of 87. Not long after Ida's death, a friend told Studs to get over his grief—he should be happy he had so many years with her. "Bullshit," was his response. He was grateful for his time with Ida but didn't believe grief should have a timetable. Considering that *Circle* was published on the eve of Terkel's 90th birthday, many readers believed it would be his final book, a fitting coda to a career that spanned more than half a century.

But in 2003 the irrepressibly energetic oral historian followed with another original book, *Hope Dies Last*, urging his readers to "keep the faith in difficult times." Ultimately, the central theme of Terkel's body of work is hope.

I met Terkel on a brisk and sunny November afternoon at his home on Chicago's north side in 2005 to interview him for The Sun, an ad-free literary magazine. He appeared frail from his recent medical battles, but his voice remained fierce, enlivened by his political and artistic passions. He spoke in stacatto bursts. A former theatrical actor, Terkel occasionally broke into impersonations of Billie Holiday and Mahalia Jackson, singing the opening of "Move On Up a Little Higher" with Mahalia's phrasing. Terkel and I spoke for two and a half hours. At the end of the interview, he offered me "a touch of Scotch." I offered him a Ghirardelli chocolate bar, which I'd brought from my home town of San Francisco. The chocolate was so tightly packaged we had trouble opening it: "I can't open half the things today," he groused, sensing another affront against the common man. "It's deliberate!"

❧ ❧ ❧

Have you ever lost an interview because of a technical problem?

I'm known for my ineptitude. That's the irony of the whole thing; they call me the master of the tape recorder, but I haven't the faintest idea. I'm just learning the electric typewriter. And I don't know what a computer is. I'm a neo-Neanderthal in technology. But the irony is my ingratitude to technology because were it not for technology, I wouldn't be here talking to you right now. Eight weeks ago, at the age of 93, I was in the hospital with a broken neck.

You've just come out with a new book . . .

The book is called *And They All Sang;* that was a phrase of Leonard Bernstein who's in the book, but the subtitle tells what it's about: *Adventures of an Eclectic Disc Jockey*, eclectic of course being the operative word. How it began: I went to the University of Chicago Law School, and it wasn't for me. Nahh, I went there dreaming of Clarence Darrow and I woke up to Antonin Scalia. By the way, he was teaching there, not when I was there of course. I graduated, if you want to call it graduated, in '34. He came years later to teach. It wasn't made for me, corporations and such, so I was a rotten student.

But I was a streetcar student—my parents ran a men's hotel. I would transfer two times to go to the University of Chicago Law School on the South Side of Chicago. Our hotel was near North Side on Wells and Grand. There was a stopover where I transferred streetcars. One stop was in Bronzeville, a black community in the '30s. It was of course segregated, but there was a life, oh, that isn't [there] now. You heard records in galli-maufry shops—you could buy everything, and they were sell-ing phonograph records in there for a nickel or dime. They were called race records: Okeh, Vocalion, Bluebird. And here I heard those blues singers: Big Bill Broonzy, my favorite, Muddy Waters, Memphis Slim, Memphis Minnie, and Tampa Red, so going to the University of Chicago Law School helped me get acquainted with the blues.

Then I got a job with the government, the Works Prog-ress Administration. The WPA was headed by a man named Harry Hopkins, and it did what free enterprise couldn't do. Free market—we call our hope, our love, our dear one—fell on its ass in the big crash of October 1929. And people didn't know what hit 'em. The wise men of Wall Street were going crazy. The WPA provided jobs for the millions of people who were unemployed, and now they're talking about privatizing!

Privatizing is what killed us then. It was all privatized—
we were saved by the government. We are suffering from a
national Alzheimer's disease. There is no memory of that.

So I had a job with a predecessor of the WPA. It wasn't bad,
and through that job I met this guy in the Chicago Repertory
Group; it was like a farm club for the Group Theater in New
York—we did *Waiting for Lefty*. So I became an actor. That's
when the director said there's work in radio soap operas in
Chicago. We had more than New York and Hollywood put
together. *Woman in White* is about a nurse; *The Guiding Light*
is about a minister—they're all the same script. They all had
the same crooks, the Chicago crooks, the bright one, the middle one, and the dumb one. And I was always the dumb one.
It was steady work.

Then some guy liked my style; I became a commentator
on the air. Then I was in the war (World War II) but only
for nine months stateside. I had a perforated ear drum—it's
called limited service. Now I came out of the Army, then I got
a job as a disc jockey. I was playing records, and you could do
anything you want. I remembered Caruso—I loved Caruso as
a kid, my father and of course Italian immigrants would buy
a Caruso record, two bucks a head, blank on one side, that's
like 50 bucks today.

An American poet from an Italian family said his uncle
used to hear Caruso all the time. As a small boy, he said there
was something about him that was about the possibilities in
the human race. He would hit a certain note—that's as far as
you could go—and Caruso would just go beyond that, and it
told me that human beings have possibilities. That all of us are
better than we may be behaving at the moment, that there is
within us certain potentialities not yet tapped. That's the way
he saw it.

So I'd put on a Caruso aria, say "Ombra mai fu" from
Handel's *Xerxes*; then comes Louis Armstrong's "West End

Blues," my favorite jazz record. It's got Earl Hines revolutionizing the piano. I follow that with say Woody Guthrie doing "Tom Joad," a Dust Bowl ballad. That record, which is a 10-inch breakable record, but two sides of it, six minutes, he did the whole *Grapes of Wrath*. He did everything, it was a ballad, it was all Steinbeck had in mind. Then I follow that with a Brazilian soprano and maybe a country song.

You could never do that today on mainstream radio stations. You could never get away with it.

That was a great experience. Since then I went to WFMT, a wonderful station—they let me do anything, and I continued this. But why can't I do that today?

Every station has its own format, whether it's rock, country—

That's right. So I did everything. But back to the disc jockey days. I'm known as an oral biographer, but I consider myself still a disc jockey. The word wasn't used then. But I'd play all these records. Now the key thing about it is, I expected [to hear from] a teacher here or there, a librarian, or those who would buy a season ticket in the balcony for the symphony. I get a letter from a truck driver, from a counterwoman, from a waitress, and suddenly you realize they're sayin' we never heard this music before. Well neither did the librarian hear that kind of jazz before or the spirituals or the blues that I played. It was divided: jazz, classical, instrumental, Andrés Segovia explaining the classical guitar.

This old man—I call him old, I'm 93—he was 80 at the time and his only prop was a footstool. And there's an audience of 5,000 in Ann Arbor hearing one old man with a guitar, the classical guitar, delicate, and they listen! And they're leaning over listening as he plays maybe one of his own transcriptions, a Bach transcription, Bach transcribed by Segovia. In fact he created much of the repertoire for the classical guitar. And one of his admirers came up to him and said, "It was wonderful, but you play so softly. I had to lean forward and listen so hard to you."

"You know what I did next time," he said. "I played even more softly. I played more softly so that he listened even more." So he's there, followed by Ravi Shankar, explaining the nature of a raga, first the sitar that he plays. It seems like there are thousands of chords. And there are ragas for every occasion, every moment of your life, morning, evening, daytime, summer, winter, sadness, birth, lust, anything.

Then you go on to jazz and Louis Armstrong's thoughts that are quite different from what you usually hear. And there is Dizzy Gillespie talking about his work with Charlie Parker, creating a new form of jazz: bop. And then we come to folk, and spirituals, and blues, and Mahalia Jackson, whom I knew.

Tell me how you came to interview musicians on your show.

I loved music as a kid. I never played an instrument, and I can't carry a tune. But I'd hear that music, the music was played by black bands—the patrons, the guests were all-white, working-class white, but the bands were Lottie Hightower and Charlie Cook; they were black. And I'd hear that slow blues when they could dance on a dime, and of course the bellies or rubbing together you know.

Folk music came about during the Great Depression. I ran into this group called the Almanac Singers, and they sang when the CIO (Congress of Industrial Organizations, a federation of unions) was being organized. They traveled in a jalopy around the country. And that had Woody Guthrie in it, and a kid with a big bobbling Adams apple, that was Pete Seeger. And a huge man from Arkansas named Lee

Hayes. And one day they came to Chicago Repertory—we were doing a play about a strike or something. We would do sketches on the strike lines—we called it mobile theater too, street theater.

I'd just got married—my wife and I had a two-and-a-half room place with a Murphy bed. She was a social worker, and it's about 12 o'clock at night. I write a note to my wife and hand it to Guthrie. I say, These are good guys; put them up for the night. Well she's asleep and the bell rings about 12:30 at night. She goes to the door. There are four guys standing there, a little freckle-faced guy, that's Woody obviously. Without a word he hands her my note. She says, come on in. And so there they were for two weeks on the floor together. One night I wake up, and Guthrie is asleep, his stuff is in the waste basket. It was about 20 pages, single spaced, and so help me if it wasn't James Joyce, *Ulysses*. It was fantastic writing, and I threw it away.

Meantime, I knew Mahalia because I heard her record one day: "Move On Up a Little Higher." I'd never heard a voice like that before so I went to the Olivet Baptist Church where she was singing. All the churches claimed her you know . . . and then we got to be friends. I hear Mahalia's voice and I start playing her records on my disc jockey show. The part that's sad is when Professor Dorsey in this book says, "Mr. Studs Terkel—he's the one who made Mahalia world renowned," he's paying me this credit. What a sad commentary this is. Much of Africa and America knew Mahalia's stuff—she'd pack a ballpark—but no white guy [knew Mahalia]. I was a white disc jockey, and it did play a role, there's no doubt, but he's giving me credit when he shouldn't be.

And Mahalia of course was her own self. There she was singing these songs and along came the civil rights movement. One day a call comes from Montgomery when the bus boycott began, and it's Rev. Ralph Abernathy calling her. By this time Martin Luther King had heard Mahalia and she became his favorite singer. When he was killed in Memphis the band below was playing, "Precious Lord Take My Hand," which was written for Mahalia. King considered that his favorite. And then I get a job at WFMT, this remarkable station. Mahalia now is internationally known—she sang at Kennedy's inauguration. Now CBS is hiring her for a network radio show down from the Wrigley Building. She said she would do it under one condition, that Studs Terkel is the host. So they trembled, but they did it.

Let me ask you about your literary career and what you did starting with Division Street: America *in 1967. That was revolutionary because you went into the streets and interviewed the common person, not the politician, not the author, not the celebrity.*

That's of course the point. You know how that happened. My publisher, André Schiffrin, calls me up; he had just finished a book, this was 1964, 1965, *Report from a Chinese Village.* André said, "How about you doing an American village during its own revolution, civil rights?" I said, "Are you outta your mind?" And he meant of course Chicago. And so I did it, and it just fell naturally into place. It was acclaimed by critics and public. And then about six months later he [Schiffrin] calls and says: "How about a book about the Great Depression? The young know nothing about this." I say, "Are you outta your mind?" And I do the Depression book. That's how it started.

When you started Division Street *you said you were looking for a single street where you could find white and black, rich and poor. Did that street exist?*

There is a Division Street in Chicago, but I meant it metaphorically. We're on Division Street. We're split, now more than ever. But there was a street, called Halsted Street, that had everything, though today it's been gentrified, almost homogenized.

You get people to share so much of their intimate life, their history, their feelings, their passions. How do you get people to be so forthcoming?

I don't know. There's nothing mysterious about it. "How's your day begin?" I gotta make it clear: I spoke of my ineptitude with mechanical things. I can't drive a car. I can't ride a bike. And I press the wrong buttons sometimes. I lost Martha Graham. I lost Michael Redgrave. And I almost lost Bertrand Russell during the Cuban missile crisis in '63. This was in a village in North Wales—I knew somebody who knew somebody—I had a half hour. If I had lost that one, I would have put my head in the oven.

I generally try to meet people as another guy meeting them. So I'm sitting there and this person says, "Hey the recorder's not working." At that moment that person feels my equal certainly, my superior probably, but most important that person feels needed by me. To feel needed is what every person wants, and they feel I need them because I'm inept. And I do this not as a gag. You know who Mike Royko was?

Sure, the Chicago columnist.

Mike accused me of deliberately doin' that. He says, "You son of a bitch, you deliberately . . ." but later on he discovered that I am inept. He says, "You know what, it's true, you are hopeless." A great moment for me was when I interviewed this woman years ago. The housing projects are still new and this was an integrated one. Poverty was the only common denominator. The woman had three little kids. And I got the mic—the mic wasn't as ubiquitous as it is today—and the kids are jumping up and down, their mommy is being interviewed, they're five, six years old. So I say to the kids, "Be quiet, and I'll play back your mommy's voice." I'm playing back her voice and she's listening and suddenly she hears a phrase.

This is the first time she ever heard her voice. And she says: "Oh my God, I never knew I felt that way before." Well that's a big moment. That's what I call my bingo moment! For her and for me. So how I do it? There is no one way. I sit down with this guy, and he might give me a cup of coffee, and I start talking. I sometimes mention something about myself as I'm talking to them. I'm just a guy who's asking questions, and they forget about the mic.

If you could invite anybody to dinner that you've ever known, who would be at the other end of the table?

Bernard Shaw or Mark Twain, I think George Bernard Shaw. This guy was everything—he was the founder of the Labour Party. Playwright, for chrissake. He's next to Shakespeare. He's a drama critic, he's a music critic, the best. He was funny; a soapbox speaker.

One last question—are you still hopeful about this country?

You know what, whether I want to be or not, I have to be. It's as simple as that. Well, I think we had a good session. I think you just about got me. Would you like a little touch of Scotch or something?

Sending Down Roots in Tuscany
FRANCES MAYES

"People are always saying, luck, luck, luck. I think you make your own luck in a lot of ways," author Frances Mayes told me when I interviewed her at the home she restored in Italy. "I think change is good; I think taking chances is good." Mayes made a long leap of faith when she and Ed Mayes bought a house in the Tuscan hilltown of Cortona in 1990. It was a deeply intentional decision; she and her first husband had ended their marriage; her new partner, Ed, was up for the adventure; and Frances believed that by changing her setting she could reimagine her life.

"I've never been averse to taking a risk," Mayes told me as we sat alongside an ancient fresco in Bramasole, Mayes' home in Tuscany. "Yeats said: 'When I changed my life, I changed my form. When I changed my syntax, I changed my life.' It was the other way to me. When I changed my world, it changed the writing."

In other words, when Mayes moved to Italy, embarked on a years-long restoration of a storied home, and kept a journal to write about the feelings it evoked within her, she reinvented her artistic life. New avenues to creativity opened as refurbishing the home helped her become part of the fabric of Cortona's community. "I was hoping for a connection with the light, something transformative, something big," she told me during the conversation for my book, *A Sense of Place*. And that's what she got.

Mayes, of course, is the author of the international bestseller, *Under the Tuscan Sun*, which has been translated into more than 50 languages, sold millions of copies, and made into an engaging 2003 film starring Diane Lane. Bramasole, the ancient name of her home, translates to "yearning for the sun."

Here's how Mayes describes the house in *Under the Tuscan Sun*: "It is tall, square, and apricot-colored with faded green shutters, ancient tile roof, and an iron balcony on the second level, where ladies might have sat with their fans to watch some spectacle below . . . When it rains or when the light changes, the facade of the house turns gold, sienna, ocher; a previous scarlet paint job seeps through in rosy spots like a box of crayons left to melt in the sun."

The book turned out to be the first in a three-volume memoir of her time in Tuscany. More recently, Mayes published a novel, *Women in Sunlight* (2018), about three women in their later years who decide to eschew living in a retirement home; instead they travel together to Italy. Mayes' latest book, *See You in the Piazza* (2019), is a nonfiction love letter to Italy's off-the-beaten-path places highlighting the delights they offer.

Born in 1940 in Fitzgerald, Georgia, a small town about 90 miles south of Macon, Mayes earned a bachelor of arts at the University of Florida and a masters degree from San Francisco State University. She crafted an appealing life in the San Francisco Bay Area, publishing poetry books and serving as chair of SF State's creative writing department. "Writing poetry is the best training for any kind of writing," she told me, "because you study imagery, you study the rhythm of phrases, you study the psychological impact of certain syntactical structures. All that translates quite easily to prose."

In 2016, a national magazine asked me to interview Mayes about what makes food in Italy, particularly in Tuscany, so appealing. This time I spoke to her when she was at her North Carolina home. Frances and Ed Mayes had recently co-authored *The Tuscan Sun Cookbook: Recipes from Our Italian Kitchen*, an ode to Italy's slow-food approach and communal dining sensibility. Growing food or foraging for wild plants and inventively preparing meals is an inherently creative act, one in which Italians engage with gusto, Mayes said. This zest for food may be something that locals take for granted, but coming from afar, as Mayes has, makes it easier to appreciate.

≈ ≈ ≈

What do you enjoy about the local food in Tuscany?

The thing I appreciate most is how local it really is. Of course we have tons of farm to table in the United States now, and so much has changed since I've been going to Italy. But there local truly means just as far as you can see, practically. I remember asking [a fruit seller], "Are these peaches local?" And she said, "No, I'm so sorry, they're from Castiglion Fiorentino." That's five miles away. There is an intense passion for local food, and it's particularly focused on what you can find yourself. That's what I see that is so different from living [in the United States].

In Tuscany, right this minute everybody is out looking for the *mazza di tamburo*, the mushroom of the moment. That means drumstick—it's shaped like a drumstick with a long stem and a big flat head, not a chicken drumstick but a drum drumstick. You cannot buy these; they're very ephemeral, so you find them on land. Everybody is looking for these, right this minute. You sauté them with garlic. They (Tuscan people) don't even want them on pasta—they just want them on little crostini because they so want to taste this wild mushroom.

And there are so many things like that; soon people will be in the forests looking for chestnuts. The *funghi porcini* will come next, but this little *mazza di tamburo* is one the Tuscans really adore. This is more of a foraged thing—they are quite plentiful. And in the spring it's strange things like the green almonds; everybody loves those crunchy green almonds before they really turn into a nut. To me that's very much an acquired taste, but local people really like them.

In August everybody is out looking for wild fennel, and they are drying the branches. This is widespread—it's not just food nuts like me. Most everybody is out getting fennel or whatever it is at the moment. Wild blackberries in August, there's a huge foraging passion and people love to get what's available on the land. Lots of wild lettuces, lots of greens that people pick, they even pull up that purslane that grows between the cracks of stones. It's great in salads, and it's supposed to be good for your liver. I tend to think of foraging in a much more limited way. Maybe a few people go out and look for fiddlehead ferns [in the American South], but it's nothing like the widespread passion for being out on the land and finding things that you can eat and enjoy and talk about all over town and sustain yourself with. To me that is the number one difference between Italy and anywhere else I've ever been: They are looking, and they find a lot of things.

It sounds like that engenders a more visceral connection with people and their food. They're finding it and harvesting it themselves; food doesn't come solely from farmers.

They're also growing it. Everybody who has even a little plot is growing some food particularly in the summer, tomato and basil, even if you have just one square of yard. I'm in rural Tuscany and everybody still has a garden. Part of the wonderful aspect of this connection with the land is that it's very involved with the generosity I've always experienced among the Italians. When you've got your garden, you share it and people share with you. I'm bringing you figs; you're bringing me melons, that kind of thing. And also putting up food for winter; I love being part of this ancient agricultural heritage. Ed is in Italy right now, and a woman had this big box of tomatoes that she had put up for us because we weren't there at the end of tomato season.

The biggest thing of all is the olive harvest. That's not foraging, but everyone has an olive grove [if they can plant one], or their uncle does or their cousin or their friend. So being able to take for granted the most sublime olive oil in the universe is just such a gift, part of that great heritage of connection with the land. We pick early, in mid-October. We have lunch in the grove; everybody gathers at a rickety old table; they even bring their coffee pots and put them on little burners. There's a lot of storytelling, a lot of singing and whistling—you're picking all day and you get really tired. You've got crates and crates of great olives. You go to the mill; that's another big community thing. People are visiting at the mill, and getting their new oil. It's just such an amazing life around food; everybody talks about food. They take a very high level of quality of ingredients totally for granted. They just have no idea what they've got.

Here in United States, in our lifetime, we've gone from consuming Wonder Bread, poor coffee, and lousy beer, to appreciating artisan breads, craft beer, better coffee, local organic tomatoes, and real olive oil. My sense is that in Italy you wouldn't eat vegetables out of a can.

It would be unthinkable. I am thrilled with what's happened in the U.S. We're really lucky that it came along in our lifetime.

We weren't meant to eat Wonder Bread; that's for sure.

No, we were not. The Tuscans eat like the gods—things taste better there—I've never figured that out. Even getting apples from the farmer who grows quality heritage apples down the road here [in North Carolina], compared to the apples in Italy, they just don't have the depth of flavor. I don't know why. I guess it's the Tuscan sun. We found that with so many things—it's just the flavor in the fruit—you just want to cry.

What do you grow on your property in Tuscany?

This year we didn't grow that much because we've been remodeling, but we're just about through with that now. We had eggplant, parsley, five or six different kinds of herbs, tomatoes, fennel, carrots, radishes.

You have lemon trees too, right?

Oh yes, we have tons of lemon trees. That's my favorite ingredient in the kitchen. It's such a luxury to have endless lemons all summer.

In Tuscany, you have a real change of seasons. Could you tell me about the seasonal appreciation of food? What's coming for winter?

The chestnuts and *funghi porcini* are the main fall things that people absolutely love the most, but everything is just appreciated in its season. You find *sagras*, these big community dinners celebrating one ingredient of the season. There will be a *sagra* of the cherry in June or a *sagra* of the *funghi porcini*. There's a *sagra* of the wild boar. All around Tuscany, if you see a sign that says *sagra*, you know something is about to be celebrated. You see the signs posted outside towns: the *sagra* of the tomato, the *sagra* of the snail—we have that in Cortona, the snail in the spring. People are out on the old castle wall in the middle of the night picking these snails; it's intense.

When we spoke for A Sense of Place*, you said that one of your first published stories after moving to Italy ("Market Day in a Tuscan Town," The New York Times, July 19, 1992) was about the nearby farmers market in Camucia.*

Yes, it still thrives. At the Camucia market you can get things from other parts of Italy like artichokes. That's a huge passion of the Italians: artichokes. As soon as they're in season in the south of Italy, big trucks come up in the night and sell the artichokes at the market. So you do get a few things from other parts of Italy, but everybody knows they're from somewhere else. The market still thrives. It's like an old medieval market except that all the goods are modern. A lot of the Italians aren't running the stands—it's people from other countries—but other than that it's still the same market as when I first moved there.

Farmers markets still thrive in Italy; I think there are many more than there ever were. It's surprising in the digital world, but these are places where people meet and greet. Old men from the country come in with their tweed suits and stand around while the women shop. That part doesn't seem to have changed, just the goods have changed.

This speaks to the close connection between food and community in Italy.

That has to do with the strong influence of the piazza in rural Tuscany, rural Italy, I would say. The piazza is still that place of community where people gather. They're talking about recipes; they're shopping; they're telling each other what they're going to do with the grapes or whatever they just bought. Food is paramount for them; it's what they talk about. So when they get together in the piazza, you hear, "Well no, you don't put it in the oven; you grill it," things like that. When you're standing in line at the meat market, somebody will always ask you what you're going to do with what you're buying and will offer how they'd do it, which is much better. (Laughs)

People sometimes have an impression of Italian food being a lot of pasta and rich sauces. Do you feel that Tuscan cuisine is healthy?

Well, Italians have great longevity and one of the best health-care systems. I think one reason their statistics are so good is that they eat well. They do not eat a lot of processed food; I think that's the big secret. And they have never ever eaten much sugar. Their desserts are, to a Southerner's taste, dry and not very sweet. When I have cooked for Italian friends and served what is considered an incredible Southern dessert, like pecan pie or coconut cake, sometimes they just take a bite and look at me like: What is this? I think the fact that they have never been into sugar has kept them fit.

Are there certain seasons you spend in Tuscany now?

We're in Tuscany about six months a year; we are quite used to coming and going. Ed is over there now organizing the olive harvest. I love the fall there; it's glorious. Of course fall is glorious most places; it's really glorious here in North Carolina. We are always there [Tuscany] in summer. I love it in winter because our little town just curls up its toes, and there's no one there. A lot of things close; it's when a lot of Tuscans go on vacation to places like Thailand. It's so peaceful and beautiful. When Ed is asked what his favorite month in Italy is, he always says, "January through December." Each season has its pleasures. The only month I don't like being there is August because everything is closed. Italians are all on vacation. There are just too many tourists everywhere so I don't stay there in August, but any other month I am happily there.

You just published the 20th-anniversary edition of Under the Tuscan Sun. *Could you tell me about the new essay you added to the book?*

It's at the end, an afterword about what it's been like to live with the book over a 20-year period. The expectation I had of it was of course minimal because I had published only books of poetry before then. You don't know when you write a book whether it's going to sink or swim or fly. It's just such a shock to me that it is still going strong after 20 years, so the essay is kind of about that.

What changes have you seen, particularly in Cortona, since the book was published? And what role do you think your book played in those changes?

Undeniably it changed Cortona because the book is in 52 languages now so people from all over the world come there. I can always tell when it's come out in a different country because we have people from Romania or Brazil or wherever. We have them coming by the house. So it's had a tremendous effect locally. I think most of it has been for the good; there are many more wonderful restaurants in town now and people can live there profitably. They don't have to go work in Milan anymore or wherever. So in those ways it's been good. Other times I think: Gosh, there are a lot of tourists here, *mea culpa, mea culpa*!

Italy really didn't change for a long time, and now it's changing rather fast. Until about three years ago, you didn't see people hunched over their computers and glued to their phones; you do now. They still talk in cafés. I don't see any Italians with their computers out in the cafés. Maybe you would in Rome or somewhere, but I haven't seen it. And I hope it doesn't happen because I find the whole thing in America with people getting more and more keyed into their phones and their devices just so dreary.

Do you still have a lot of people coming to Bramasole?

We do. People come and look at the house, take a picture. The house is above the road so they don't come in the gate. It's been fine. Sometimes I open the window in the morning in my nightgown and I think, oh God, there are 40 people down there.

Looking for Diane Lane, I imagine.

Right.

Can you tell me about the novel you just completed?

It's called *Women in Sunlight* and it takes place in Italy. It's about three American women who are slated to go into an active, over-55 retirement center. They meet there and over a few months become friends. They decide to go to Italy together for a year and lease a house. It's about reinventing yourself later in life. And it's about friendship and the complications of being a parent, lots of things.

I know you're from Georgia. Are there some similarities between the U.S. South and Tuscany?

Living in North Carolina now, I'm often reminded of living in Tuscany mainly because that old sense of Southern hospitality still exists. I live in Hillsborough, a town filled with writers and artists, photographers and playwrights. It's just a fabulous place to live, and the social life could kill you. It's party party, all the time, and the Italians are that way too. They think nothing of having people over on Wednesday night when they have to get up and go to work the next morning. It's just an open door—let's have dinner—let's gather around the table. That's common to both places.

You have your grandson Willie spending time with you in Italy.

Yes, that's such a joy. He loves Italy; he's been there every summer his whole life. For the past three summers, he's been taking Italian from a tutor in Cortona, and we travel around so it's become part of his life. We're planning to be in the Dolomites this summer and all over northern Italy. Willie is 14. I just have one daughter and she has one child.

In your cookbook you say: "Tuscan food tastes like itself. Ingredients are left to shine."

Recipes have very few ingredients. So many times I see Italian recipes here [in the U.S.] with 40 ingredients and I think, no way am I making that. It's because [in Italy] the ingredients are so good; you don't really need to do a whole lot to them. The classic example is the Caprese salad. What could be simpler then tomatoes, mozzarella, basil, and olive oil? It's just that each one of those things is primo, so when those four things come together, it's magical, and there's not anything else that you need to do to it. Italians keep it simple. Whether it's meat or vegetables, they tend to leave them alone.

Are Tuscany's restaurants preserving the tradition of simple whole-some food?

Most of the trattorias and restaurants are. People believe: "What *Nonna* (grandma) made was good for us then, and it's good for us still." In Cortona we have so many fabulous trattorias and restaurants. You can't really go wrong. There is now a good bit of innovation all over Tuscany, particularly in Florence. It's just kind of exploded in the past five years with more creative, innovative chefs coming in and opening restaurants that have edgier decor. They are a lot more hip, really fun. I think the two coexist quite well. These innovative chefs are not throwing out babies with the bathwater. They are bringing traditions along and still using the great Tuscan ingredients; there is not a lot of silliness around the innova-tion. They're not just innovating for the sake of it. It's genuine and really exciting.

What advice would you give people to appreciate the local food?

One thing I usually do when I get to a town is start up con-versations with people and say: "Where do you eat? Where would you go on a special occasion?" Not necessarily relying on magazine articles and guidebooks. I think it's fun to follow your nose and try and make a discovery, not just go where Mario Batali said he went. Look at the menus posted on the streets; look inside the door. I like that sense of discovery in travel and not that everything is mapped out for you. There's just so much to discover in every town. I like to discover by walking the town. When I get someplace, that's what I do first, just walk and walk and walk.

The Minstrel in the Gallery
IAN ANDERSON

J ethro Tull frontman Ian Anderson, like many famed
performers, has been interviewed more times than he
can count. He's so eager to avoid the same old queries that
Jethro Tull's website has a section called "All Too Frequently
Asked Questions." So in 2016, before I interviewed Anderson
in advance of his theater show about the band's namesake, the
18th-century agricultural pioneer Jethro Tull, I reviewed the
oft-asked questions.

I didn't want to commit the sin of boring Anderson, whose
quick mind I sensed wouldn't find questions like "Are you
too old to rock 'n' roll?" to be clever. The band released an
album called *Too Old to Rock 'n' Roll: Too Young to Die!* in
1976; the title song became a classic. At the end of some Tull
shows in the years that followed, Anderson, who was born in
Scotland in 1947, would theatrically collapse onstage.

Jethro Tull launched in the late 1960s, an era of bound-
less possibility and creativity, especially for musicians. Like

the Yardbirds and Rolling Stones, the musicians of Jethro Tull were deeply influenced by American bluesmen such as Muddy Waters. While rooted in the blues, especially early in their career, Jethro Tull found a unique niche in rock: a flute-driven band with highly developed imagery that, in many songs, evoked the mystical folklore of the Brothers Grimm. Around the same time, Chris Wood was doing magnificent flute work with Steve Winwood's band, Traffic, but the difference in Jethro Tull was that the flute solos took the lead.

After Tull's eponymous debut gained some notice with its "Song for Jeffrey," the band released *Stand Up* in 1969. About a decade after it came out, I found *Stand Up* at a used-record store called Recycled Records in San Francisco's Haight-Ashbury and bought it for its pop-up art. When I put the record on the turntable, I discovered early Tull gems such as "A New Day Yesterday" and "Nothing Is Easy." The flute solos were refreshing, but that wasn't all that appealed. Listening to Jethro Tull, I felt transported to another time and place; I could imagine a mysterious English wood where I might come across a hermit who'd invite me into his hut for a cup of mead.

Jethro Tull hit its stride in the early 1970s with the release of a pair of albums that garnered worldwide attention: *Aqualung* and *Thick as a Brick*. The latter was a response to the former. Critics viewed *Aqualung*, about a down-and-out streetperson, as a concept album. This was news to Anderson—he didn't see it that way. So Tull made *Thick as a Brick* as a spoof of a concept album, taking a satirical jab at progressive bands that Anderson viewed as excessive or overwrought.

More critically acclaimed albums followed throughout the '70s: *Minstrel in the Gallery, Songs from the Wood,* and *Heavy Horses*. By this time Tull was playing at big festivals and 20,000-seat arenas; Anderson's exuberance reached up to the rafters. Jethro Tull may not have had the virtuosity of guitarists such as Jimmy Page or Jeff Beck, but man could Anderson put on a show. He'd hop around on one leg, evoking Kokopelli, the hunched Navajo flute-playing deity, whimsically telling tales and singing his heart out. Anderson is a born raconteur and was as entertaining in the banter between songs as he was while wailing on his flute.

Speaking of his flutes, in a 2019 post on JethroTull.com, Anderson wrote that he came to the instrument when he traded in his old Fender Stratocaster guitar for whatever the music shop owner would allow him in exchange. "The only thing that caught my eye was the shiny Selmer Gold Seal student flute hanging on the wall, glistening in the sunlight. 'Come hither,' it seemed to say. Well, at least Eric Clapton didn't play flute so it seemed worth a try." Anderson said it took him several months to "coax a wobbly, insecure note of G out of the thing."

As an aside, he said the Selmer Gold Seal was the first flute played by classical flautist Sir James Galway. "I think I liked mine better than he liked his, since he is often disparaging about the poor quality of his original instrument," Anderson wrote. "I later bought for him a hard-to-find Gold Seal for a recent birthday. I had it cleaned and restored and he managed to get a few notes out of it."

Through 1968 and into 1969, Anderson played his Selmer until it was lost or stolen while touring the U.S. He hurriedly replaced it with an Artley flute, a marching band instrument made in Indiana, and he used a slew of Artleys into the 1980s. Of course Anderson could have afforded a more expensive and higher quality flute, but given his untrained approach to the instrument, he didn't see the need and has said he liked a less polished sound.

Anderson spoke to me by phone from his estate in the English countryside. He's been married for four decades, has two adult children, and spawned a salmon farm in his native

Scotland that at its height employed 400 people. But he left aquaculture after realizing he couldn't be both a touring musician and a fishmonger. "More fun being a flute player than a fish-salesman," he said. A half century after Jethro Tull began, the band had played more than 3,000 concerts in some 40 countries, and had released 30 albums with sales topping 60 million. And proving he's not too old to rock 'n' roll, Anderson continued to tour, celebrating Jethro Tull's 50th anniversary.

I spoke to Anderson just before his fall 2016 tour of the western U.S. For the first few minutes of our interview, he railed against the minimal payments artists receive from music services such as Spotify and Apple Music, and said he had no idea whether he was receiving the tiny royalties he was due because those services are impossible to audit with any sort of assurance. Then he targeted his ire at rich companies that pay no taxes, saying wealthy people and corporations should be proud to support their societies, suggesting they could wear T-shirts reading "Taxpayer." Eventually the conversation turned to music and how Jethro Tull consciously chose to be unique.

≈ ≈ ≈

I'd like to ask about the new album and the show you're touring that tells the story of your namesake. Has learning more about the man Jethro Tull given you a greater appreciation for your band's name?

First of all the name Jethro Tull was not the choice of me or any other members of the band at that time. It was an agent who gave us the name. We said, "Yeah, all right, we will be Jethro Tull this week and see what happens." Having not studied that period of history as a schoolboy, I didn't know we had been named after a dead guy who invented the seed drill, so I didn't appreciate until a couple of weeks later what the significance of the name Jethro Tull was. By that time we had received our first positive reviews for the band, and we felt we had to keep the name, to change it again would have been folly.

So Jethro Tull it became. Over the years I rather avoided knowing too much about the original Jethro Tull until about 2014 when I looked up Jethro Tull, his life and times, and tried to find out a bit about him. As I was reading the different accounts of his life, I was just struck by little points of coincidence. It just threw up titles of songs that I've written over the years, so I started making a list of songs that seemed to apply to his life. And suddenly I have a setlist of essentially the best of Jethro Tull. I was surprised in a rather spooky kind of a way that so many of these things just seemed to fit elements of his life.

I decided that this might be a suitable topic to tell the narrative of his life from the songs of Jethro Tull. Rather than place it in a historical perspective, I thought it would be more interesting to put it in the present day or near future, so I wrote another five short songs to round out the story and give it a little bit more relevance to the world of today. That's the basis of the current production, the concert tours that we are doing around the world. Another tour, another excuse to play the best of Jethro Tull, but in the context of a production show with big video screens, special guests, and things going on that make it a little more of a theatrical event.

Did you modify some of the songs for this tour, lyrically or musically?

Musically they're hardly modified at all. In most cases they're the same arrangements, same instrumentation, as the original recordings. Lyrically, because I have some guests who sing (on screen) in character, they're going to be singing in the first person, so there are a few changes in pronouns at the very least. In the case of two or three songs, there are some changes to the lyrics. When I'm singing, I have to remember that sometimes an "I" becomes "he"—or "we" becomes "they." In a couple of cases there's a whole new line, and one case where I wrote a whole new verse, in "Heavy Horses."

You're taking on some of the signature issues of the day, such as genetically engineered food. Are you showcasing your opinion or trying to imagine what the historical character Jethro Tull would think?

We're in line to have our third agricultural revolution. The first one goes back almost 5,000 years when our ancestors in the confluence of the Tigris and Euphrates learned to plant crops and grow food. That expanded dramatically during the next couple of thousand years as things went on using very basic methods of sowing and growing crops without really understanding anything about the technology or science behind it.

Jethro Tull lived around the time of the second agricultural revolution. In the 18th century Jethro Tull decided, and he wasn't the only one, to look at (farming) with a bit more of an analytical and scientific mind. He got some good ideas—unfortunately on some quite principal ones he was completely out to lunch.

Now we are looking at the need for a third agricultural revolution. We know that looking forward 30 years or so that we'll be experiencing very meaningful levels of climate change and its effects on crop-growing areas will begin to become quite a major event. There will be more droughts, more problems producing food in areas of the world where to some extent people are already under pressure of producing food. I am thinking of pretty much the entire African continent . . .

We should really be very concerned for those poor Canadians to the north of you because looking ahead 50, 100 years from now, we'll be seeing a lot of the traditional grain-growing areas of America no longer being able to produce anything like what they produce today. To some extent that will move northwards, and the Canadians may find that their winter wheat is going to be much more prolific. But they will have the North Americans knocking on their door. The Canadians may be wanting to borrow from Donald Trump, his ideas about building a fence, to keep you guys out of Canada.

Going back to your early days, Jethro Tull sounded quite different from your contemporaries. You were growing up in an era of guitar gods but you chose the flute. Why?

We were always thinking about a point of difference—you've got to have something that sets you apart from everybody else if you're going to sell fish or breakfast cereals or arguably even music. Without having studied marketing or commerce as a youngster, I inherently knew that there was not much point in me being another, probably very second-rate, guitar player in the face of such overwhelming competition from Eric Clapton and Jeff Beck and Jimi Hendrix and Jimmy Page.

I looked around for something different to do, and the flute just happened to catch my eye in a shop window. I thought, well, I'll give it a go. It's not like a cello or a tuba to have to carry around; it will more or less slip into my pocket, so I decided to get a flute. For a few months, I didn't get a note out of the thing at all. It was much harder than I thought. Then suddenly it kind of clicked and I managed to get a couple of notes, and then an hour or two later I got a couple more. A day or two later I managed to play a couple of octaves of scales, and the day after that I managed to play a couple of tunes and do a bit of improvisation. The next week I was playing it live onstage.

It caught on pretty quickly. It was the thing that set Jethro Tull apart from the many other blues bands playing around the pubs and clubs of England. At the time, we were the only band that had a front man who played the flute. It was the point of difference; it was what people noticed. I gratefully accepted the mantle of being the flute player in rock music.

But at the same time, of course, I play a bunch of other instruments, most of them even worse than I play the flute. I enjoy doing it. I am a comfortable guitar player doing the thing that I do. And I am a comfortable flute player doing the thing that I do. But if you asked me to stand up next to James Galway and do a flute recital, forget it. He's someone, who like most classical musicians, has studied for years and years and took lessons. He's done it the correct way, whereas I just picked the thing up and made noises until some of them made a bit of sense. So that was always my approach: to be self-taught and find my way through to doing something that had an individualistic approach to it, but at the same time was not too studied or too considered. There was a bit of a rough edge to it that I think was important. If you're going to be a rock musician, you've got to retain that rough edge to give it credibility. And to this day, I maintain my rough edge without too much difficulty.

I think another thing that has attracted people to Jethro Tull is that your songs tell stories. What's the key to telling an effective story in a song or do you try to do that?

I less often tell a story than paint a picture. If you look at the whole repertoire of (Jethro Tull) music, for 48, 49 years now, it's not usually narrative; it's more observational, more like painting a picture. If I were to describe what I do musically and lyrically, it's to present a musical equivalent of a piece of pictorial artwork. I am trying to paint a picture for you using words. If anything, I suppose I paint people in a landscape. I'm not so often concerned with close-up portraiture. I'm also not concerned with just the general landscape. I like to have people inhabit my landscape, and I want to tell you about these people.

They're not me. Very rarely do I write in an autobiographical way, even if I use the first person to sing a song. In that way, I'm a bit like an actor. I'm taking on a character role; sometimes I will express things in song lyrics which are not my views at all. And not my personal experience or emotions, I'm singing in character. People are interesting, but somehow the closer you get to them, the less interesting they are. You got to put them in a context. Where does this person live? Where did they grow up? What are they doing? Why are they doing it? To me, it's important to see them in a context.

And do you have sympathy for people who are down and out or ignored by mainstream society?

"Aqualung" is very much a person in a landscape. Yes, there is a social context. It's a disadvantaged person; in that song I'm expressing the response of the individual to that homeless person, that disadvantaged person. That response is a little bit of fear, a little bit of discomfort. It's something that I guess we all experience when we see somebody sitting in the street, begging, panhandling, and looking up at us. We're a little embarrassed. Sometimes we cross over the street so we don't have to walk past that person and cope with it. Sometimes we just stare fixedly ahead or these days pretend that we're checking our emails. And sometimes when we feel empowered or brave enough to do so, we reach in our pockets and fish out a few coins and put them in a tin cup.

On the rare occasions when I write a piece you might describe as a love song, that's usually based on something that is more personal because when you're talking about emotions of that sort, you have to draw them from yourself. It's rather difficult to imagine from the standpoint of somebody else.

I'm not saying I couldn't do it, but I don't think I've ever written a song from a woman's perspective. I would feel a little awkward about that in the same way as I would feel awkward about singing the blues, because I am not black; I am not American. I wasn't around experiencing the trials and tribulations of racist America in the early '60s. So I would feel a bit of a charlatan if I were to try and be a blues singer in the same way I would feel a bit of a charlatan trying to write a song about menstruation.

Yet some of the blues legends here in the United States were more popular and better treated in the U.K. and Europe than they were at home.

Indeed, I think what you're describing is the reverse engineering of a musical culture; it was something that Britain did play a part in. Those artists in the late '50s and early '60s were being appreciated in Europe as cultural assets. That was a very important thing for people like Muddy Waters; they came as part of the blues festivals that were organized in Europe. They weren't playing in clubs; these guys were playing in our finest classical concert halls. Indeed I went to see J.B. Lenoir, Buddy Guy, and a whole bunch of other folks playing at the Manchester Free Trade Hall, a classical venue.

The fact remains that these guys came over to Europe and found themselves celebrated in a way that they never were back home. They were treated like royalty. It gave them for the first time a sense of cultural and artistic dignity to be appreciated in the same way as classical musicians, in many cases towards the end of their performing lifetimes. They had an iconic value. As you probably know, Jimi Hendrix had to become a hit in the U.K. before he could go back to the USA and claim any kind of crown as an aspiring contemporary rock guitarist. He had to come here to make it first.

I grew up at that time, at the end of the '60s, when suddenly we were hearing not only black American blues musicians doing the real thing. We white, middle-class, pasty-faced, art school students were able to pick up guitars and tried to emulate our heroes, even if we didn't really understand the background and indeed much of the angst behind the music. We just liked the sound. And by and large, we did a fair imitation. I don't mean me or Jethro Tull, but that huge plethora of British artists that came about in the latter part of the '60s. We were being imitative, but we were learning the job on the job, by getting in front of an audience even if we didn't really understand what we were performing.

Whether you were in Led Zeppelin or Deep Purple or Jethro Tull, we learnt our stuff by badly imitating in many cases black American blues artists. And then we found some other kind of an angle. We found that point of difference by incorporating elements of European classical music, of European folk music, and perhaps even elements of church music. But if we hadn't had our grounding in trying to sound a little bit like Muddy Waters, we would never have got off the ground. Or we would have just turned into more Beatles.

You grew up in Scotland; did you have music in your home and around you?

Not really, no. At school we did a little bit of church music, and some elements of folk music. At home there wasn't really any music in evidence other than my father's small collection of wartime big band music on 78-rpm discs, which I was allowed, begrudgingly, to play when I was eight or nine years old. By the time I was nine, I heard Bill Haley and the

Comets and then, a year or two later, the early Elvis doing "Jailhouse Rock" and "Heartbreak Hotel." Some elements of that sounded weirdly familiar from a couple of years before when I was listening to Benny Goodman and Duke Ellington and big band jazz. I didn't understand what it was, this strange little commonality between those music forms, and of course it was the blues scale, the flattened fifth, the elements of what we call blues.

I didn't understand it musically back then, but something sounded familiar. The bit of Elvis that I did like, before he got into the ghastly white satin jumpsuit with the rhinestones, he did have that somewhat impassioned background in essentially black American blues, along with a bit of country and white-boy stuff from Memphis. It's always worth remembering that the early Elvis, when he played at the Grand Ole Opry in Nashville, they told him: "Don't come back, son; you're not cut out for this."

When I was in the Ryman Auditorium (in Nashville), the third or fourth time I played there, a few months ago, I noticed they had actually removed Elvis' picture from the backstage area. Elvis was the true originator of shaky-leg rock 'n' roll, but it didn't go down too well with the good ol' country boys who ran the Nashville musical mafia. They didn't like Elvis one little bit. At that point, he was still a revolutionary, a kind of punk, an avant-garde musician. That's the first Elvis we got to hear about back in the U.K.

So after half a century, what keeps you on the road, touring and performing?

It beats the hell out of going to the gym, doesn't it? You're gonna get some exercise and do some aerobics and generally jump about a bit. Better to do what I do than pay good money and go to the gym and be shown up by a lot of bronzed, hunky, six-pack youths. It's part of keeping fit, mentally fit too because part of being a musician is you really do have to keep your marbles in play. You really got to exercise those brain cells. Part of it is memory, memorizing huge amounts of words, of lyrics, of musical notes. There may only be 12 of them, but you got to remember to play them in the right order.

That's something I think is quite healthy. You know you're pushing yourself to the limits physically and mentally every time you do it. It works for me. That's a big part of the pleasure, knowing you can still do it. When I was in my twenties, I had a lot more bad nights than I do these days. It was sometimes excruciatingly bad—a lot of it had to do with technical issues that these days we've managed to iron out with modern technology. We can always remember there are personal-best standards that we've set that realistically we're probably not going to surpass in what remains of our careers. But we can probably get pretty close. And that in itself is quite rewarding, so don't expect us to give up the crown until we're well and truly ready.

To Boldly Go
JAKE SHIMABUKURO

Hawaiian ukulele player Jake Shimabukuro says he didn't know what YouTube was when people began telling him they'd seen a video of his transcendent version of the Beatles' song, "While My Guitar Gently Weeps." Posted in 2005, the video shows Shimabukuro sitting in New York City's Central Park, backed by trees and rocky landscape, playing an otherworldly rendition of George Harrison's timeless song. That video, which by 2019 had more than 16.4 million views, helped Shimabukuro develop an international fan base and launch his touring career.

Until Shimabukuro came along, the ukulele was typically considered a quaint folk instrument—now it's viewed as a source of epic jams. Just listen to Shimabukuro's take on Queen's "Bohemian Rhapsody." It's true to the original yet takes the song places it's never been. At press time, Shimabukuro's most recent album was 2018's *The Greatest Day*, which combined covers of classics such as the Beatles' "Eleanor

Rigby" and Leonard Cohen's "Hallelujah" with original compositions. Yet even Shimabukuro's covers are original because the way he plays the ukulele makes all his interpretations fresh.

His love affair with the instrument began at age four when his mother, also a musician, gave Jake her Kamaka ukulele. He gained notice in Hawaii as a member of the group Pure Heart and soon developed a local following. His humble, low-key demeanor hasn't changed as he's gained international renown as the master of the ukulele. Shimabukuro has collaborated with legends from Yo-Yo Ma to Béla Fleck. He's been compared to guitar wizard Jimi Hendrix for his incendiary riffs and covers Hendrix's song "If 6 Was 9" on *The Greatest Day*.

"This is the underdog of all instruments," Shimabukuro said as he opened his 2010 TED talk. "I've always believed that it's the instrument of peace because if everyone played the ukulele, this world would be a much happier place." A 2018 profile in Glide, an online arts magazine, says of Shimabukuro's ukulele: "One minute it can sound like a lush lullaby, like the waves hitting the shores in his native Hawaii, while the next it can rock out with all the rascally tonality of an electric guitar."

Married to a Hawaiian physician with whom he has two young sons, he typically plays 120 to 140 gigs a year, and seemingly everyone who attends one of his shows is astounded by what they hear. "When I'm onstage all I'm trying to do is just connect with people, and I want to be as sensitive as possible so that I can feel what they're feeling," he said in the 2012 documentary *Life on Four Strings*. "Music communicates the purest form of emotion."

In 2018 Shimabukuro helped found Jake's Clubhouse at his former elementary school in Honolulu. Working with the Music for Life Foundation, he equipped the school with 100 ukuleles, 12 guitars, 4 pianos, about 15 percussion instruments, a recording studio, and a repair workshop, according to the Hawaii State Department of Education. "Everything in there belongs to you. Get in there. Get inspired," Shimabukuro told students gathered in the cafeteria at the opening of the clubhouse. "Whether or not we know it, we are all musicians. Music is the language of the universe. It helps us to communicate with each other. It helps us to connect with each other."

I interviewed Shimabukuro by phone twice, in 2017, shortly after he released *The Nashville Sessions*, and in 2019, nine months after *The Greatest Day* came out. Shimabukuro was relaxed and genuine, without a trace of conceit. After his 2017 show at Santa Rosa's Luther Burbank Center, no one needed a backstage pass to meet him. As he typically does, Shimabukuro came out to the lobby and graciously greeted everyone who wanted to say hello or get a CD, or even a ukulele, signed. Then, ukulele in tow, he drifted off into the night.

꙳ ꙳ ꙳

I'd like to start by getting your take on your most recent album, The Greatest Day.

With *The Greatest Day* we really wanted to bring in all kinds of players and instrumentation. We just wanted to be open to bringing in different sounds, horn players, string players, keyboard players. We just went all out on this one. I learned a lot because I love working with different studio musicians.

It seems that there is a growing appreciation for Polynesian music. Could you say what this music offers during a time when there's so much strife in the world?

I definitely think that the popularity of Polynesian music, Hawaiian music, has been growing tremendously. I have a lot of buddies who do slack-key guitar on the festival circuit. Of course I'm biased because I grew up in Hawaii, but I think that the traditional music we have is some of the most beautiful music in the world. I can see why more people gravitate toward Hawaiian music now with so much going on in the world; that music is almost an escape for me.

Would you tell me about your creative process? How do your songs come to you?

It just depends. Some days it's great; I'll just have an idea right away, and other days it's like, where is it? Sometimes changing scenery helps a lot. If I'm trying to write music in my studio and nothing's happening, then I'll go and drive to the park or the beach or sit on a bench, and that puts me in a different headspace. Being in the right environment helps when you're trying to create or write stuff. It's always fun. Usually I'm sitting with my instrument, and I'll have an idea spontaneously. I'll write it down or sing it into my phone.

So do you seek a quiet space away from distractions so you can hear the music that wants to come in?

Sometimes it's nice to be in a quiet place; sometimes just the opposite will do the trick. It's the extremes that pull different things out of you. So if I go to a live concert and it's loud and crowded, but it's exciting and fun, it's like, wow, you leave feeling so inspired, and you just want to go home and practice. But then I could do a short hike into a valley and be out there completely by myself in super-quiet nature, and you can get inspiration from that as well. It's the extremes, either extreme happiness or extreme sadness, that's going to pull very strong creative content out of you.

What led you to play non-Hawaiian songs, such as "While My Guitar Gently Weeps" or "Bohemian Rhapsody" on the ukulele?

I definitely wasn't the first. There was of course Iz's (Israel Kamakawiwoʻoleʻs) version of "Over the Rainbow." I grew up listening to his music. That made me realize that you can take any kind of song and really make it into something beautiful but still capture the essence of the instrument. When you hear "Over the Rainbow" on a ukulele, it puts you in a different headspace. I think that was the magic of that recording and why it was so loved. So for me it was just continuing in their footsteps. I'm just trying to keep pushing, not just the instrument but pushing myself to learn as much as I can and just try different things. Sometimes it works, but most of the time, it's like, oh maybe not. It's a matter of using your own personal judgment and figuring out if something works or doesn't work. If it doesn't work, that doesn't mean that you give up. You just take a different approach.

How do you know when it works?

For me, it just feels good. If the instrument doesn't sound like it's struggling, then it's good. When I say struggling, a lot of times your fingers can be struggling so you gotta practice, but if the instrument doesn't sound like it's struggling and it sounds like the voice is being carried, then you know you just gotta work on your part. Sometimes it's just changing your hand position, or changing the voicing or the technique. And then, all of a sudden, it works.

   It was such a struggle to try to make "Bohemian Rhapsody" work for the ukulele. When I was working on that arrangement, I went through so many different key changes, trying to approach the different parts in different ways, and it's still a work in progress. I'm still tweaking it, and it's been almost

10 years since I arranged it. At some point you've got to know when to stop adding and let the song breathe. But every once in a while, you find a subtle line or a subtle movement that could add to the song and doesn't take away from its character or essence or spirit. Whenever you find those, it's like yeah, that's really cool.

How old were you when you started to play the ukulele?

I was four.

As a kid, could you have imagined that you would be touring the world playing the ukulele?

Oh God, no, no way. Not even when I was in high school could I have imagined that. I didn't think it was possible. When I was in high school, I played in a couple of bands, and we had some success in Hawaii. But I never thought it would carry outside of the islands. All that changed in the late '90s and early 2000s. I started touring in Japan, and I spent almost half the year there doing concerts, TV shows, and radio stuff. That's where my career started. I had my first record deal with Sony Music in Japan in 2001. So I was spending a lot of time there.

It wasn't until 2005 when there was a viral video on You-Tube of me playing "While My Guitar Gently Weeps" that completely opened all these doors for me to tour outside of Japan and Hawaii. That video changed my life. I'm so grateful for it.

What's the story of the making of that video?

It was from a TV show. I was in New York playing at a Hawaii festival there. While I was there, a group of guys who

were really into the ukulele found out I was in town. They
wanted to interview me for a little TV show they had called
Ukulele Disco. We met in Central Park; they asked me a few
questions; then they asked me to play a song. So I played
"While My Guitar Gently Weeps."

I was working on that arrangement around that time,
and I think it aired on TV. Then it was all over YouTube,
but back then it didn't have my name on it. It said something
like "Asian guy shreds on ukulele." I didn't think much about
it, and a few weeks later my manager started getting tons of
calls from all kinds of industry people and other bands who
wanted me to open. It was pretty insane how that all came
together.

*You're well known for some of your early covers, but your 2017
album,* The Nashville Sessions, *is all original. How did you
approach this record?*

It was very spontaneous. The nice thing was we didn't have a
deadline or really any plan, so there was no pressure. We just
wanted to approach it like a jam session. I would write some
basic melodies, and we would figure out a form and then just
play. In the middle we'd improvise and just let whatever happened happen. Just by luck, we were able to finish everything
in that session. We had more material than we needed, about
13 or 14 tunes, and we chose 11 of the songs.

We weren't really thinking about genres or styles. We didn't
try to write something jazzy or bluesy. When I was writing a
lot of the tunes, I would take basic elements, for example just
rhythm, and ask, What can we do to make it interesting? I
would do a lot of odd meters and obscure time signatures, a lot
of meter modulation, moving things around. We were experimenting with the sound of the ukulele. I'm really happy with
what we came up with because I think the ideas were so fresh

and so new that you can feel the inspiration behind them. It's not like we wrote the tunes two months prior to going into the studio. That's what I appreciate most about it; you can still feel the excitement in the music. It's not perfect, not perfectly played or executed, but the feeling is there, and I think that's the most important part.

The bassist, Nolan Verner, was a longtime collaborator but the drummer, Evan Hutchings, was someone you had never played with before, right?

That's true. I had just met the drummer the night before we went into the studio. The first time we played together was the first day of the recording session. You never know how it's going to turn out. When you're playing music with people, it's not just about your skill level or how good you are, it's the personality too. You have to be able to read each other; you have to be able to respect each other, and you have to trust each other. I can venture out and I know that the drummer and bassist are going to be right with me. And they have that kind of trust where they can feel something and just go for it and know that I'm going to dig that and go with them.

Usually that relationship takes years and years of playing together all the time. It was just lucky. Now we call each other, we text each other; we're best buds, but we spent just those six days together. Sharing that experience, we feel like we know each other so well. Those kinds of things don't happen often.

Is experimenting and pushing boundaries what most interests you?

I love experimenting. I love trying new things, and I feel like with this album I really dove into some uncharted territory. On this album there were a couple of pretty out-there pieces.

We had one based on a contemporary classical piece, "Tritone," and there's a song called "Kilauea," the last track, that was definitely not what you'd expect from a ukulele record. It's very abstract, but it was fun exploiting a different side of the instrument, getting interesting sounds and tones and these weird intervals to create tension and release.

Jeff Beck was one of my heroes growing up, and I think on that particular track you can hear his influence. A lot of times he'll use the guitar as more of a sound-effects maker rather than playing melodically. With that track I dove a little into that headspace, trying to create emotion and feeling with sound rather than just with something very melodic. I've played it live a couple of times, but it's different hearing it without the drums. And the thing with "Kilauea" is that it was completely improvised. It was a one-take piece, which for me made it more special. It was that one moment in time when the three of us just played, and something pretty cool happened. We were able to capture that.

When you play that song live do you try to recapture that moment, or do you continue to improvise onstage?

When we first started playing it, I transcribed it. Because it was all improvised, I had to go back and learn how to play it, so I transcribed it and I started trying to play it like the way it was recorded. But it lost something; it just lost that vibe. So then I took a more improvisational approach. I took a couple of licks from the song that were pretty established, and I utilized those lines throughout the piece. Then in the middle I would just freely play, and that made it work a lot better. One of the key elements in that piece is the improvisation and spontaneity. So we kept that there while quoting a few recognizable lines, melodic lines from the track, so people could say: Oh, that's "Kilauea."

Because we were in the studio and not in front of a live audience, we weren't afraid to go for something and have a big train wreck. We had several train wrecks when we were in the studio; it would fall apart, but then we would try again. It was fun to have that freedom to just go for it. You've got this safety net under you—if it doesn't work, you just try it again. The idea was to not play it safe. If you hear something, go somewhere, as you're playing; try to get there and see what happens.

For a few years, you were using all these wild effects and kind of became the ukulele's Jimi Hendrix. Then you gave that up. Why?

I thought I was getting too dependent on my pedal board because when you add a lot of delay and echoes and overdrives and all these different things, you rely less on your technique and more on the electronics to shape your sound or to express something. I wasn't focusing so much on my fingers anymore. I was focusing more on the different sounds: This pedal does this, and that pedal does that. I wanted to go back to the pure, natural sound of the ukulele. When you take all those effects away, you feel so naked because now it's just you and your instrument again.

All the little things, like if you're moving from one note to another note, or your fingers are sliding off the strings to go to the next chord, you hear all those things. So now you have to be *very* careful how you move around the fingerboard, even the way you pluck the strings, your tone. You have to be so aware because there aren't all these other things to distract the listener from what you are actually doing. Sometimes it's easy to hide behind the echoes and the delays because everything just sounds so good. You play one chord and wow, that's beautiful.

When you strip away all the effects, it's how can I make it sound beautiful without all that stuff? I'm glad I did that because I started to develop more finesse toward my strumming and my picking, just being more aware of the tone. How can I get a smoother sound? How can I get a warmer sound? And just being more aware of the subtle nuances in your technique. When you start focusing on those things, you really start to home in on those bad habits and start to realize what you need to improve on, what you need to work on.

It seems that you've had the gift of knowing what you wanted to do all your life, like you got a message from the universe saying this is what you're supposed to be doing.

I'm not sure this is what I'm supposed to be doing, but it's definitely what I love doing most. I've never looked at playing music as work or career or anything like that. It's always just been my passion. I'm so grateful that I can do this all the time, and I can spend every minute of every day thinking about music and focusing on it and taking these opportunities to travel and to learn. That's the best way to learn, you gotta expose yourself to new experiences. Once I started traveling and left Hawaii, I realized that there's so much great music out there, so many amazing musicians that you can learn from. So touring became my college experience. When I got to go out with different bands and meet different artists in Japan or in Europe, that was kind of like studying abroad.

Could you mention a couple of the musicians you learned from or were excited to collaborate with?

Yo-Yo Ma was one, Béla Fleck, Tommy Emmanuel, the great bass player Victor Wooten, Jerry Douglas, Chris Thile. Growing up in Hawaii, Hawaiian music was always my passion.

That's my roots, so people like Eddie Kamae, the first ukulele virtuoso. He recently passed away, and he was the godfather of the instrument. He was probably my biggest inspiration. Gabby Pahinui, the Sons of Hawaii, Ohta-san, Sunday Manoa, Israel Kamakawiwoʻole, all these traditional bands. Hawaiian music was my biggest influence because it was my earliest influence, all these traditional bands.

You play a Hawaii-made Kamaka ukulele. Why?

They make a signature line for me; it's the one that I play now. They've been making ukuleles for over 100 years. They are the inventor of the modern-day ukulele. All my heroes played Kamaka ukuleles, so it was always my dream to play one of those. I remember saving up my money, saving, saving, saving, saving until I could afford one of my own. To this day, that's all I play. I don't have a contract with them; I just love their instrument.

Do you feel that to be a real ukulele, it should be made in Hawaii?

No, I think there are a lot of great makers out there, but for me it's the sound. There's something about those Kamaka ukuleles; they just have a different sound. It's the sound that I grew up hearing on all those Hawaiian records. There are some ukuleles that are beautifully made, but if you strum them, it almost sounds like a classical guitar. It doesn't have that twang, that ukulele twang that I'm used to hearing. That's what I love about Kamaka ukuleles; they have the traditional sound, that twangy character, but still you can get so much emotion out of them, so many different timbres and colors. They're just incredibly versatile.

Do you remember how much your first ukulele cost?

Oh yeah. The first ukulele I ordered from Kamaka, I paid $2,500 for it. Every two weeks, I would stop by the shop and drop off $100 here, $100 there. It took about a year to build, so it was perfect. It gave me time to save up the money because I was still in school, working a part-time job.

At your elementary school, Ala Wai in Honolulu, you created a center for music education called Jake's Clubhouse. What inspired you to do that?

Back when I was in elementary school, everyone in fourth or fifth grade learned to play the ukulele. When I was a student at Ala Wai, the school lost the funding for their ukulele teacher, so my mom volunteered for a time to come down to the school to teach ukulele. About 10 years ago, I realized a lot of the schools now, because of all the budget cuts, don't have their ukulele programs at all, so that's when I started working with a few nonprofits trying to get ukuleles back into the school program.

Whenever I'm in town, I'll try to go in and sometimes I'll do stuff with the kids. But mostly I help the teachers so that they can teach the students. There's a little portable recording studio set up in the corner and a little stage area where kids can practice, and a little ukulele instrument repair workshop area so they can learn about building and repairing instruments. Ala Wai was always dear to my heart because that's my alma mater.

The Impresario
WARREN HELLMAN

It was an idea hatched on a chairlift around the time of the millennium. San Francisco financier Warren Hellman had gone to Lake Tahoe to ski with a friend and shared his dream about launching a bluegrass festival in Golden Gate Park. Hellman loved bluegrass music and had a special fondness for the banjo. After tremendous success in the financial world—he'd become the president of the New York investment bank Lehman Brothers at age 39—Hellman added philanthropy to his portfolio. He wanted to create a festival that supported his love of music while giving something back to San Francisco, the city that for generations had provided so much for him and his family.

Hellman's great-grandfather, Isaias W. Hellman, was an immigrant from Bavaria who landed in California in 1859, found a job in a dry goods store, and over time became one of the state's top financiers, serving as president of Wells Fargo bank. (The Hellman family story is chronicled in the book,

Towers of Gold by Frances Dinkelspiel, and in the documentary, *American Jerusalem*.)

Back to the festival dream: Hellman was seeking direction on how to make his fantasy real. Rather than think about all the reasons this couldn't happen, Hellman sought people who could help him bring his vision to life. He contacted two women who'd worked in San Francisco concert production for decades, Sheri Sternberg and Dawn Holliday; they met with city officials and got to work. The free concert would be called Strictly Bluegrass, which Hellman had envisioned in Golden Gate Park's Polo Grounds. Those with experience in concert production suggested the park's Speedway Meadow, Hellman told me, "and that's where it's been ever since."

The first Strictly Bluegrass concert took place in October 2001. After two years, the concert was expanded and the name changed to Hardly Strictly Bluegrass, opening it to all types of music. Now held the first weekend in October, by 2018 the three-day festival had grown to more than 80 bands on six stages attracting about 750,000 people during the three-day event.

Staging a free concert isn't cheap. Though the Hellman family and organizers don't release cost figures, it probably requires several-million dollars annually to pay for talent, staging, security, and so much more. But Hellman liked to say that money is like manure: If you pile it all in one place it stinks, but if you spread it around you can make a thousand flowers grow. Some of his maxims are displayed on wooden boards at the festival. Here's one: "I always say, a Monet or a festival; if you had the money, which would you rather own?"

Musicians enjoy Hardly Strictly, as it's become known, because they're treated well and love the outdoor setting, playing in meadows surrounded by trees as red-tailed hawks soar overhead. "It's my favorite place to play," said Robert Earl Keen, an alt-country troubadour. "There are no sponsorships, no signage; it's like going to heaven." The silken-voiced singer Emmylou Harris agreed; as she closed the festival a few years ago, she called it the "eighth wonder of the world."

Keen said that before he met Hellman, he was "fascinated by somebody who had the vision and generosity" to create a free weekend of concerts in Golden Gate Park. And the better he got to know Hellman, he said, the more he liked and respected him. "This is as good as it gets," Keen said. "It's our favorite show of the year for everybody in the band and myself . . . It's the perfect camp, our home away from home. What a gift that is."

Warren Hellman was born in New York City in 1934 and spent his youth in San Francisco and Vacaville, California. He graduated from the University of California, Berkeley, where he played on the water polo team. Hellman was also a long-distance runner and expert skier. He graduated from Harvard Business School in 1959 (in our interview the ever-humble Hellman didn't mention Harvard but said, "I went east to business school.") He soon joined Lehman Brothers, the investment bank. (As an aside, Isaias Hellman's wife had a sister who married Mayer Lehman, a co-founder of Lehman Brothers in 1850.)

Hellman left Lehman in the late 1970s, well before the subprime mortgage crisis that led to the firm's bankruptcy in 2008. He spent several years working in Boston before returning to the San Francisco Bay Area in the early '80s, and in 1984 founded the investment firm Hellman & Friedman. Hellman strongly believed capitalism and philanthropy should go hand in hand, and the Hellman family funded the San Francisco Foundation and San Francisco Free Clinic, which provides medical services. His wife, Chris Hellman, served as president of the San Francisco Ballet's board, and the Hellman family donated generously to support the city's ballet and symphony.

Warren Hellman shepherded the building of an underground parking garage in Golden Gate Park that enabled the California Academy of Sciences and the de Young Museum to remain in the park. In 2010, Hellman funded the short-lived Bay Citizen, dedicated to public service journalism. "He worked until the day he died," Mick Hellman said of his father. He understood that the private equity industry was viewed as a den of iniquity and worked hard to bring his unassailable ethics and values into that business, Mick said, but "he never un-sold-out to capitalism."

Into his seventies, Warren Hellman woke around 4:30 A.M. to run 5 to 15 miles and still got to the Park Hyatt hotel for his legendary 7 A.M. breakfasts, where he'd meet with local union leaders, the city's mayor, other politicians, or family members. In his younger days he ran 100-mile ultra-marathons (nearly four times the length of a standard marathon). He was a five-time champion in a sport called ride and tie, which involves horseback riding and cross-country running. While financial management came easily to him, it was bluegrass music that sparked his creativity and enlivened his soul. Hellman's aspiration was to become a capable banjo picker in a bluegrass band, and like just about everything he set out to do, he achieved that goal.

Hellman told me he'd approached Pete Seeger and asked the folk icon to give him lessons, but that Seeger said he had no interest in working for bankers. However, Don McLean, best known for his 1971 song, "American Pie," did offer lessons to Hellman, according to Mick. During his final years, Warren Hellman performed as part of the Wronglers, a band he co-founded in 2006 whose music he described as "simple tunes played by complicated people." The Wronglers played not just at Hardly Strictly but at venues such as the esteemed South by Southwest in Austin, Texas, and on *A Prairie Home Companion,* the NPR show hosted by Garrison Keillor. The

Wranglers' second album, *Heirloom Music,* featured Jimmie Dale Gilmore.

I had the pleasure of interviewing Hellman twice, once by phone in 2009; a year later we had a more in-depth interview in person at his One Maritime Plaza office, 12 stories above San Francisco's Financial District. Dressed in a colorful striped shirt and khakis (no jacket or tie), Hellman welcomed me into his office and made me feel like he had all the time in the world. He had a jaunty sense of fun, his attitude a sense of wonder and amazement that he was in a position to create a festival that had given so much joy to so many people, including himself.

At times Hellman became confessional, saying that he found it excruciatingly painful to see his wife, a former ballerina and artist, struggle with Alzheimer's. Chris often sang with the Wranglers, taking lead vocals on the song "Gold Watch and Chain." Now Frances Hellman, dean of mathematical and physical sciences at UC Berkeley (and Chris and Warren's daughter), sings that song with the Wranglers, Mick said, as a tribute to her late mother.

During our 2010 interview, Warren Hellman's mood picked up as he told me about his late-in-life bar mitzvah. Though his Jewish roots ran deep, Hellman wasn't raised in a family that observed religious traditions. But when he was 75, he and his daughter, the physician Tricia Hellman Gibbs, had a b'nai mitzvah (the plural of bar mitzvah and bat mitzvah) at Congregation Emanu-El in San Francisco.

"After 75 years, I have come home," he said of completing the ritual traditionally held at age 13 that marks a Jew's entry into adulthood. At the ceremony, Hellman wore a Cal yarmulke, a nod to his alma mater in Berkeley. Afterward, he picked up his banjo and joined the Wranglers for a bluegrass interpretation of "Ein Keloheinu," an uplifting Hebrew song beloved by congregants far and wide because it typically signals the end of a service.

As our interview concluded, Hellman played me a recording of a song composed by a Hardly Strictly enthusiast that captured the spirit of the event. A woman sang about "bluegrass for no admission fee, brimming with the spirit of joy for free." I asked if I could photograph Hellman with his banjo. With the instrument around his neck, he asked me if I'd like to hear him play. So more than a hundred feet above the streets of San Francisco, one of the city's most influential financiers, on the eve of Rosh Hashanah (the Jewish New Year), performed for an audience of one. Three weeks later, after my story ran, Hellman sent me an email that revealed his wry, self-effacing humor: "Terrific! You nailed it! If I could play like you write, we would be on one of the larger stages."

In October 2011, the Wronglers with Hellman on banjo took the Rooster Stage at Hardly Strictly Bluegrass for the final time. Wearing a denim jacket made by his granddaughter, Laurel, with sparkling Jewish stars (composed of rhinestones) on the sleeves, Hellman played beautifully and savored every moment. He was already suffering from leukemia and died less than three months later, on Dec. 18, 2011, due to complications from treatment of the blood cancer. A week before, San Francisco honored him by changing the name of Speedway Meadow, the HSB festival site, to Hellman's Hollow. Thanks to Hellman's bequest, the Hardly Strictly Bluegrass festival is on a firm financial footing and set to continue for many years to come.

≈≈ ≈≈ ≈≈

Let's talk about the festival. How many people did you have at the first one?

Surprisingly, way more than we thought. We had no idea whether anybody would show up. We had two stages, I think 12 bands. I said, do you think maybe 1,000 people would be there? And there were like 20,000 people. I may be making that up, but that's my recollection. And it's grown by orders of magnitude since then. But like most things, there's no profound thought as to why I did it. Did I ever dream it would be as large as it is? Absolutely not.

So tell me how this got started.

I was skiing with a guy named Jonathan Nelson, who has been a partner in this thing forever, not a monetary partner but a partner. I said, "Jon, I've always had this fantasy about putting on a bluegrass festival." So he said, "Why don't you do it?" I said, "OK, but I don't have the foggiest notion of how to do it." He said, "I used to work for Bill Graham Presents." He knew two of the top people there, Dawn Holliday and Sheri Sternberg. So Jonathan and the two of them had lunch, and he asked, "Is this something we could do?" And they said, "Sure, why can't you do it? There have been festivals in the park forever." That was sort of the Genesis—we are not to Exodus yet.

Year one, I really wanted to get Hazel Dickens and Emmylou Harris. Hazel was fine—the problem was that Emmy wasn't playing bluegrass anymore. I thought if we called it Strictly Bluegrass, it would shame Emmy into playing bluegrass. Of course, as with most things, she completely ignored it. So after two years we changed the name to Hardly Strictly Bluegrass. And since then it's been ecumenical.

Through the festival you've really brought this type of music back to prominence.

Thank you.

Bluegrass is cool again. People are playing more bluegrass—there are more bluegrass shows in town. Like blues and jazz, it's genuine American music. As country music has become so polished and squeezed through this very narrow tube of what's acceptable in Nashville, bluegrass has managed to escape that.

I think that's valid. It really fascinates me when people say, "That's just old-time music, old people's music." So I always say, "The next performer is Ricky Skaggs: Take a look and tell me that's old people's music when there are several thousand people in the audience under 40 dancing, just having a great time." Maybe it was (the 2000 film) *O Brother, Where Art Thou?* that moved it back; maybe the festival helped. It's just really interesting playing at these small festivals now, how young the audience is. There are obviously a fair number of superannuated people like me, and I hope we can keep it going. The interest seems to be compounding. People are coming from all over the world, which I sure as hell didn't expect ever. God I love talking about this. I'd so fucking much rather talk about this than [about] collateralized loan obligations or convertible debentures.

Can I tell you one story and then we'll go on? We played at South by Southwest this year; the day after our performance I was listening to Buddy Miller's show. And this guy comes up and says: "Hey, you're with the Wronglers, aren't you?" I said, "Jesus, man, I was an investment banker for 40 years and not one person recognized me." And he said, "Yeah, that's fine, what's your name?" And I said, "Man, you've made my life."

I know you were the head of Lehman Brothers. What led you back to California?

I was from here [San Francisco]. I went east to business school, and then I went to New York for 18 years and back to Boston.

Most of my kids were living out here so we moved back to San Francisco in [the early 1980s].

So at South by Southwest, you were recognized as a bluegrass player.

As a member of the band. There have been two experiences like that. Should I tell you the other one and then I'll quit? Emmylou Harris is the biggest baseball fan, bar none, I've ever met. She said, "I don't see why Molina is the starting catcher for the Giants. I think his brother's better." So we go to the baseball game, just the two of us together. And on that huge jumbotron in center field, there are the two of us. I said, "Emmy, this has happened to me before. A long, long time ago in New York there was a picture on the front page of the New York Times, and it said, 'Prince Charles with unidentified man.' I've waited all these years and I've become the unidentified man again."

Did you personally know Emmylou before Hardly Strictly?

No, one of my fantasies was trying to get Emmylou Harris [to play in Golden Gate Park]. Now she and Hazel quarrel over who is the mother of the festival. We are going to make a presentation to Emmylou and Hazel [to honor them as the festival marks its tenth year]. I don't want to die that day. I want to live another few hours anyhow (laughs).

So through the festival your musical heroes have now become your compadres.

Well, they're still my heroes.

Sure, but you get to hang out with them and probably pick with them a little bit.

I get to play with Earl Scruggs again this year.

The festival typically invites bands no more than every other year, but you have a few exceptions who you invite every year.

It's really hard to enforce the rule. We do pretty much, but Emmylou and Hazel, Earl Scruggs, Doc Watson, Ricky Skaggs; there are about 10 or 12 that are just automatic.

Let's talk about the evolution of the festival, which has gone from relatively small to huge. The word has gotten out.

That's true, but a lot of these people have become big stars. Ricky Skaggs was well known, but was he as well known 10 years ago? We've had our share (of well-known musicians). Paul McCartney's manager called last year and said, "Gee, Paul would like to play your festival—it'll be a million bucks." And I said, "Well, I wonder what else he can find to do that day." We've had T Bone Burnett. Robert Plant is off the charts—he and Alison Krauss played two years ago. He just phoned and said "Can I sit in with some of the bands; you don't have to pay me."

I don't like to have superstars that just dial in. All the big names pretty much hang around all weekend. When they're not playing, they're hanging out backstage or sitting in with other bands. Emmy probably plays with six or seven other bands. Elvis (Costello) plays with a whole bunch of other bands. T Bone Burnett does. Buddy Miller is everywhere. And that's as important as anything, the family feeling among the musicians. I think we treat them well. I think they love it here and they all hang out.

I am insanely fond of Jimmie Dale Gilmore. I was sitting next to him at dinner and I said, "Jimmie: Everybody in the world . . . has to give me a CD [to audition for HSB]." He said, "I know, it probably drives you nuts." Five minutes later I said, "Oh, by the way, Jimmie, the Wronglers just made a CD." And I said, "Oh shit, I've done it myself."

So tell me a little bit about the Wronglers. How long have you been playing together?

We've been playing close to six years. Except for Colleen Browne and Heidi Clare Lambert, we all have the same teacher, Jody Stecher. Before we became a band, he said to us all at the same time, "You ought to be playing with other people." So we started playing together. Ron (Thomason) from Dry Branch Fire Squad said: "You guys rehearse more than anyone on Earth." I said, "But we don't know anything. You've been playing all the way back to Bill Monroe; of course you don't have to rehearse."

We've never been asked to play the Grand Ole Opry, and we've never been asked to play at the Shoreline Amphitheatre. But we played at Strawberry [near Yosemite in Central California], six terrified people standing on the main stage at the Strawberry Music Festival. We had a good set. We do a lot of Bread & Roses Presents concerts [free shows for people in institutions]. We played at a Chinese retirement center, which we didn't know (in advance) was a Chinese retirement center, singing "Long, Skinny, Lanky Sarah Jane" in front of two dozen Chinese people who didn't speak one word of English.

The festival has grown to more than 700,000 people over the course of the three days. How are you going to manage growth?

I have no idea. The city keeps asking, What are you going to do to control the crowds? And I say, nothing. There are ways to cope with it, but we've had almost no incidents. Pot doesn't make you obnoxious. We have had some drunkenness but not very much. People have been really nice, polite, and concerned about each other. But there is stuff you can do. Some people say, I can't get from stage to stage. I say, OK, let's pick a stage. Would you go to a concert that had only these bands? And they say, oh god yes. So sit down at one stage and stay there all day. And discover some bands that maybe you never heard before.

Is financing this festival your tzedakah *(the Hebrew word for charity or giving back to one's community)?*

Yes, it's also the gift I give to myself. It's just an unbelievable *mitzvah*—that's one of about 11 Yiddish or Hebrew words that I know—to be in a position to do this. I'm just so blessed. People keep saying, thank you, thank you, thank you. I'm happy about that, but it is the world's most selfish gift to spend three days with people that I adore and musicians that I'm nuts about. I'm so privileged to be able to do this, and my family doesn't object.

Why would they? You mean the money?

Ya. It's so not my character, as you can tell. How many things in this office do you see that are worth more than about 200 bucks. We once bought a Hopper [an Edward Hopper painting]. We had it for about five years. Then I thought, I don't ever look at this; why do I want to own this? So we sold it. We had two, so we sold one, and I now pretend that I look at it [the Hopper they kept] all the time.

I want you to listen to this. This is so much about the heart of the festival, the soul of the festival. (Hellman plays a song composed by an HSB fan with the lyrics: "Blue Angels booming through the sky, wish they could turn into butterflies.

Hackysackers landing moves; Earl Scruggs got 'em in the groove. Climb a tree for less occlusion; everyone gets a soul infusion.")

Isn't that amazing, for that to just come out of the blue.

That's the kind of stuff that makes it all worthwhile, isn't it?

Yes, absolutely, people having a good time, people committing themselves to it.

The Godmother of Soul
SHARON JONES

Interviewing soul singer Sharon Jones may have been the most difficult assignment of my career. Her music had inspired me for years, maybe because I grew up during the 1970s, the heyday of soul music. In the early 2000s, Jones and contemporaries Charles Bradley and Lee Fields sparked a soul music revival. By 2010, when I saw Jones play to thousands of people at the Hardly Strictly Bluegrass festival in San Francisco, she was finding her audience and was on top of the world.

Jones was a firebrand, sometimes introduced as "100 pounds of soul excitement," who'd been dismissed by mainstream record companies as "too short, too fat, too black, and too old," Jones says in the 2016 documentary *Miss Sharon Jones*, made by Oscar-winning director Barbara Kopple.

When Jones was about 40, she found a home with Brooklyn's Daptone Records and formed a band called the Dap-Kings. Her shows were a revelation—it was almost impossible not to get up and dance or clap your hands and stamp your feet. Her albums were recorded on vintage equipment, and her band played instruments from the '70s when soul was king, giving the music an authentic sound.

But Jones bristled at the "retro" label and was outraged that the Grammys didn't have a category for soul music. "I'm not some kid from the doggone past," she told Rolling Stone in 2014. The Grammys "just don't recognize me. I'm sitting at home every time there's a Grammy . . . But I ain't retro. Don't call me retro." (There is a Soul Gospel category at the Grammys, and though some of Jones' music was influenced by gospel, this category doesn't fit her.)

Jones' powerful and muscular soul evoked the sound of James Brown—both Jones and Brown were from Augusta, Georgia—some even called her a female incarnation of Brown. When Jones was three years old, her mom and she moved to Brooklyn. As a young woman, Jones worked as a prison guard at New York City's notorious Rikers Island Correctional Center. Prisoners there often insisted that she sing a song for them before they'd go to sleep. Sometimes she'd oblige, and she'd bring the Big House down, leading one prisoner to tell her she should be singing in theaters, not working in a jail.

In 2013, just before Jones released her highly anticipated album, *Give the People What They Want*, she was diagnosed with Stage 2 pancreatic cancer. She underwent the Whipple procedure, a devastating surgery that in Jones' case entailed the removal of her "gall bladder, the head of my pancreas, and they took out a foot and a half of my small intestine," she told Rolling Stone. "Then they built me another bile duct and connected it to my stomach. They had to cut me right across my diaphragm, all the way down to my navel. That was hard. I didn't do any sort of singing until October [2013]. I sang 'In the Garden' for my pastor, and my voice came back slowly after that."

Jones had what she thought would be her final chemo-therapy infusion on Dec. 31, 2013. Weakened by months of treatment, she initially didn't want to celebrate New Year's Eve, but changed her mind and paid $200 to attend a gala. "I had so much fun, man. I got to dance," she told Rolling Stone in January 2014. "Then a DJ came into the room and started playing Aretha Franklin's 'Respect.' I grabbed the micro-phone and started singing. You can't play no 'Respect' and not let me sing. It was amazing, even though half the people there didn't even know who I was."

Throughout 2014, Jones gained strength during her trium-phant return to the stage. One of the most powerful moments of Jones' shows that year was when she and the Dap-Kings, with their stellar horn section, played "Retreat." Jones' song, about using one's strength to keep demons at bay, was written just before she was diagnosed with cancer. She was too ill to make a video for "Retreat," so a director created an animation. In the video, packs of menacing wolves represent the cancer that pursues her until the animated Jones finds the power to repel the attackers and prevails.

At the 2015 premiere of the Kopple documentary in Toronto, Jones announced that her cancer had returned. That's why it was so hard to interview her—I knew her energy was limited and didn't want to impose. I found it astounding that she was touring in 2016 after all she'd been through. But Jones' agent said she wanted to talk in advance of her show in Santa Cruz, California.

When we spoke by phone, Jones was recovering from a chemo treatment, trying to find the strength to headline a rig-orous tour after being on the road with Hall & Oates for much of that summer. No matter how much time she had left, Jones wanted to do what she was born to do: sing her heart out. Cre-atively expressing herself mattered more to her than ever; it was a matter of life and death. Until her final days, Jones said:

"I have cancer—cancer don't have me." She died on Nov. 18, 2016, at the age of 60, just 10 weeks after we spoke.

෴ ෴ ෴

How are you feeling and how is the tour going?

We're near Seattle. It's a pretty intense tour, I am really looking forward to these next couple of weeks. I am going to be tired but hope my body can stand up to it. I just had chemo Wednesday the day before I left (two days before this interview). I had to get radiation for a tumor that was in my back. You hope to hear something good, but it's always something—that's the way it's been with me.

So I just gotta stay positive, you know. I'm on the road, and I've been feeling good, but my tumor count has been going up in my blood. They stopped giving me one of the chemo medicines because of the neuropathy in my foot, and my hands were hurting so bad. So they stopped that for the past couple of months, but the tumor count has gone back up. I don't want them to hurt me again. I take it one day at a time—that's all I can tell you. Like right now I'm getting ready to go onstage tonight and my feet are totally numb, like little pins and needles. But I got to do what I got to do.

Once I get on the stage and the band gets playing, I can deal with it. I can't wear my heels like I used to wear. I gotta wear little flats, and they put a carpet down on the stage. I got to adjust. I'll find out in the next few days what I need, what I don't need, and how much I can do, and what I can't. But I am so happy to be back out here right now.

What happens when you're onstage that makes the pain disappear?

The adrenaline and the endorphins get me up—that's what soul music is about. That's what me and the Dap-Kings have had all these years. We know that stage; we all feed off of each other. If I feel like shit, they're going to feel like shit, excuse my language. That's not what it's about so I want to go on with my best. When Binky [Griptite, the band's guitarist] says, "Please welcome Miss Sharon Jones," I try to go. That's what I do.

That's fantastic. You're an inspiration to so many people; it's really a gift. What's it like to talk with the audience about what's going on in your life?

It's a little hurting that I have to, but I feel I need to because I know my energy is not like what it was three years ago. I have to let them know how I'm feeling in order for me to finish my task. It gives me more energy. I use everything, the bad along with the good. I've never shared that before, but that's what it is. I take the bad, and I turn it around. I talk about it and get it on out the way.

It sounds like audiences have been very supportive when you share your story.

My fans, they inspire me. I get on that stage, and they're standing up. That's like, well, we appreciate what you're doing. I am so glad to be back out here on the stage. I am so looking forward to tonight. In a few hours we'll be out there, giving people what they want.

Performing without a wig, you haven't covered up that you now have short hair. It reminded me of the scene in the TV show, How to Get Away with Murder, *when Viola Davis' character is going to confront her husband about his infidelity and—*

She takes her wig off.

Yeah, revealing who she really is.

I saw that—that was intense.

Could you tell me what it's like to go out in front of an audience totally as you are?

It's weird, it's funny, but it's me. It's just me without hair. Putting on a wig or trying to hide it is stupid. You can't hide it. I don't like it; now don't get me wrong, but I got to deal with it, so I do.

Some people say soul music is '70s music. What do you say to people who think soul is music of the past?

They don't know any better. Soul music is not music of the past. Our music is what I call the new old soul.

Being part of Daptone Records, could you put out the music you wanted without commercial pressure?

I want people to know who I am. I grew up on that stuff, the '60s and '70s was when soul music was pop. Like the Jackson 5 went from soul singers to pop. If people can't tell the difference between a new record and one that came out in the '60s and '70s, then you hit it on the nose. If they say, "That sounds like it was done back in the . . ." yeah, that's the whole purpose. We still use 8-track recording equipment like they recorded back in the '60s and '70s. You know that mono sound.

Your voice sounds fantastic. Has the disease or the treatment affected your voice?

Well the air, they cut me across the diaphragm straight down when I had the Whipple [procedure] so it feels like I can't take in all the air that I used to take in. But to me my voice still sounds strong. It still sounds pretty good. I mean, I'm aging. I'm 60 years old.

How has it been opening for Hall & Oates?

For one thing you're on a time schedule, and you only have so many minutes. So you have to go out and do your minutes. When we are on our own stage, we're up there an hour and a half or two hours, but when you're on with these guys, your 40 minutes is your 40 minutes. Being out there for 40 minutes is great for me. I don't overexert myself too much. It's enough for me to get out there and put out and still do well. If I have to do an hour and a half or two, it would be a little too much right now. The body is still weak. You pick those great eight or nine or ten songs and you do them.

How do you decide what songs you'll sing each night?

Gabe, our bandleader and the president of the company, he calls the songs. Sometimes he might call a song and I say, no, I don't want to do that one. They might have 15 or 20 songs on the floor, but they're not in any order. He just calls songs. But if Gabe is not there and we have a sub, we'll have a setlist.

I've heard you say that for you singing is therapy. How is singing like therapy for you?

Well, it takes the pain away. When I'm out there, I don't think about pain. I don't think about anything else but the music. I'm on the stage to sing, to perform. Once I get up on the stage, that's what I'm there for, to perform.

There was a musician, Warren Zevon, who, like you, was publicly open about being diagnosed with cancer. After a 25-year career, The New Yorker asked him for an interview. He had two words in response: "Too late." He wondered why he hadn't heard from them years before. Do you feel that way, or do you appreciate the attention that's coming to you now?

I've learned in my faith and my beliefs, you don't question God. He may not come when you call him, but He's right on time. To get to this stage and then to get sick and get all the media attention, if this is what it took to get me out there, then it was meant to be. There's nothing I can change. I'm not making up the cancer. It's just something that happened.

Right now I wish I had all my energy and that I was not in pain so I could just go out there with everything, like I did four years ago. But it's not there. I just have to deal with what I'm dealing with. I'm really looking forward to the day when these tumors stop growing and just fade away into remission, and I heal. That's what I want to see. All I can do is think positive.

Circus of Life
KINKY FRIEDMAN

Kinky Friedman couldn't sleep. He was at his ranch near Kerrville, Texas, watching *Matlock* at 3 A.M., he says, when he got a call from Willie Nelson, the man he refers to as his "shrink."

"What are you doing, Kinky?" Willie asked, and when Friedman told him, Willie said, "That's a sure sign of depression. Turn *Matlock* off and start writing." Friedman hadn't written a song in "35 years maybe, but something inspired me about the fact that Willie at his age was actually interested in helping and encouraging others." Friedman says he then began "writing frantically." Soon he had about a dozen new songs, which he considered calling *The Matlock Collection*. Instead the 2018 album is aptly named *The Circus of Life*. Friedman believes the collection is "arguably the best stuff I've ever done" because the songs "have been percolating through a lifetime."

Born in Chicago in 1944, Richard Samet Friedman got the nickname Kinky thanks to his hair's curly ringlets. He spent his early childhood in Chicago; when he was 10, his family moved to the Texas Hill Country to open a summer camp called Echo Hill Ranch.

His life has been a circus of his own creation, and Kinky is the self-appointed ringleader. As a musician and social critic, he's known for his sardonic humor and has earned the wrath of some country music fans for songs such as "They Don't Make Jews Like Jesus Anymore," a scathing takedown of a "redneck nerd in a bowling shirt" who believes Jews killed Jesus.

After making a splash in the early 1970s with irreverent but finely crafted songs, Friedman and his band, The Texas Jewboys, opened for Bob Dylan during Dylan's Rolling Thunder tour in 1976. The band name may have been a riff on Bob Wills and the Texas Playboys. Starting in the 1980s, Friedman began writing detective novels and has had a successful career as an author. He's railed against political correctness, saying it would be impossible to make *Blazing Saddles* today. "George Carlin, Richard Pryor, and Mel Brooks," he said, "probably wouldn't make it today."

In 2006, Friedman ran as an independent for governor of Texas saying he'd repeal the death penalty. He got 12.6 percent of the vote, losing to Republican Rick Perry. Campaigning with the slogan, "Why the hell not?" Friedman would say to voters: "Wouldn't you rather have a governor who can tell a joke than a governor who is a joke?" After the election, he said, "I won everywhere, but Texas." He deconstructs the word politics as "*poli*, more than one, and *tics*, blood-sucking parasites."

A child chess prodigy, Friedman was a Peace Corps volunteer in Borneo and a popular columnist for Texas Monthly, a highly regarded magazine. He founded an animal rescue facility near Kerrville and says he was the first Jew to take the stage at the Grand Ole Opry in Nashville.

Known for his black cowboy hat and prodigious cigars, he is the subject of a biography: *Everything's Bigger in Texas: The Life and Times of Kinky Friedman* by Mary Lou Sullivan, for which Friedman wrote the foreword. In the short preface, Friedman confessed that he hadn't read the book but said he was pleased to show that he's not dead.

Sullivan reported that his father said Kinky began talking at seven months and could speak in complete sentences when he was a year old. Though anti-Jewish prejudice was rampant in 1950s Texas, Friedman doesn't recall much anti-Semitism from his youth. "Texans were preoccupied with picking on the Mexicans, so the Jews did pretty well," he says in Sullivan's book. But had he been picked on, he says, "I certainly wouldn't have been a victim. I liked being an underdog, being in the minority, being on the outside looking in."

Though he enjoys the attention of women, Friedman never married. "Kinky is devoutly single," says his former manager Cleve Hattersley, "with no children of his own, thank God. He always seems to have three or four women in whom he is intensely interested."

Friedman rants about not being able to smoke anywhere anymore, even in Irish pubs. He got kicked out of Vienna's Sigmund Freud Museum for smoking a cigar, he says, pausing for a moment to let the listener inhale the irony. "The thing is, a cigar kind of defines you," he says. "There are going to be people who love you because their grandfathers smoked cigars; it's kind of subconscious. No question smoking cigars puts you in a good frame of mind." In Cigar Aficionado magazine, Friedman cited Mark Twain's comment: "If smoking is not allowed in heaven, I shall not go."

Friedman's quips have often obscured the seriousness of some of his songs, such as "Ride 'Em Jewboy," a tribute to the everyday heroes of the Holocaust. He says Nelson Mandela interpreted the song as a call for freedom and listened to it as he drifted off to sleep while imprisoned on Robben Island.

One of Friedman's passions is animal welfare. Twelve years ago he opened the Utopia Animal Rescue Ranch, which takes in abandoned animals and tries to find homes for them. "We take animals from death's door—we're the defender of strays," he says. "We're trying to open the gates of heaven a little bit wider." Of hunting, a popular pastime in Texas, he says sarcastically: "What a wonderful sport, to send a tiny little projectile through the skull of a peaceful, harmless animal."

Unlike some other musicians of a certain age, Friedman doesn't use an iPad onstage to scroll song lyrics as he plays. His comment on using tablets for lyrics: "As Kris Kristofferson says, 'I don't fuck with any of that shit.'" But sometimes Friedman will forget a line. When he does, he typically swears, takes a shot of what he calls "Mexican mouthwash" (tequila), and soldiers on. Looking back, Friedman seems at peace that stardom and a big fan base have eluded him. Recalling a Willie Nelson maxim, he says: "If you fail at something long enough, you become a legend."

≈ ≈ ≈

Is the Willie Nelson and Matlock *story true?*

It is true, yes. I started writing frantically, having fulfilled the first prerequisite of being a songwriter: I was miserable. I wrote 12 songs and called Willie; I wrote them all in about two months. I told Willie, I got these songs, and he said, "Well, send them to me." I asked Willie how he was doing because there were rumors about him not doing well, healthwise, and he said things were a little up little down, the usual. Then he said: "By the way, Kinky, what channel is *Matlock* on?" I don't think it was a joke, but if it was, only one person in the universe could have understood it, and that was me.

There's a lot of wisdom in it [the *Matlock* metaphor] because we all have a *Matlock* in our lives. I don't mean heroin or something like that, but there's something you're doing that keeps you from what you could accomplish. And the minute I turned *Matlock* off, really turned him off, it opened up a lot of things: "Jesus in Pajamas," "Circus of Life," and the other songs unrolled pretty quickly. Arguably they're the best stuff I've ever done. These songs must have been percolating through a lifetime. They sound to me like echoes of early Kristofferson or Leonard Cohen. When you hear this, you're going to say: Where the hell did that come from?

A guy who sits down and says, "I'm gonna write a great song," or "I'm gonna paint my masterpiece," he never does. It's always done obliquely; it's done by a guy who was trying to pay the rent, like van Gogh, starving to death someplace and disowned by his family, living with a prostitute and a little kid, and winding up in a sanitarium with nothing but a stray cat as his friend. And you'd think that somebody would buy a van Gogh, wouldn't you? This guy's pretty good, but it never happened [during his lifetime].

Some people don't take you seriously because they think the Jewish cowboy with the cigar is a schtick, but if you listen to songs like "Ride 'Em Jewboy," there's heartfelt emotion.

You just can't worry if people think you're a comedian. If I am a comedian, I'm about the only one who is funny these days. There are very few. This is a really politically correct time. Political correctness has seeped into everything. That's why all the hit records today, you can't tell if you're listening to Taylor Swift or Beyoncé or Miley Cyrus. You just can't tell which is which because they are totally sanitized and homogenized.

My greatest honor brought to me by virtue of country music was the fact that Nelson Mandela chose "Ride 'Em Jewboy" to listen to in prison on Robben Island. It was on a smuggled cassette tape; he would listen to "Ride 'Em Jewboy" as the last song every night for the better part of his last three years on Robben Island.

That's quite a tribute.

That is one you can only consign to your heart, Michael. You cannot put it up on the mantelpiece; it's not being nominated for a Grammy or anything like that. It's better than that.

So how did you find that out?

When I was in South Africa in '96 on a book tour, I did a national TV show with a guy named Dali Tambo, the son of Oliver Tambo, who was Mandela's mentor and who died while Mandela was imprisoned, as did just about everyone in his life. There was another guest on the show named Tokyo Sexwale, Mandela's right-hand man. He's the guy who told me, "Kinky, you know Mandela is a big fan of yours." I said, "Really, amazing, which book is it?" And he said, "It's not the books, it's the music." He proceeded to tell me that Mandela would get these smuggled tapes and, late at night, like a private pirate radio station, he would play certain songs. And Tokyo said, as his right-hand man, "They put me in the cell right next to him so I could kind of monitor him." They were trying to kill Mandela, the Boer prison guards; when he was freed from prison and won the election, the Boers were in the pubs chanting, "Viva Mandela!" He had turned them. He was quite an amazing man.

In 1973 in Nashville when Chuck Glaser of the Glaser Brothers was producing this record, he and I were talking about "Ride 'Em Jewboy," and would the stores stock it, would the radio stations play it, what would the disc jockeys really think? The last thought on my mind was that Nelson

Mandela is gonna be listening to this in his prison cell. And then Tokyo said there were occasions when Mandela played it multiple times, played "Ride 'Em Jewboy" like it was speaking to him, bringing him comfort, he would play it twice, three times maybe. Quite amazing. It's also amazing that this is a song about the Holocaust, not about Africa. This shows that Mandela really had a spiritual reach.

It's what they say in Nashville: When you make your first record or any record, you never know who's going to hear it. It's out there, into the universe, and there's no telling who is going to be listening.

How did your family feel about their bright Jewish boy who chose to be an itinerant musician?

My parents were terrifically supportive; they were great. But my father felt that Kinky Friedman and The Texas Jewboys was not a very attractive name. Jewboy was something that cost us a lot. I will never forget that Joe Smith of Warner Bros. loved our quasi-legendary living room tape, songs that we brought to him back in 1971 maybe. And he turned it down. He said, "I have to turn this down. What would my mother say if I signed a band called The Texas Jewboys?"

Did you ever consider changing the name?

Sure, we considered a lot of things. But around that time Vanguard Records picked us up and we went ahead with it. They're the ones that turned down Bob Dylan when Joan Baez tried to get him a record deal. This is a very strange time to operate in, if you're in the music business, because the record companies really have become obsolete. They're dinosaurs, and there's no reason to be on a label. Nobody knows what label Beyoncé is on; nobody cares; the songs are all written by committees.

What they call country music sounds like background music at a frat party. So this is very different. *Circus of Life* is probably the best thing I've ever written. If I pumped a bunch of money into it and had a staff working on it, we could be nominated for a Grammy. That's one way to promote the record these days, and it's hard because the audience has become the show. Americana music, I think their heart is in the right place, but unfortunately there are probably more people in bands and agents and management types who are in Americana than actual fans.

I am Frisbee-ing this record out into the universe, *Circus of Life*, believing that there are people out there who will understand and relate to it. And that means the record will have very long spiritual legs, and very strong ones, that it will be around longer than this ADD [attention deficit disorder] culture. In the music business they will listen to the first 30 seconds of every song and make a decision on that. What would a poor guy like Tom T. Hall do? I've always said, I love all of his songs and both of his melodies. But a guy like that would be shit out of luck, if they listen to the first 30 seconds, because all of his songs were stories.

These aren't like that, but I have consciously and unconsciously broken every possible rule I can break about making a record and putting it out and writing the songs. I am doing that because I'm 73 years old, though I read at the 75-year-old level.

Do you reach a point when you say: "I'm 73, I don't give a shit; I'm just going to do what I want"?

That's exactly what I am doing now. There's something about the liberation, the freedom. Maybe I'm a serious soul who nobody takes seriously, as [Texas country music singer] Billy Joe Shaver said. The people who come into contact with this record and these songs will take them seriously. I really think there is a Willie Nelson inspiration here because Willie, the first half of his life he was not only a rogue and a scoundrel, but he was just scratching to get by, leaving ex-wives in trailer parks with kids in poverty. His career was going nowhere, mostly because the Nashville good old boy network didn't really approve of Willie even though he had written some great stuff.

I am employing a lot of Willie's methods. This California tour is nine shows in nine nights in nine cities. It's a solo tour all the way. In today's world, at age 73, it wears you out. And pretty soon you're running on pure adrenaline. You're very raw. And you can imagine that you're hearing things when you're onstage. You can hear Jesus Christ or Lenny Bruce or Hank Williams singing to you or talking to you when you're sleep-deprived enough and when you travel enough miles in a short period of time, and you get out of Dodge that night. In other words when you play San Francisco you don't stay over; you move to the next town and arrive there at four in the morning.

I told Willie: "Find what you like, and let it kill you," which Charles Bukowski was using before he fell off his perch. Bukowski had a poem about find what you like and let it kill you, [Note: Some credit Bukowski with saying, "Find what you *love* and let it kill you."], which I've been saying for 35 or 40 years. There's a little thing on the internet about who stole it from whom. I did not steal it from him; I borrowed it from Leon "Slim" Dodson, a black man who washed dishes here at our ranch for many years, a real philosopher.

I know you have some shows in Europe. How do foreign audiences respond to your music?

One thing I like about the German young people who come to my shows, they look to America, and the people they like here are not the mainstream success stories at all. It's people like

Gram Parsons and Tom Waits and Shel Silverstein and Iggy Pop and Hunter Thompson and Abbie Hoffman. They think these people are the troublemakers who didn't make it to the level of Justin Bieber.

Not to put down people who sell millions of records. Garth Brooks is important to his publisher and his fans, but I don't think he's significant. These guys coming out of Nashville are not really significant, but if some of them record my material that may well change my mind. It's not the way Hank [Williams] did it or Waylon [Jennings] or Merle [Haggard]. You just about have to go see a geezer to get inspired. There's nothing inspirational about country music today.

Merle was a beautiful writer. There is a story about Merle and Willie walking around Nashville back when Kris Kristofferson was the most talented janitor in Nashville. He was a janitor on music row. Merle was breaking big and he said, "I guess Kristofferson is the greatest songwriter in town right now." Then he said, "After me and you."

Did you ever get any response from Merle about your performance of the song, "Asshole from El Paso," [songwriter Chinga Chavin's parody of Haggard's "Okie from Muscogee"]?

Yes I did. I traveled with Merle for a little while—he invited me aboard. He was very supportive, very helpful. He was very happy with my version of it.

Are you content with how your career has gone?

It really was a quixotic adventure, The Texas Jewboys. There never was a chance that this band could make it with songs like, "They Ain't Makin' Jews Like Jesus Anymore." It [commercial success] was not gonna happen—I didn't really know that. I do now. I am a folk hero, not a celebrity. If I were a celebrity I'd be richer. But it's fun being a folk hero.

Hero's Journey
PHIL COUSINEAU

A modern-day Renaissance man, Phil Cousineau is an author (*The Art of Pilgrimage, The Olympic Odyssey,* and many other titles), documentary filmmaker (the Academy Award-nominated *Forever Activists: Stories from the Abraham Lincoln Brigade*), and host of the PBS interview show *Global Spirit*. His guests on what he calls the "internal travel" television show have included Carlos Santana, Deepak Chopra, Joanna Macy, Jean Shinoda Bolen, and Pico Iyer. And he is interviewed in a set of documentaries about Major League Baseball legends.

A lover of language and its components, Cousineau is the author of *Wordcatcher*, in which he writes about the origin of words, and more recently *The Accidental Aphorist,* a book of reflections that he calls "a curiosity cabinet of aphorisms, maxims, epigrams, pochades, gnomic sayings, laconics, notebook jottings, . . . and afterthoughts."

Yet his numerous credits barely describe what he brings to the table. Cousineau is a captivating storyteller and agnostic preacher, deeply versed in the work of mythologist Joseph Campbell. He wrote the screenplay for the 1987 film *The Hero's Journey: The World of Joseph Campbell* and leads tours to mythic corners of the world, including Greece and Ireland.

Cousineau grew up just outside Detroit in the 1950s and '60s, when the city, sometimes called the "Paris of the Midwest" but better known for its car-making prowess, was at its apogee. While studying journalism at the University of Detroit, he moonlighted at a steel factory to pay his tuition.

Hard work has defined his life—he often toils hours past midnight then gets up early the next morning to pound on his keyboard or prepare for an interview. A former semi-pro basketball player in Europe, Cousineau remains an imposing figure, with an accent that makes him sound a bit like fellow Michigan documentarian Michael Moore.

Cousineau now lives in San Francisco's North Beach neighborhood, just a couple of blocks from Coit Tower and a short walk from poet Lawrence Ferlinghetti's City Lights bookshop. For our interview we meet at Francis Ford Coppola's Cafe Zoetrope, which occupies the northern tip of a triangular block in North Beach. The cafe is decorated with film posters; its strong cappuccinos and espressos perfectly suit this traditionally Italian neighborhood. Our conversation is occasionally halted by the hiss of spritzing seltzer bottles.

As our interview begins, Cousineau shares a story about reading that 1999 would be the final season for Detroit's legendary Tiger Stadium "where I grew up, my father taking me, his father taking him, where my great-grandfather Charlemagne Cousineau took my grandfather to see Ty Cobb play against Babe Ruth. So I had to take [my son] Jack, although he was only three years old."

But Cousineau was "broke" and his credit cards maxed out so he threw himself "on the mercy of United Airlines." He called them and said, "I've been flying with you all these years, I'm good for it; I need to take my three-year-old son back to

Detroit." There was "dead silence on the phone. I realize I'm turning beet red; it's such a ludicrous thing to throw yourself on the mercy of a huge corporation like that, but instead this little squeaky voice came back. 'That's so sweet, Mr. Cousineau,' and she gave me two round-trip tickets to Detroit on credit. You probably couldn't do that now."

After the interview, I take Cousineau out to the ballgame. We walk more than a mile and a half from North Beach to the San Francisco Giants' ballpark—only later did he tell me he was taking meds for knee pain. We sit in the upper deck watching Giants ace Madison Bumgarner shut down the Oakland A's while Buster Posey leads a rare (for 2018) hitting outburst, propelling San Francisco to a lopsided victory.

During the game, Cousineau shares insights such as: former Giants slugger "Barry Bonds never got what he needed from his father" (Bobby Bonds, who also played for the Giants), and that the scorecard symbol for strikeout is "K" because it's the most memorable letter in the word "strikeout."

A lifelong seeker, Cousineau doesn't pretend to have all the answers. He'd rather ask penetrating questions, which continued as we watched the ballgame. Early in his book *Stoking the Creative Fires,* he asks the reader: "What are you waiting for? Why are you avoiding the real work? What will it take for you to go deeper?" Those who are born to make art face a simple choice, he says: "You create or you die." Not literally of course but perhaps spiritually. "You either take that first step or you are stuck. Your task in life is to express yourself—to make a mark, as boldly, honestly, and as often as you can."

❧ ❧ ❧

Could you tell me about taking Jack to Detroit?

Tiger Stadium was built in 1912 and had these long ramps that led up to the bleachers. That moment when you walk out of the concourse and see the great expense of green in front of you, if you've gone with your dad as you told me you did, it's very emotional. My son starts crying: "Pop, Pop, you promised, you told me you were going to take me to a park."

"Jack, it's a ballpark."

"I want to go to a park." It ended up being so sweet. I asked myself this huge question: and now you know you are in the creative moment because something new is happening, something original, there's a new thought—you're not on the treadmill of thinking the way you ordinarily do. This is something creative people have, a built-in detector for the new thought, the new emotion, the new feeling that arouses the imagination, so I took notes on the back of my hand of everything Jack said. Old friends congregating around the bleachers and I asked them why—why are we here? Well, we're here because we're old friends, but what it came down to was fathers and sons. So I end up writing this whole essay about taking my boy back for these last games, and then I track it all the way back to ancient Greece.

The traditional date of the Olympics is 776 B.C., one of the few dates anybody remembers from high school, but now it's traced back to at least 1200 B.C.; the earliest games were probably around 1200 or 1250 B.C.. And the ancient Greeks were every bit as obsessed about sports as us, with one exception: There were competitions for everything: oratory, sculpture, poetry, history. So Herodotus of the famous histories, he writes the first draft of the histories in Olympia in ancient Greece. Every statue we have, every mosaic, the paintings, the poetry, that have come down to us, they were all part of competition.

The reason you can hook back into our theme of creativity is in ancient Greece, they believed that inherently human beings are lazy, that unless you're challenged, unless you have a model in front of you—which gives us the word mime—I swing a certain way because I saw (Tigers slugger) Al Kaline and still, to this day I bat like Al Kaline. If you watch Robert

De Niro, you probably have a tick. The Greeks knew that so they use the same word for actor as they use for athlete. And the ideal life was the life of excellence. It wasn't just the life of creativity. It wasn't just the life of competition; it wasn't just the life of war. There's a beautiful Greek word, *arête,* which means excellence. That became the heart of my book on the Olympics.

It's not just the marketplace. It's not recognition, the New York Times bestseller list, or a gallery showing here in North Beach someday, but can you strive to be your excellent self. John Wooden (the legendary UCLA basketball coach) said that if you teach people only to win at all costs, they turn out to be monsters. He said he didn't use the word "win"; he only used the word "excellence."

What you said made me think of Mongolia, which has what they call the Naadam games every July. It's wrestling, archery, and horseback riding. It's all martial—it dates back to the time of Genghis Khan and it's all about winning wars. But it seems the Greeks had a broader view of athletics and what it meant to be human.

Sophocles wrestled in the Olympics. Euripides, Aeschylus, Socrates himself, he was a wrestler. They were constantly working out with mind, body, and soul. The tradition was you had three statues in every gymnasium. You'd go to a gym to work out, and it would be a statue of Hercules and a statue over there of Hermes, and in the middle was Aphrodite. She's a reminder of beauty. It's not enough just to be a brute—you have to be proud of your body.

So you exercised your body in the morning, then you'd go to a temple, maybe say a prayer to Aphrodite. Every athlete dedicated his entire career to one of the gods. You could choose any god you wanted. You also went to the theater, which was free in ancient Greece. It was actually considered a duty of all citizens. You want to know what's happening in the world? You have got to go and see a play. If you've just had a war with Sparta, somebody's going to write a play about it. Imagine that in this culture today because that's where you're going to find the truth.

It sounds like theater was the media of the day.

It was but with a little twist. I just came back from France where 17 percent of every movie ticket you buy goes to a fund for filmmakers all over France. There are 3,000 bookstores in Paris. Some only specialize in one author, like Jules Verne. Why do they have all this? Because France believes it's good for the public weal, it's good for the public soul to have people thinking, creating. It's a very different way of looking at things, compared to America where we arguably have been suspicious of intellectuals since the founding of the country. If you wear glasses, if you have a college degree, if you travel to Europe, if you lived in Paris, you are suspect in certain corners of the country because you are creative. Creative since Prometheus has meant rebellious.

Look at what the Khmer Rouge did: If you wore glasses, if you were a teacher, if you traveled, more often than not you were killed or put into a forced-labor camp.

April 15, 1975: They burned people, but they also burned watches and clocks. It was a symbolic way of saying, we are starting the world over.

They outlawed money—how do you run a society without money?

My mentor, Joe Campbell, used to say, "The sin of the 20th century was literalism. When you can't look at things like time and creativity symbolically; if you look at everything literally, you have to kill it eventually."

Why?

Because imagination is very threatening to the fascist mind. The fascist mind doesn't like nuance. The whole world is black and white. And the world of creative people knows nuance.

Creative people are sometimes in lethal danger in fascist countries because they're independent. They can't be controlled by the state. I've been working at newspapers since I was 16, growing up in Detroit. By the time I was 21, I'd written for many newspapers all around the metropolitan area, and I did photography. I got out of the University of Detroit with a journalism degree in 1974, after Columbia it was the best journalism school in America. It was a sexy time to be studying journalism because Watergate had just hit. We were proud—we weren't ashamed—to be studying this. But Detroit was also the most violent city in the world, and I realized that I was going toward the arts for freedom. Although it's very, very difficult to be a freelancer as you know, what's beautiful about freelancing is that you're free.

I remember the exact moment when I punched my timecard at this steel factory in Detroit after four years, after going to school for 20 credit hours at U of D, working 60 hours a week at the Detroit steel factory. It gave me enough money to go to Europe. When I hit that card, it's a big-headed thing to say when you're 22 years old, but I swore I would never work for anybody again because working in a steel factory was a form of slavery. It was very violent, extremely competitive, territorial, who owned what machine, and so on. And I think this whole realm of working on books, film, radio, television, teaching, it's not only creative, it's free, I'm free to be who I am. I'm not really in tow to anybody unless I sign a book contract. And that's still my life.

So after you left the steel factory you began to forge stories.

That's the other beauty of it. When you are writing, know the story behind the words you use. Give those words the dignity of knowing how long they've been around, how many times they have shape-shifted over the centuries. Words change meaning, right. So I had to look up the word "create," which goes back to the old French *créer,* to grow, and the secondary meaning is to find order where there's chaos. And that's part of the beauty of being someone creative. I don't start a story or a film or a radio show with all the answers. Those tend not to go anywhere. If it's boring for me, it's going to be boring for you. So I pursue things that I would say I'm haunted by, provoked by. And if I can put my heart and soul into that, you as the reader or viewer, you're going to feel some of that charge. But if I have all the answers up-front . . .

There's no suspense.

No tension, no payoff.

No evolution.

That's a good word for it.

Sometimes I think of the creatives in our society as dreamers, and you talk about daydreaming and being open to dreaming, but I think some people discount the hard work that goes into making a book or song or painting. Can you talk a bit about the dreaming and the hard work?

Most cultures don't have words for artist. Even in Greek there isn't a word for artist.

Because it's taken for granted that everybody is one?

That's Bali; everybody is creative in some way. In Greece the closest is the goddess Techne, who gives us the word technique. She is a goddess of skill or craft. So it was believed: You could be a sculptor, a stonemason of some kind, you work on craft, you work on skill, and maybe a god will look upon you and enthuse you. Enthusiastic means to have a god suddenly fill you up. So when you come out of that reverie: where did that come from, where did those words just come from? Something else came in. The Greeks knew that. It could be fire, it could be water, it could be one of the sexy muses, but it's not you and your ego.

It was skill and craft, until the Renaissance, until these notions of divinity. Leonardo is divine. How could you possibly paint that unless God, now with a capital G, looked upon Leonardo or Michelangelo or Botticelli with some kind of favor. So two things for me: One is you have to begin with a dream; you have to know in some way that you are different. All creative people do. There's a moment when we are told we are different, even special.

Jerry Seinfeld said something quite amazing: At some point creative people want to be seen, seen in the broadest possible sense of the word. You want to see your name in the paper. Up until 1962, '63, no articles in Time or Newsweek had bylines. No photographs were attributed until Cartier Bresson; he was the one who finally got permission for photographers to have credits. They were shooting without credits since the 1880s.

I remember when I was starting out how thrilled I was to see my byline in a newspaper. The first time I got a story in The Washington Post, I was writing for Woodward and Bernstein's newspaper so I was really proud of that.

This is one of the X factors in the arts: You have to care. What's that great Dorothy Parker line? "I hate writing; I love having written."

Sure, that's because writing well is hard. I think Truman Capote said of Jack Kerouac's work, "It isn't writing at all, it's typing."

And sometimes you hear that as the criticism in the movie business: If someone says, "You can hear the typewriter clacking," it means it's too literary. It isn't dialogue like people would say around the bar right here. So there are different ways to be creative but in the long run, without bastardizing or prostituting yourself, can you communicate your deepest thoughts, your finest thoughts, to somebody and move them?

The last thing Tolstoy ever wrote was an essay called "What is art?" And in there he makes a startling case for emotion and feeling being the X factor in the arts. If I told you: "I took my son to see the last game at Tiger Stadium. I interviewed my mom about what it was like to have me as a baby in an Army hospital in Columbia, South Carolina, in the 1950s," those are facts. But if I layer in some feelings: "My son cried because I didn't take him to a park. And my high school coach comes up to me and almost crushes me with a hug at the end of the game, the last pitch ever in Tiger Stadium, and shakes his head and says: 'Go make us proud.'" He wants me to tell the story. Now I'm giving you some emotion. Now it's a real story, bordering on art.

This is an important thing for me because feeling and emotion aren't generally conveyed, emphasized, or respected. It's mostly craft. I did interview Gary Snyder years ago. He wrote a beautiful book called *The Real Work*.

Poems?

Essays. You can write about North Beach on Saturday night, he said, but the real work is finding the spiritual vibe, what's the soul of the neighborhood? Don't tell me that Carol Doda is all lit up tonight or you saw Ferlinghetti walk into City Lights bookstore. The real work is finding what's happening spiritually. I don't mean in a religious way. The Greeks talk about *genius loci*—that is the spirit of a place or the genius of the place. You've got to go into deep feeling, and most people are not prepared to do that or they're not encouraged to do it. But it's what we remember.

So why does creativity matter? Why isn't it enough to farm a plot of land, make a living, come home, and entertain yourself?

A couple of things: I remember once asking Joe Campbell, my teacher, what about all the people who don't know ancient myth? It's something a 32-year-old would ask his wise old teacher. In his avuncular way he would slap my knee and say, "Phil, you just can't worry about all those people" (laughs). I was expecting him to quote Nietzsche, or Schopenhauer, or the Upanishads. The way I've come to understand that is you get different sensibilities in life. Some people can hit a fastball; some can hit a curve.

In real life, if there are people who only want to plow their field, cultivate their garden as Voltaire would have said, that's fine. But there are others, as T.S. Eliot said, who are provoked to disturb the universe. Isn't that a great phrase? And disturbing the universe means playing with what's traditional. Traditional literally means "to hand down." That's just their sensibility. It's enough for them to survive, to get by.

For others who are disturbed by the iniquities of the world, you begin to tell a story around the cave fire, so creativity is a response to the world. You make a comment, did you see the woolly mammoth that just came across the tundra yesterday? It begins with an observation. At that moment you are different than the people around you. But creative people do one other thing. They act on it. You actually have to make something. The origin of the word poetry is "to make"—originally that's all it means. So if you have a poetic impulse that means, I want to make a story, I want to make a dance out of what just happened. I am not content, I can't live with myself by accepting the way that things are. I have to make something else. I have to render it.

Meaning tear it apart?

You have to tear up the fabric. People say, just leave it alone, calm down, things will be all right, or you can't mess with fate. I'm writing about Sisyphus: Creative people wrestle with an enormously important distinction between fate and destiny. Ordinary people leading ordinary lives believe wholeheartedly in fate: This is what was given to me by God. Or if you're scientifically inclined, you might say this is in my DNA. I can't help it. This is what came down to me. Fifty years ago or 100 years ago they would have said, that's fate.

So your three-year-old was run over by a car—this is what God wanted? My grandfather ran over his son, my father's youngest brother, three years old, he was playing behind the car in the driveway. My grandfather ran over him. What did my grandmother say? God wanted him first.

So he died.

(Nods.) Creative people, if fate is what's handed to you—they talk about the hand of fate—the lines of fate in the hands, if you have worked on hitting a curveball, if you have worked on memorizing five hours of Eugene O'Neill, if you have worked on your craft to publish a story with The Washington Post, you believe in a lot more than fate. You believe in destiny. Creative people take fate into their own hands and they make something out of it.

The making of it separates, as we used to say, the men from the boys, the girls from the women, and so on. I am not content to just say, Trump's our president, let things fall as they may, this is God's plan, and things will sort out later on. Or, the Giants don't need to trade for anybody, this is God's plan, we are where we should be at the All-Star break. Do you feel the bile rising right now? Creative people do. It rises up in them.

Ric Burns, Ken Burns' brother, did a magnificent film on Eugene O'Neill, who was preternaturally talented early on. I think he [O'Neill] won three or four Pulitzers before he was 40 years old. And yet he was ferociously unhappy, and ferociously insecure because he felt he still hadn't done his real work yet. This is what separates *deeply* creative people from everyone else. They say he was the most photographed person in America until the 1940s because he was a star. But he was miserably unhappy: he felt, and he was right, that he hadn't written about the biggest issue in his life.

Depression?

His mother's alcoholism. And this is what deeply life-committed creative people have to ask themselves: Why are you here? Have you really written about what you're supposed to write about? Have we written about, have we painted, have we made the film that we're supposed to? And that's a little hint that we have something loftily called destiny: I have the capacity to grow this much, but what have I done here? I've written this book, I won these awards, who cares if I go . . . my soul cares. And my soul is biting all the time.

That's a great way to own it. Instead of saying I was always pushed as a kid, if you feel there's something in you that wants to be expressed, then you can say more easily, yes. Yes! I need to go there.

That's beautiful. The Greeks had this amazing preternatural sense that we had two souls. And the second soul was called the *daimon*. It's not the same as demon. Christianity took that same word and they made it demonic, devil-like.

Deeply creative people are imaginal. They think in images, not just words, which can be traps as beautiful as they might be. Socrates is actually a general in the war I think against Sparta. There's a story that Xenophon tells about him. They've been fighting all day into the night. Then he leaves the battle and walks up onto a ridge where the enemy could easily have killed him at any point all that night. He was standing there in an absolute trance, in a reverie. No one touched him, including the enemy who could have killed him. Why? He later said he was in conversation with his *daimon*. And everyone knew it. They also respected this notion that you and I have this second self, maybe the deeper self, and this is where the deep creativity lies.

It's not enough just to think about it, the creative person needs to make something. I feel that every day. If I haven't made something, a new photograph, a new story, a poem, I go to bed guilty. I can't sleep.

Do you feel like you wasted the day?

I have wasted the day. I think of it as soul rust.

And the accretion starts with just one day?

I can ameliorate it in some ways. As you can see I have my own postcards. This is my way of personally responding to people to get out of the whole electronics business, which can be so distancing. If I handwrite something, I'm trying to talk to somebody. I'm reaching out. By the end of the day I've written five or six postcards, maybe two handwritten letters to somebody; I've published a couple of photographs for a photography book that I'm creating. I have to do something. Why? Because there is this other self that says you're not living up to the gift.

Last week I gave a commencement talk to The Marin School. They brought me over to talk to the journalism class and I was really on fire that day. I've learned that's what kids want. They don't need theory. I'm telling stories about The Dude (the real-life Jeff Dowd who says the character in *The Big Lebowski* was based on him), so I'm talking about guys like that to connect with them. I told them: Find what you're passionate about. Don't worry about the money; don't worry about society's approval. Find something creative to do. Be passionate.

And 72 hours ago, I was sitting at Café de Flore in Saint Germain des Pres, where Sartre and Camus and de Beauvoir used to hang out. There was a huge argument that they had when the Nazis occupied Paris: Camus decided it wasn't enough to be a philosopher; he had to join the French Resistance. Sartre and de Beauvoir met with him at Café de Flore and said: We're going to ride our bicycles out in the countryside until the Nazis leave. They had an enormous tiff and de Beauvoir said, "Why can't we still be friends and disagree politically?" And Camus said we have to be *engagé*.

Engaged.

Politically engaged. You can be creative, artistic, write your philosophy, write short stories and poems, but the other half of life is being *engagé*. I turned (to the class) kind of dramatically and said: "Find a way to be *engagé* in the world. Follow your passion, but find some way to be engaged in the world. Do something, be part of the response to the day." And the teachers and the parents, they came up to me shaking my hand, because they knew that the school was good academically and they had won athletic awards but what everybody needed because we are in a crisis point culturally is to be *engagé*. At some level this is what creative people feel in their heart of hearts. I can barely sit still. I want to talk about this because it's not enough to be passive. Creative people are active. You make something.

(We pause as our server spritzes seltzer into our glasses.) I grew up with seltzer—remember those blue glass bottles?

We did too in Detroit. My grandfather ran a pharmacy.

I took the ferry over to San Francisco today. As we were going by Angel Island I was thinking that on the walls of the buildings there are poems and memories inscribed by Chinese and other immigrants. That made me think: We need to express ourselves, we need to let people know what we're going through.

The Cousineaus came from this little area called Périgueux in the Périgord region of France, five miles from the Lascaux caves. If you've gone to any of those Paleolithic caves—maybe 36 of them have been found in France, Portugal, and Spain—they are renowned of course for beautiful paintings, often three-dimensional, using the outcrops of rocks to show cavorting gazelles and mammoths and saber-toothed tigers.

But the image that has stuck with me from my visits there: handprints on the wall. They would use probably eagle bones and dip the eagle bone in some kind of a sulfurous powder and create a stencil, a Paleolithic stencil of hands. What does that mean? I was here. Not just that mammoth was here,

that's another impulse of creativity. We have images of sha-
mans probably having taken some kind of mushroom and
been on some kind of spirit journey. But why the hand? The
hand is primordial; if I touch you, now we have connected
here, we shake hands. We have made a connection. To put
that handprint there says: I was here. I matter.

Recent research shows that 90 percent of the handprints
were made by women and some small children. So the men
are making their statements by painting the animals, but the
women are saying: I was here too. And the children: I was
here too.

The New York Times a few years ago said the average
poetry book sells 500 to 1,000 copies, and yet we are in an
efflorescence of poetry, rap, hip-hop, poetry in the schools
movements.

Poetry slams.

Even if only a few thousand people are reading the work and
hearing the work, now we can hear more of it. We can see
more of it because of YouTube or elsewhere on the internet.
Does it matter, does it change the world? We don't know. I
asked Gary Snyder this once at a conference at the Palace of
Fine Arts, I think in 1982, it was a whole conference on words.
Shaking like a leaf on a tree, I asked one of these late twenties,
early thirties, questions: "Mr. Snyder, does poetry change the
world?" Of course I would never ask that now.

He turned around and he looked like a samurai warrior to
me. He just turned and said: "It doesn't change the world, but
it changes the poet, one half of one percent every time he or
she writes a poem. And it changes the person who reads that
poem one half of one percent, and if we have enough people
writing enough poetry, we can change the world." Isn't that
something? Not being grandiose, just trying to put creativity,

poetry, all the arts in some kind of proportion. He's saying it's the doing of the thing that shifts consciousness somehow.

Do you feel most alive when you're creating?

My first answer is resoundingly yes. I'm more alive because time has stopped. Two, three, four hours can go by and I don't know what happened, I don't know where I am. I'll look at the prose—sometimes it's garbage that needs to be rewritten—but other times it comes from somewhere else. This was, I think, the whole inspiration for the notion of the muses, for the Greeks. But that is dangerously close to narcissism if we just love that dopamine fix: Man, I painted for seven hours, and I'm high! The other half though is that when someone out there in the world responds to what you did in that reverie and you have touched them, you have moved them. So it takes two. It's a two-part answer: The first half is what I live for. It's very similar to the rush I had playing ball.

Basketball?

Yes, basketball, some baseball, running too. The word ecstasy is Greek for being outside of yourself. Standing next to yourself: ex-stasis. Actors look for it, athletes, artists all live for this because in some ways it's unnatural to be only head-bound in our life, to only be body-bound. To find a way into reverie through the arts or sometimes in nature, a seven-hour hike gets you out of yourself. It's healthy to be an artist. Why? It takes you out of your head. It takes you out of your body.

I wrote a short story in my *Book of Roads,* something like at midnight standing in front of my father's grave. I went back to Detroit for a school reunion, met with some old friends at a local bar outside Detroit. On the way back to the hotel, I stopped at the cemetery where my father was buried. Pouring rain, 2:30 in the morning. It began as nostalgia. I try to see him every time I go back to Detroit, but that one night something was aroused. Something was released, maybe because of the nostalgic conversations with my high school friends. I couldn't get in the cemetery, but I could see his grave. I stood there, shaking the fence, and this is what I wrote:

"Why the fuck did you die so early? There were so many things that we did not talk about." I wrote up this whole story and four or five times in the middle of it, I said: "You can't write that. Good sons aren't supposed to say these things. Who's going to want to read this?" What Joyce called the biting of your conscience. "Don't say bad things about your mom; don't say bad things about your president." I wrote it anyway—I had to write this because I had written a lot rhapsodically about my dad and what an influence he had been. This was another part of it, and it's been one of my most anthologized pieces. I usually hear from men, but also some women, all around the world saying: "I never thought I would see this in print." This is an aspect of creativity that's unpredictable. I didn't know I was going there. I didn't intend to go there, but you and I follow that *daimon*, that second soul, that second voice. Somebody's got to say this, man. Somebody has to paint this. Somebody has to tell this story.

André Gide, the French novelist, once said that to only create off the top of your head is confessional—it tends to be sentimental—but go deeper: "Why was I really screaming at my dad that night? Why have I never said this to my mother?" The first part, generally speaking, is easy, but the art comes when you keep spiraling down. You say, I haven't gotten it yet; I haven't felt this frisson, that shiver of truth. OK, this is the 39th draft, it doesn't matter. I'm not there yet. I've got to go again.

But you know when you hit it, right?

Absolutely. You know the minute . . . it's in your body—it's not just intellectual. James Hillman once told me that our word aesthetics, which we think of as the study of beauty, is more than that. In ancient Greek, it's the gasp; it's the thing that takes your breath away, like hearing a Van Morrison concert or seeing a Tim Lincecum curveball. Something takes your breath away—that is the hallmark of art. That's the difference between entertainment and art.

I think those moments are hard to reach.

To get there takes work. Inspiration moves you out of the ordinary moment, but it's the actual work, going back and trying to get to the essence of the thing. The famous image of Michelangelo looking at the block of marble and saying: I stare at it until I can see the finished statue—then I just cut away everything else. It's something like that with the story too. You know generally where you're going.

I remember writing *The Art of Pilgrimage,* which was inspired by seeing this one little piece in the New York Times travel section. I'm reading this in 1997: By the year 2000, travel is going to overtake the armaments industry as the number one business in the world. That really hit me. And then I saw a piece that said pilgrimage was at an all-time high, or at least since the Middle Ages, more people going to Jerusalem, Santiago, Mecca, but there's got to be more than that too. I realized I had taken people on a pilgrimage to James Joyce's house in Dublin. I had taken people to Cooperstown (site of the National Baseball Hall of Fame) on a pilgrimage.

What I loved about that book was your thesis that every trip can be a pilgrimage. Your summer in Europe can be a pilgrimage. Your trip to an island in Greece can be a pilgrimage; it can be spiritual without being religious. I remember when you wrote about Egypt's pyramids—what made the greatest impact was not the pyramids themselves but your interaction with a Bedouin who made you tea.

I thought maybe I'm going too far with this, but I realized how many times I heard versions of this from other travelers. Well, Stonehenge was cool but it was really being in a pub five miles away where Stonehenge came alive. Maybe by definition art is active versus static.

And creative people don't want to do what they just did. After Bill Bryson wrote A Walk in the Woods *about the Appalachian Trail, he was asked to walk the Pacific Crest Trail and write a similar book. But he wanted to do something different. Look at Picasso, the stages of his career, he was always moving on to the next thing, always trying some new form or exploring a new way of looking at the world.*

That does seem to be the core of it. Creative people are restless.

You've talked about how creative people are sometimes not the most mentally stable. Or like Picasso, for example, not very kind to the people in his life.

Two aspects of it for me: one is that there is a huge and critical difference in the urge itself. Some people are compulsive, which essentially means you continue to do something and you don't know why. You can drink, you can have a sex addiction, you can have a music addiction. But obsession is different. Obsession is fierce, ferocious focus and concentration. Arguably nothing great has ever been achieved without obsession. Maybe a fascination would get you there, but obsession is single-mindedness. You are focused on one thing. Talk to a ballplayer. They don't know what's going on in the world. They are fiercely focused.

Olivier apparently did not have a very good social life or family life. It's single-mindedness, but that's the only way you can get something done that's original, things that have not been done before. I've had students who don't want to rewrite. They say, I believe in Allen Ginsberg: first thought, best thought. OK, that works for Buddhist meditation practice but not for writing practice.

The other half I can illustrate again by story. Joyce, who was hugely important to me growing up French Irish Catholic, writes in the famous last lines of *Portrait of the Artist as a Young Man*: "Welcome, O life! I go to encounter for the millionth time the reality of experience and to forge in the smithy of my soul the uncreated conscience of my race." He's fighting the smothering influence of the family but also the corrosive pressures of the Catholic Church of that time in Ireland. He had to leave.

So he goes off and writes all his great books in Europe. And he has two children. His daughter was clinically mad, and he went to Carl Jung—this is a play that's waiting to be written—because he felt guilty about his daughter. Is she crazy looking for attention? Or is she crazy because somehow my obsession—12 years over *Ulysses*, 17 years obsessed over *Finnegan's Wake*—rubbed off on her? Often artists leave in their wake a terrible toll.

The story goes that Joyce was so troubled about his daughter Lucia's schizophrenia that he visited the famous psychologist to ask him to explain the illness. Jung's response still takes my breath away. First, Jung cited Plato's famous comment that madmen and geniuses are kindred spirits, and then he told the novelist that the difference was, "You dive, she falls."

What you just said about diving and falling—diving is a choice.

That's right.

And falling you can't help yourself. She can't help herself.

Apparently she was a good dancer. She wrote some poetry; she was trying to follow in her father's footsteps, but she did not have the artistic discipline, the practice. This is the other half of the creative process: Are you disciplined?

I had a great talk with the humanist psychologist Rollo May. His book, *The Courage to Create*, is one of my favorites. In that book he says: Courage is the capacity to go on despite your circumstances. Despite it all. You're sick, you've got money problems, you got laid off, your wife left you. I'm not trying to be glib here—creative people find a way despite the circumstances. In the end you are courting madness. Put the book down, forget the movie until you reconcile with your brother or your wife. The artist has to go on anyway. It's not just selfishness. Part of it is: my wife is not going to take me back until I am my better self.

There is something ornery at the heart of someone who's creative. I've got to finish this. Sweetheart, trust me, I will be a monster unless I finish this. I was given this much bandwidth, this much capacity, this much of a gift, and I've only lived up to this. I will not be myself until I get here. I won't be a good father, a good husband, a good buddy until I finish this.

There's certain amount of Nietzschean will that you have to have if you're going to create something. But if it's only Nietzschean will, you can become closed; originality won't creep in unless you learn how to trust serendipity. Sometimes you're more flexible; you play with time. The great example is Joyce, who had 14 eye operations, 12 in one eye, two in the other. He couldn't even read. So he hired this young writer who had come off the boat from Dublin, Samuel Beckett, to be his secretary. And Beckett helped him finish I think the last part of *Ulysses* and most of *Finnegan's Wake*.

One afternoon, there was a knock at the door; Joyce said come in. It's the maid with the afternoon tea, very Irish, she sets the tea down. "How are you, Mr. Joyce, Mr. Beckett, how do you like your tea?" Then she leaves and slams the door. Joyce says: "Where were we? Read back to me the last few things we were talking about."

"There's a knock on the door, the man walks in, and says 'Mr. Joyce, how's your afternoon been with Mr. Beckett? How would you like your tea?'" Beckett was in a reverie; he just wrote down everything that happened. And he looked up at Joyce who said: "Leave it in." Joyce was superstitious/mystical. He believed there were reasons that sometimes the unexpected bleeds in from left field. Are you and I creative enough to let some of those moments come in?

I've got short passages and stories from [my son] Jack when he was little. "Pop, what are you doing?" And inspired by Joyce, I would leave it in the story. Or there's one little word there because Jack had just said it. It's playing with words.

There's another aspect of creativity that I don't want to forget. The man who first hired me, 32 years old, to help rewrite the whole Campbell film, Dr. Stuart Brown, he had been a world expert on serial violence. He became a specialist on why certain kinds of men become serial murderers. The element that he found was play. They never learned how to play. Or they were resolutely prevented from playing. So they were fierce literalists, no humor, no sense of play.

And that's our earliest experience of creativity.

Creative people play with time, play with space, play with words, play with color. His book *Play: How it Shapes the Brain,*

Opens the Imagination, and Invigorates the Soul is about play as a trigger for human evolution. Didn't you use the word evolution when we started out? The ability to play; that means open-ended. We are about to see a baseball game, which is competition, but pure play has no goal. It's for the joy of it.

And yet baseball is one of those rare sports that can conceivably go on forever. We could be there until midnight.

I hope they never change that.

The Long View
KYLE CONNAUGHTON

Creativity is often viewed as a flash of inspiration or sudden insight. Yet for Kyle and Katina Connaughton, the co-owners of the phenomenal SingleThread restaurant in Healdsburg, it was a nearly lifelong plan. The couple met during high school at a punk rock concert and consciously plotted a course that took them to culinary schools, farms, and restaurants around the world. They cultivated their vision for more than two decades before opening SingleThread in the heart of Sonoma County's wine country in late 2016.

Less than a year later, SingleThread earned two Michelin stars, and in autumn 2018, the restaurant garnered Michelin's highest ranking, three stars. Only 15 U.S. restaurants that year earned this level of acclaim. Yet the Connaughtons' goal isn't recognition or kudos, it's perfectly executed hospitality and cuisine with a connection to the people who provide everything from the earthenware pots to the Japanese miso.

Reviewers have praised the restaurant for opening with a fully realized vision. "Every aspect of the experience was buttoned down and polished," San Francisco Chronicle restaurant critic Michael Bauer wrote in 2017, just a few months after SingleThread opened. "I've never seen that before in a restaurant shooting for the stars. But then I've never seen a husband-and-wife team with such a focused and well-formed idea of what they wanted and how to get there."

Kyle trained at the California School of Culinary Arts in Pasadena and the California Sushi Academy in Venice. He refined his culinary sensibilities working at Spago Beverly Hills, Lucques, and Hama Sushi, all in the L.A. area. Next he worked with renowned French chef Michel Bras in northern Japan and Heston Blumenthal at The Fat Duck in Bray, near London. Connaughton helped develop the curriculum for the Culinary Institute of America and is co-author, with Naoko Takei Moore, of the 2015 book, *Donabe: Classic and Modern Japanese Clay Pot Cooking.*

Katina began farming while she and Kyle were living in Hokkaido, Japan, and gardened on a Victorian estate in England. She and Kyle moved to Sonoma County where she studied sustainable agriculture and served as greenhouse manager for Santa Rosa Junior College's farm program. Katina now oversees the five-acre farm just seven miles from Healdsburg where much of SingleThread's produce is grown. While in Japan, she worked on a strawberry farm and learned about the Japanese concept of 72 micro-seasons, each five days long. Attunement to these natural rhythms enables her to harvest produce at its peak. (We dined there during a late autumn period described as, "North wind blows the leaves from the trees.")

For our interview, I met Kyle at SingleThread on Halloween Day in 2017, three weeks after a fire that devastated much of Sonoma and Napa counties. There were still ash particles floating in the air. Though their restaurant closed for several days, the Connaughtons and their team had been working to provide meals for people displaced by the fires. Evacuees probably didn't know that their biscuit-and-gravy breakfasts and lasagna dinners were prepared by chefs from Northern California's most highly esteemed new restaurant.

Relaxed and soft-spoken, Kyle has the quiet confidence of someone who knows exactly what he wants to do and how to do it. The restaurant occupies the site of Healdsburg's former post office; the commanding white building looks like the prow of a ship, formidable without being foreboding. It includes a small hotel, five guest rooms on an upper floor. Showing me the elegant yet understated entry hall, Kyle noted that no touchscreen gets between the staff and the guests. There's a view directly into the open kitchen where a dozen chefs work rhythmically with theatrical, almost choreographed, precision.

"We want you to feel that you're coming into our home," Kyle told me. Part of that is the Connaughtons' connection with just about everything in the restaurant. The nine-foot-tall wooden dining room door was made at Sonoma Millworks in Healdsburg, a mile and a half away. On the kitchen shelves are *donabe*, clay pots made in Iga, Japan, by the Nagatani family, master potters for eight generations. "It's special clay," Kyle said, "very porous, so it fires and cooks evenly."

The interior of the 55-seat dining room is an earth-tone masterpiece of understatement with hidden touches, such as the tan fabric screens. Each screen's pattern, a server explained, is based on the DNA sequence of a vegetable at its peak at that time. The November screen, for example, reflects the DNA pattern of kale. It's a hidden message, similar to what's known as an "Easter egg" in a video game.

When guests arrive, if the weather is good, they're ushered up to the rooftop garden where they sip cocktails or bubbly and nibble on canapes. They're free to explore the herb garden, take in the view of Healdsburg and the surrounding hills, or sit around the octagonal gas fireplace. There's no menu—based on diners' preferences, the chefs prepare for an 11-course selection of Japanese-influenced California farm-to-table cuisine.

While on the roof, I asked about the herbs growing in tall wooden planters, and Kyle pinched off a bit of pineapple sage. "Try one of these red flowers," he said. The scent of pineapple hit my nose before I tasted the piquant flower. Nearby, the citrus aromas of lemon verbena and kaffir lime leaf (often used in Thai cuisine) drifted by. In the greenhouse, spicy red peppers from SingleThread's farm are dried on racks. "It's nice," Kyle said, "because chefs can just run up and get some herbs."

The wow moment comes when diners arrive at their table where they find an edible work of art, a stylish array of more than a dozen delicacies—in small shells, atop little wooden planks, and on handmade ceramic plates—garlanded with greens and flowers from SingleThread's farm. The tablescape's beauty is ephemeral, every item emblematic of the late autumn season and arranged with the precision of a Japanese garden.

"These are beets, roasted in the hearth with shaved purple cauliflower from our farm," said our server when we dined there to celebrate my wife's birthday. "This is a salad of lotus root with silken tofu. There's also some mustard greens from our farm. This is golden-eye snapper wrapped around braised *kombu* and sea palm. We have some sesame-dressed young broccoli from the farm with a broccoli blossom," she said. "Moving on to the boards: Fort Bragg sea urchin, which is just beginning its season here in Northern California, served raw with some ahi tuna and a little bit of tamari dressing." And that was just part of the first course.

The tablescape and dishes in the procession of Japan-meets-California cuisine were custom-made for us after conversations with Kyle and his crew about what we liked and whether we had dietary issues. The guiding philosophy is the Japanese concept of *omotenashi*, the spirit of selfless hospitality, anticipating needs without being asked. You don't see a menu until you leave, when you receive an elegant paper folder, listing each of your courses, along with some sprigs from the garden and a packet of seeds. Every moment, including the farewell, has been thoughtfully considered and planned, well in advance.

↝ ↝ ↝

There were two big pieces of news for you this month. First the fires that burned through parts of Sonoma County. A couple of weeks later you heard that you earned two Michelin stars. Such good news after such bad news. So how are you doing?

After the fires, we had the closure. During that closure, we went into volunteer mode and started producing food for the shelters. And that's something we've decided will be ongoing. We were up to several hundred meals a day. Everyone just started contributing. And through the reopening we kept doing it; now it's part of our routine. That's going to be our long-term thing. We said, why not? We have this huge team; we have lots of food, lots of ingredients, our own farm, great suppliers who are willing to work with us. Let's just continue to produce a hundred meals a day or a couple of hundred every other day, whatever the need is. The silver lining has been that it's really brought together the community. People mobilized very quickly to help.

Being awarded two Michelin stars so soon is phenomenal. (As mentioned above, in 2018, SingleThread would receive three Michelin stars, the highest award.)

It's been great that we just got the two Michelin star recognition within less than a year of being open. It's very rare; this is only the fourth time it's ever happened in the world. Obviously it's a great accolade for us and the team—we are super proud—it's something the team can really celebrate. It's been a tough year, opening into floods, then the fires, so this has come at a really great time. Everyone can celebrate it. And it helps in the process of welcoming people back to Sonoma because it's put us on more people's radar. Now hopefully more people will come. When they come here they will go to Flying Goat and have a coffee, they're going to buy a book at Copperfield's, and visit some wineries. We want to be a part of that community support.

It's not the first time you were part of a restaurant that earned Michelin stars.

Well, it's the first time owning a restaurant, so that's great. The Fat Duck had three stars all the years that I was there. So it's an exciting time, though a difficult and trying time.

It seems you came out of the gate with a fully realized vision. Could you tell me about the years that went into creating SingleThread?

I think a big part of what allowed us to do that is that we opened this restaurant when we were 40 rather than opening it when we were in our late twenties. We took a lot of time in our careers to work everywhere we wanted to work and take the time to really plan and think about what we wanted to do. We also took the time to find the right project with the right group of investors, the right design team, all of those elements.

Oftentimes what happens with chefs opening restaurants is we have a limited budget; we have to lease a space; we don't have a lot of time to spend on a build-out; everything's got to move kind of quickly. You get somewhere with something and then say: Over time we'll evolve it to what we want it to be in the end. We kind of did that in reverse so that when we opened, it was exactly what we wanted it to be, and we didn't have to compromise on anything.

Speaking of compromise, how is working with your wife day and night in such a demanding field?

First off, Katina and I have been together since we were 15 years old so we've had all of this time to live and travel all over the world and dine. We've looked at farms and worked in places, and can now say: We like this; we don't like that. We had hotel and dining experiences, and we would say: What did you think about the timing of this, and how did that make you feel? That's been an ongoing conversation for us for over two decades now.

How did you and Katina meet?

We met at a punk rock concert in Southern California, east of L.A. where we grew up, a band called Face to Face. I transferred to her high school after sophomore year so I could be with her. I lived in Redondo Beach at the time, and she was in East L.A. I had a lot of friends who were at her high school, and I convinced my parents to let me go live with one of my friends so that I could be in her school district.

We worked in L.A. for a couple of years, then moved to Japan and then to the U.K., always with the goal of coming to Wine Country. I went to culinary school in Southern California and in Japan. She went to horticulture school here (Santa Rosa Junior College), but she first started farming where we lived in Japan. She was the greenhouse manager for Shoan Farms, run by Santa Rosa Junior College's agricultural program.

How did SingleThread get started?

There used to be a post office on the site that burned down in 2009. The Seghesio Winery family is one of the oldest wine families up here. They bought the site and their plan was to make a *salumeria*, a meat market, tasting room, and rooftop event space. They built the basic structure of what this building is now and in the middle of that, they sold their winery. Overnight they didn't need this anymore. We put together a group and took over the site. We stopped construction for eight months and brought in our design team; then we completed the building and interior based on what we wanted to do.

Could you give an example or two what you do differently now than when you opened?

We use the Japanese term *kaizen,* which means good change. It's about constant improvement, always looking for ways to refine. Just because we have been doing something one way doesn't mean that that's the way it has to be. We can look at ways to refine our routines and find a better way. Everyone is looking for ways to refine and improve.

We have this thing called the Kaizen Award. Management doesn't decide who gets it. It's the team who will write a note saying so-and-so has really been working hard and improving this particular system. When you have 50-something staff and the majority of those people are constantly looking for ways to improve the things they are doing, then you can have rapid improvement.

In terms of the food itself, what have you brought from the different places where you trained or worked? And what is the meaning of the name SingleThread?

It's really more the approach to hospitality. When we were first describing this project to people, we found ourselves saying there is the farm component and the gardens component and the rooms and the restaurant, and the breakfasts in the room and a little winery. And all these things are connected through this single thread that runs through all of them, this interconnectivity of, first and foremost, hospitality.

We have our structures and our menu formats, but within that we create maximum flexibility for our guests. So if someone doesn't like seafood or shellfish or they're pescatarian or vegetarian or vegan, or they have a nut allergy, we create and tailor the experience for them individually. But we also want to know what are you celebrating, what you like, what you're into, and we do all those things within what it is that we do.

It's the spirit of making things. We like to do things ourselves or have a connection with the people that do them. So we grow our own vegetables. We grow our own flowers and things we collect to reflect today and this moment in Sonoma County. Our menu reflects what's happening on the farm. We make our own wine—we have a very extensive wine list—but with the team making something themselves, all day we're talking about wine and pouring wine. Usually sommeliers just talk about what other people do, and now they actually get to do it themselves.

So it's very hands-on?

Yes, they have that connection with the winemaking process, not just from a book or going to observe other people doing it. We work with the artisan producers on all of the earthenware. Different people make our dishes or our knives; there are very few things here that we don't have a direct connection with the people who make them. The artists who make our weavings, the people who make our furniture, the people who make our knives, our clay pots, our dishes, the people who make all of our ingredients.

The ducks that we use—that's one of our main courses—are raised for us by Oz Family Farm. We went to them and said, "We really want to have this breed of duck called the Duclair duck; are you interested in raising them for us?" We're involved in that project, in their feed, in their life. We are in communication with this farm, visiting all the time; it isn't just calling up and people dropping stuff off in the back. It's understanding craftsmanship and the investment that it takes to make great things. So supporting that community is also part of the single thread.

Could you give me a couple of other examples of ingredients and where they come from?

Most of the vegetables that we use here come from our farm and other local farms. There are very few things we order from the outside world. It's why we came to Sonoma. We can have everything right here; there's very little produce that comes to us that is not generated from Sonoma County, and if it is, it's something like huckleberries that come from Oregon. We are buying direct from those farmers. With fishermen it's kind of the same, whether it's crab or black cod or wild salmon.

I have relationships with Honda Miso who were the miso makers to the Imperial family in Japan. Our *kombu* (edible kelp) producer that makes *kombu* for all of our *dashi* comes from Hokkaido. We used to live near the coast of Hokkaido in a place called Kombu Mori, which means "kelp forest," so we use *kombu* from there. Our vinegar producer called Iio Jozo is the only vinegar producer in Japan that grows their own rice, organic rice, to make their own vinegar so they're in control of the whole supply chain. We go to them, and they come out here and visit us, so there's that connection.

The pioneering food writer M.F.K. Fisher lived in Sonoma for many years. Was she an influence for you?

I read a lot of her work early in my career. I went to culinary school and started my career before the introduction of the internet. Now I can see any chef's cuisine all over the world and what they're doing just by launching Instagram, but at that time you had to get people's cookbooks. We were reading more actual food writing, not just blogs and those kinds of things. So I got turned on to M.F.K. Fisher, especially since I knew that she lived where I wanted to be.

Early in my career, her writing was definitely one of those things that helped me to understand that there was more to hospitality than just the food on the plate. I think what happens oftentimes with chefs is they're so focused on the food, it's easy to lose sight of the people, the human element, and the multi-sensory aspects of what's going on during the dining process. I feel very fortunate to have been shaped early on by food writing that got to the hospitality and the adventure and the more sensual side of food, rather than just the hard-core cooking.

That seems so natural. When I go to a nice restaurant, I like supporting local farms and feeling taken care of. With your commitment to your guests, how do you and Katina take care of yourselves?

Neither one of us is high-strung. We are both very low-stress and compassionate people so we don't let things get to us. And everyone here is incredibly well organized, so it's not this white-knuckle ride every day of "are we going to make it?" There are a lot of details. It's the farm and the restaurant and now it's a lot of charity fundraising, outside dinners, which adds a whole other layer. But we just take it in stride. We certainly are exhausted, but we also are on the same team. And we knew what we were getting ourselves into. We've been in the industry so long; we had absolutely no illusions as to what this was going to be.

Speaking for the Seas
SYLVIA EARLE

W hen Sylvia Earle was just three years old, her parents took her to the beach where she got knocked over by a wave. "The ocean got my attention," the future oceanographer and marine biologist said. Shortly after she turned 12, her family moved from New Jersey to Florida, where to her delight her backyard was the Gulf of Mexico. As a young scientist during the 1960s, she joined exploratory expeditions to the Indian Ocean and the Galápagos; on one far-flung mission she was the only woman among 70 men. In 1970 she spent two weeks underwater on the Tektite II expedition with four other female scientists—the press called them "aquababes."

But discrimination never got in the way of Dr. Earle's mission: working tirelessly to protect the planet's oceans. After logging more than 7,000 hours underwater (more than a year's worth of waking hours), Earle, who was in her early eighties when I interviewed her, knows how high the stakes are. "The most important thing we extract from the ocean is our existence," she says. "Our very lives depend on a healthy, stable ocean."

Born in 1935, Earle has become one of the world's fiercest advocates for preserving the planet's blue regions, an aquatic Lorax who speaks for the seas. She creatively crafted a life becoming what so many said a woman could not be: a leading scientist and widely respected voice for preserving Earth's oceans. She has been called "Her Deepness" by The New Yorker and named a "Hero for the Planet" by Time magazine, which put her on the cover—on a beach wearing a wetsuit—of a 2017 issue celebrating the achievements of trailblazing women.

The first woman to serve as chief scientist for the U.S. National Oceanic and Atmospheric Administration (1990-92), she later founded the advocacy group Mission Blue. A National Geographic Explorer-in-Residence for more than two decades, Earle is the author of many books including *The World Is Blue: How Our Fate and the Ocean's Are One* and *Sea Change: A Message of the Oceans.* Her gorgeously photographed *Blue Hope: Exploring and Caring for Earth's Magnificent Ocean* was published by National Geographic.

Earle's 2009 TED talk has been watched more by more than 2.4 million viewers. Her goal is to create a planetary network of what she calls Hope Spots, aquatic refuges, or as she more poetically says, "a blue necklace of protected treasures, to preserve 30 percent of the planet's oceans by 2030. Just as French oceanographer Jacques Cousteau did in the latter half of the 20th century, Earle has worked globally to raise awareness about the necessity of preserving oceanic health.

The 2014 Netflix documentary *Mission Blue* chronicles Earle's quest to explore and protect Earth's oceans. "I see things that others do not, a different world, a world that's changed enormously just in my lifetime," she says in the film.

Another recent documentary featuring Earle is 2017's *Sea of Hope: America's Underwater Treasures*, produced by National Geographic. In it, Earle says environmental preservation isn't "a liberal or conservative challenge—it's common sense."

Even after more than 60 years of diving, Earle is entranced by what she finds below the surface. Navigating through an undulating forest of yellowish kelp, she says, "I felt like a dancer, these golden scarves surrounding me." Earle suggests Hope Spots can be an aquatic version of what has been called "America's Best Idea," its national parks.

U.S. presidents from across the political spectrum have bestowed praise on her. "I want to thank Sylvia Earle," said George W. Bush when he dedicated Papahānaumokuākea National Marine Monument protecting the seas surrounding Hawaii. "She sat me down and gave me a pretty good lecture about life." President Barack Obama, as he walked along a Hawaiian beach with Earle, said: "I'm in awe of anybody who's done so much for ocean conservation."

Coincidentally, I met Dr. Earle on the 101st anniversary of the founding of the National Park Service, August 25, 2017, at Deep Ocean Exploration and Research. That's the laboratory she founded in 1992 in Alameda, California, on the shores of San Francisco Bay, to build state-of-the-art submersibles and other equipment to traverse the ocean's depths and bring back samples for scientific inquiry. DOER built the arm for the Deepsea Challenger capsule that film director James Cameron used to descend more than 35,000 feet below sea level.

Earle, who has turned over management of the lab to her daughter and son-in-law, was being forced to relocate the facility when we met because the Alameda Marina was being turned into condominiums. "This is a working waterfront," she said indignantly. "We have sailmakers here. San Francisco has lost its waterfront; here it prospers. Where will people put their boats? For a really good cause we'd put up with it, but to destroy this for something that will decrease the quality of life and be a burden on the community—does that make sense?"

Wearing a black top with a cobalt blue jacket that evoked the color of a healthy ocean, Earle brought me into her second-story office at DOER. (The acronym fits as Earle is certainly a do-er.) With the thrum of motors from the lab below, Earle, despite the calamities befalling her beloved seas, was relentlessly hopeful. Her precise language and passionate voice make everyone around her pay attention. But she doesn't lecture—she wants you to discover the wonders of the seas for yourself. Irrepressibly optimistic, Earle made a fervent plea for saving Earth's oceans, not just for the sake of fish and its other creatures, but for the preservation of the human soul.

➷ ➷ ➷

It's been more than 60 years since you started exploring the ocean. It's such a short time in the history of the Earth, but so much has happened. What have been the most significant changes to the ocean?

I tell people sometimes that I come from a different planet. My friends say, oh yeah we knew that. But actually I did come from a place that doesn't exist anymore. Earth has changed so much in the last few decades, even little kids, 10-year-olds, can see changes that are almost geologic in their timescale of impact on the planet. You see it especially in coastal areas because people have tended to occupy coastal regions throughout our history, for good reasons. It's transportation, quality of life, for some it's been food. Whatever it is, people love to be near water, rivers, lakes, but certainly the ocean.

Can you tell me how you felt when you moved to Florida and started exploring?

I think I took for granted the amazing nature of the Gulf of Mexico. When my family moved there, I was 12 years old. We lived on the Gulf; my backyard was this big beautiful blue body of water that was shallow enough so that at low tide I could go out and explore the grassy meadows and see all the creatures that were there. At high tide I'd often go out just with a face mask and sometimes an inner tube so I could float along. It was calm, no big currents, a very safe backyard for a kid.

I got acquainted with so many creatures that I could not find in books. I'd ask my teachers at school what those little crabs were—they didn't know. The books that I could find couldn't tell me. There are spider crabs that are common, and there are little snails, we call them bubble snails, and I couldn't find out what they were. I thought that libraries were full of everything that I needed to know and my job was to digest all that information, but I realized that for the ocean we have so much left to explore. Maybe 10 percent has been seen, let alone explored. So even kids can come up with questions, with discoveries that no one has made before.

We've been to the moon; we've sent vehicles deep into outer space, and yet the vast majority of the ocean hasn't been—

Seen.

Is the ocean the last frontier in some ways?

I think there will always be frontiers. The idea that we've made all the discoveries there are to be made is just nonsense. You make new discoveries and then you see how much more there is to discover. Every new way of looking and seeing and understanding leads to new questions that need to be answered, even with our own bodies. Who knew, who really understood, the importance of what we now refer to as our microbiome, the many creatures who share space within our skin and on our skin that make our lives possible? Think of all the creatures in the sea; think of the microbiome that the ocean has. We're talking many millions of living creatures that grow very fast, adapt very quickly. There is constant change. If we change the ocean, we change the nature of that microbiome that in turn changes the chemistry of the planet. So we're just beginning to understand what we're getting into when we alter the nature of nature.

Sometimes we think more about the larger creatures, but the whole foundation of the ocean seems to depend on tiny things like plankton that we don't notice until half the plankton are gone and the species that depend on them are tremendously affected.

We've learned more in the last half-century than in all preceding history. We can see for example the consequences of carbon dioxide in the atmosphere, the correlation between burning fossil fuels and emission of CO_2, the release of methane, the greenhouse gas phenomenon; that was unknown when I was a child. It might have been suspected in some ways, but now we have evidence, clear evidence of the cause-and-effect relationship of what we're doing and what the impacts ultimately are on polar ice, on ocean currents, on what kinds of creatures can live where, on the generation of oxygen, the capture of carbon. We can look at the trends and say, hmmm, now we know, now we can see what the smartest people who ever lived in times past could not see because the evidence was not there.

The world is tuning in to the knowledge that could not exist before, but now we have it, maybe just in time to save us from ourselves. This is good news. You can be frightened by the trends, and it's easy to say, "Wait a minute, unless we do something we are headed for real trouble." Extinction for ourselves is a real possibility based on what we are doing to ourselves, what we're doing to the planet that keeps us alive. We're not going to manage nature, but we can certainly manage ourselves to give nature a break. We've seen evidence that when we back off and stop killing, stop poisoning, stop the way that we obstruct the processes that keep us alive, recovery, at least in some cases, is possible.

We'll never be able to go back to the way things were when I was a kid, let alone go back to (how Earth was) a thousand years ago. But we can make things a lot better than they otherwise would be. It's not a matter of believing or disbelieving, just look at the evidence and consider: What are the consequences if we don't do something? Look at the way things are going. We may not be able to turn this rush toward a warming planet in time to avoid some really terrible consequences for humankind, but we can make things a lot better than they would be if we just coast along and deny that there's a problem.

There's a lot we can do to soften the blow and maybe even to see, within the century, a turnaround. We have the power to do that; it comes with knowing what the problems are and getting enough people motivated personally—locally, nationally, and internationally. If we just inspire individuals to do what they can, that's a powerful force that transcends laws, rules, regulations. It just means that we are all committed to surviving, that we are all committed to having reasons for hope. I certainly do.

Could you share a couple of recovery stories? If you create an ocean sanctuary, it seems to come back in a robust and vibrant way.

The reason is that for now much of the ocean is still in pretty good shape. I think about the Exxon Valdez spill; it was horrendous, 1989, I was there on several occasions. It looked just devastating, those poor sea otters, and the impacts are still being felt. The oil is still there. If you dig down in the cobblestone beaches, if you go down deep enough, the oil trickled down while it was liquid, and it's still there. It's not just going to, whoop, disappear. Bacteria do act on oil and turn it into other compounds, but it's a long-term effect, maybe a forever effect, because you've set in motion a new set of circumstances. Things were moving along as they were over millennia, thousands of millennia actually, and then abruptly there's a change. Everything changes thereafter.

It's like a war. Think about Europe after the war. Things now look pretty good but if the war had not happened things would be very different. We recovered but with a new pathway, new buildings, new societies, new genetic pathways of the families that have been disrupted. There's always change, storms come, diseases come, but humans as the agents of change, we are, some say, like the comet or asteroid that struck the Earth, 65 or so million years ago. This marked a notable change, including the end of the era of dinosaurs. So people are calling this the anthropocene, [the current geological age, viewed as the period during which human activity has been the dominant influence on climate and the environment], which started in about 1950. It's a remarkable time to be alive.

We know so much now, but we still have such strong constituencies working against environmental stewardship. Even people who are spectacularly wealthy like the Koch brothers seem to be arrayed against trying to reduce carbon emissions. How do you reach people who say: We need jobs, we need the development. Or they say: Well, it's all God's will.

I love the thinking of E.O. Wilson with respect to the religious aspects here. If, as many religions would have it, the higher power created Earth and all the creatures who live here including us, isn't it arrogant to think that we should be destroying the creation? That's arrogance, the arrogance to think that we know better than God. Whatever, whoever, however you think of the creation, we have methodically, willfully, unraveled the amazing fabric of life that we now know is vital to our existence.

This is not a guess, not a matter of religion, not a matter of belief. We know where oxygen comes from. We can measure it and see it. Green plants generate oxygen and capture carbon. It's a process that began 2½ billion years ago. And we can see that most of the action is still taking place in the ocean by phytoplankton, bacteria, organisms that generate oxygen and take up carbon, just as happens within leaves, within grass, within ferns, within moss. It's the glorious green mantle of Earth that captures carbon, generates oxygen, creates the food that animals, including us, rely on for their sustenance.

Many religions speak of something equivalent to a paradise, a Garden of Eden, that we began to destroy in ways that on one side have created our prosperity but on the other side, taken to extremes which we are now doing, undermine our capacity to exist at all. Listen to Pope Francis, the pope of hope, who embraces nature and is willing to look at the evidence and say we have to respect the natural world and care for it as stewards.

This is not about jobs. Jobs come where there's prosperity. When we destroy natural systems, poverty, scarcity, and wars follow. We need clean water; we need places to live; we need a quality of life that causes people to feel good, to be happy, to feel secure. Protecting the natural world is a security issue, first and foremost. We need trees to foster our prosperity, generate oxygen, take up carbon, provide homes for creatures. We need the birds; we need the squirrels; we need the bacteria; we need the natural systems. It's our life-support system.

Ask any astronaut, What does Earth require to support life? And you'll hear them say: We need life to support life. We need a living planet. Think about any big city: San Francisco, London, New York, Miami. That's where it looks like humans are really prospering, right? Think about the buildings, where did all the materials come from? The food, the water. Now put a wrap around it, just take a dome and plop it down on top of New York City. Don't let anything out, don't let anything in, just wrap it and imagine how long it could last. Where is the oxygen going to come from to replenish that which is being consumed? Where is the water coming from? Where will the emissions from all those taxis go? Where's the food coming from?

So just try to imagine what we're doing to our life-support system, all of it, the whole world. In just a few decades we've managed to change the chemistry of Earth, the atmosphere above, that's a big change, increasing the amount of carbon dioxide and methane and nitrous outside, the pollution. The ocean has been a great buffer for the amount of CO_2 that's been generated in recent times, but it's turned into carbonic acid. The ocean is becoming measurably more acidic in recent decades.

So this is not good news if we want a planet that continues working in our favor. We have microbes in the ocean, phytoplankton, zooplankton, fish, whales, the whole spectrum of life in the sea. All those invertebrates, the mollusks, the sponges, the starfish, each one like a piece of a giant computer doing its thing, like an orchestra just working away, working away. It's taken 4½ billion years to get this orchestra to play in our favor in ways that shape the world over many ages, and we come along and consciously disrupt it. What are we thinking? Why would we do such a crazy thing?

We came very close in the 20th century to killing whales to the point of no return. We were armed with technologies that made it really efficient to capture whales and reduce them to oil and the ingredients for fertilizer. Until we became more technologically capable of killing, we were bumbling along with gradual extinctions, gradual depletion, but whether we're talking trees or songbirds or ducks or geese or tunas or swordfish, you name it, we are so good at killing on a scale that is unprecedented on the planet.

And thus the Anthropocene, where our impact is changing the chemistry of the planet. The evidence is so clear now. We can still breathe—it's hard until you are falling over dead, until people are gasping, for people to think about what tomorrow is going to be. Today we still have a planet where it's kind of comfortable. We have a big storm right now welling up in the Gulf of Mexico (Hurricane Harvey would flood Houston the following day). There have been other big storms of great magnitude in times past, but the evidence is clear: more storms of greater intensity, greater impact, and we have more to lose because of our infrastructure concentrated in coastal areas. Why is this happening? Look in the mirror. We are altering the nature of the basic processes that govern planetary functions.

On land, when there's a strip-mining operation, you can see the desecration. In the ocean we're not seeing it because it's not happening on the surface.

Meanwhile there are things we can do to soften the blow. We can plant a lot of trees; we can stop cutting trees, stop the deforestation. We need to treasure marshes, treasure forests, treasure every bit of wild. National parks, some say this is the best idea America ever had, 101 years ago, putting in place this framework of protection as safe havens. President Teddy Roosevelt and others at the time who loved nature could see that unless we took action proactively and embraced wild places, they would be turned into farms and cities. The trees would be cut; the wildlife would be gone.

It's beyond our capacity to create a Yellowstone or the Grand Canyon. We didn't do that. We could not do that. We could not create the flow of rivers. These are things that people were inspired to protect. What we did not know a hundred years ago and now can see is: it isn't just because they're beautiful, it's not just because they are aesthetically pleasing. It's because now we know we absolutely require wild places for our existence.

Here's the thing: The ocean comprises the great majority of our life-support system. It shapes climate and weather, holds the planet steady with respect to temperature, distributes the flow of temperature around the planet in ways that are favorable to us, a planet that's not too hot, not too cold. Why? Because we have the ocean as the great swirling, stabilizing factor. Perhaps most important, it's where most of life on Earth exists. It's where most of the oxygen is generated. It's where a great amount of the carbon is captured. The atmosphere above, the ocean below, it's one big system, and until recent decades the ocean had been largely unaffected by us. Yes, we had taken whales; some fishing had taken place, but altering the nature of the chemistry of the ocean is something new, truly new.

I'm not talking oil spills. Of course that's a factor, but it's tiny compared to the effects of ocean acidification, burning fossil fuels, causing excess carbon dioxide to be absorbed. And it's not just the acidification of the ocean; it's setting in motion other processes; you create an increase in organisms that favor an acidic environment and you depress the organisms that do not like more acid circumstances. So you've got new ecosystems arising in the ocean as a consequence of our actions. We have seen and measured a sharp decrease in oxygen in the ocean in the last 50 years, the de-oxygenation of the ocean. So if the ocean has less oxygen, less is going into the atmosphere as well.

We can still breathe, but I don't want to mess around with my oxygen-generating system. Ask any astronaut: Would you sacrifice your oxygen-generating system casually? Wouldn't you take care of it as if your life depends on it? Wouldn't you do everything you can to stabilize your oxygen-generating system, your carbon-capturing system? Wouldn't you really be mindful of what you're doing to the very spacecraft that keeps you alive? And shouldn't this be the highest priority of every living human being—every man, woman, child? We like to breathe. We like water that falls out of the sky; we like to have something to eat. We like a planet where we don't have to walk around with a tank on our backs just to be able to breathe.

Shifting gears, when you were in college, working women were thought to be teachers or nurses, but you didn't let anything stand in your way. Could you give me a sense of what the atmosphere for an aspiring woman scientist was like in those days?

I have become more philosophical, I suppose, over the years that everybody faces challenges in trying to achieve whatever it is they want to do with their life. You're too tall, too short, too fat, too thin, too old, too young. You can't hear as well as some others, or you can't see. Everybody has something that either serves as an advantage or as a barrier. One way or the other, people over the ages from the beginning of time have found ways to either not get to do what they would love to do or overcome obstacles, or turn obstacles into an advantage.

Being a woman in a place where men typically dominate is mostly not an advantage, but there are times when if you're the only woman in a place, you get noticed. If you're doing a really good job, maybe it's not so bad that you get noticed, that you stand out. You're not just doing a good job, but you're a woman doing a good job. And maybe you are special because you had to do as Ginger Rogers did with Fred Astaire. She did everything Fred Astaire did, but she did it backwards and in high heels.

So I didn't consider it a particular disadvantage being the only woman as a scientist, except that when it came to looking at a career path, clearly it was a man's world. As a student at Duke University, I was told that even though I was well qualified, I would not be considered for a student assistantship that paid pretty well because the young men would have the responsibility of providing for a family and making a living, and I was just going to get married. That's what women did; I'd be relying on a man for economic security. For me it was considered a nice thing to do to be a scientist. For them it was a profession. It was just the attitude of the '50s, and it's still an attitude that persists. Women are not expected to be as professionally motivated or stick with a job the way a man would.

One thing that seems to be a common factor for those who do succeed is they really love what they're doing and won't let the reasons that people give for why they can't do something stand in the way. You have to have a sense of humor. The suit of armor that you wear is called "laugh at it, and shrug it off, and turn it to your advantage." Make a joke of these idiots who want to put you in a box.

Are there any comments you remember or any anecdotes you could share about men's attitudes toward women decades ago?

Well, headlines. When I joined an expedition to the Indian Ocean, I was the only woman. I was there because I was trained as a botanist, and they needed a botanist. So I was invited to join this group: 70 men with the ship's crew and the scientific complement. When the group gathered in Mombasa [Kenya] at the beginning of the expedition, we were interviewed by the Mombasa daily newspaper. Because I stood out as a woman, the reporter took particular interest in interviewing me. The headline the next day was: "Sylvia Sails Away With 70 Men." The subtitle was: "But she expects no problems." It wasn't about the science; it wasn't about the nature of the International Indian Ocean Expedition. But I did not have problems largely because of that suit of armor called a sense of humor and because I did not expect favors. I really wanted to be there as scientist, first and foremost.

The big problem all of us shared was: How do you explore the Indian Ocean from a little ship? It was 220 feet long but still a tiny speck in the middle of this vast ocean. We were armed with scuba, which was a gift because scuba was new for science in 1964. But to get deeper than that, we did not have a submarine. We had nets; we had hooks; we had dredges that would scrape the ocean floor. We were trying to figure out what was going on by dragging a net. In San Francisco, if you dragged a net through the streets from an airplane high in the sky, and you can't see what's below but you grab little bites out of the bottom and you bring it up and try to figure out, what's the nature of San Francisco? You know nothing of the music or the arts or Golden Gate Park.

Like trying to put together a puzzle with just a few pieces.

Right, and you have no idea what the picture is supposed to look like. Later with the Tektite project—this was 1969, 1970, it wasn't that long afterwards. Astronauts were walking on the moon for the first time in 1969; they were heroes. So the idea of being an *aquanaut*, living under the water, caught the public's imagination. I was at Harvard University at the time. There was a notice on the bulletin board that announced the opportunity to live underwater for two weeks, and scientists could apply.

There had been a previous expedition in 1969 when four men lived for two months at 50 feet in this underwater laboratory, breathing a mix of nitrogen and oxygen. They did fine, no obvious health problems. So they put out this notice to the scientific community. There was no mention that this was for men only. Nobody said women could not apply, so some of us did. It came as a surprise to the powers that be in Washington. The head of the program, Dr. James Miller said: "Well, half the fish are female, half the dolphins, half the whales, I guess we could put up with a few women." And they did.

But they did not like the idea of men and women living together. Remember this is 1969, 1970, no women [astronauts] high in the sky. And the restrooms for men and women were clearly separate, except on airplanes. They were just concerned about the social appearance of having unmarried men and women living together. So they rewrote the script and selected four women. They called us aquabelles, aquachicks, aqua-babes, aqua-naughties; that was the best one. We didn't really care what they called us as long as they let us go. And they did.

We were there as scientists, not to set records, not to be better than the guys. All of the aquanauts, we weren't trying to be superstars. We were just trying to do what we were there to do. For the women's team to do what we set out to do meant we needed to be out in the water a lot, watching the fish in their natural state. It turned out that we spent more time actually using the ocean as a laboratory, days spent outside [the living quarters], 10 to 12 hours a day, day and night. Some people took this to mean: Oh, they are just trying to show the guys up. C'mon, this is just, errrhhh, you know you have to laugh, or cry. Better to laugh.

That sounds like the way Jane Goodall studies chimpanzees in Tanzania.

Yes, you go out and watch the animals.

And sit with them until they get used to you.

Yes! One of the things that changed for me was I got to know individual animals, individual fish. I guess I knew that like cats and dogs and horses, and all living things, there aren't any two exactly alike. There are gazillions of cats, but no two exactly alike. That's one of the wonders of life. I just hadn't thought to apply it to fish.

That an eel, for example, could have a personality?

And a face. There are a number of eels, but this eel has a face and an attitude and a behavior different from that eel 50 yards away. Fish have places; they're homebodies. They may swim around, but they come back to the same little place repeatedly. Parrotfish: some fish cover themselves with a blanket of sand.

I've heard an octopus will decorate its den with shiny little shells.

For sure, you know when you've found an octopus lair because they roam around, find a tasty morsel and bring it back to eat, and they put the shells outside. So maybe it's like a trash heap outside. But maybe they do also select pretty pieces of glass or shiny shells and not just the remnants of their lunch. For me it was a personal revelation to get to know those parrotfish, those grouper, that barracuda that made an appearance right by the picture window that was at one end of the underwater laboratory, the Tektite Laboratory.

Jane Goodall was given a hard time by some loftier-than-thou scientists who said: "It's anthropomorphizing; you can't personalize these creatures." But her response was: "That's nonsense." That's my response too. Why should we doubt that we have characteristics in common? Our DNA is largely the same. We have so much in common across the fabric of life, whether we're bacteria or elephants or pine trees, the basic recipes for the chemistry of life are the same. And we are very much part of it. We share more than 96 percent of our DNA with chimpanzees.

Back to the personality issue, the emotional life of sea creatures such as eels or dolphins or whales.

Do they feel pain?

I'm sure they feel pain.

But a lot of people excuse themselves from their bad behavior with fish because they say, oh they don't feel pain, they don't have the capacity to feel pain. That's nonsense. They have all of the equipment that we have to feel pain. Don't try to spare your conscience about inflicting pain on creatures—you're doing it, so just get over it. You either choose to do it or choose not to do it.

Do they feel pain? Of course they do. Do they have emotions? Do they have alliances? Do they have a social structure? Do they bond, one with another? Absolutely. It's a smallness on our part, a narrowness of spirit and mind and heart to think that we are so special. Why not embrace it and be thrilled that we have so much in common? Humans today are empowered with knowledge that could not exist even 50 years ago and that gives us the gift of responsibility, we have an opportunity to not lose this amazing extraordinary gift, a living planet.

I like that phrase, gift of responsibility, because you're saying it's not onerous but an opportunity we should be grateful for.

Absolutely. Imagine if we did not know. Most people have access to knowledge but they are choosing not to take advantage of this most precious thing that we have that no other generation before us could have. It's the key to survival. It's the opportunity that will never come again. It's ours—why aren't we just excited about being able to take what we've got and turn it to our long-term advantage. We can be the saviors of humankind. Life will go on with us or without us. It did before and it can after.

It won't be the same assemblage of life—we're already altering the pieces of the puzzle. We've lost a lot of them owing to our actions. We blow up a coral reef—there are residents, unique species that occurred there and nowhere else in the universe. There are some species of stomatopods, shrimp creatures with unique eyes that have the ability to see a spectrum of light, of color, that is much broader than humans have. It's the broadest spectrum that we've been able to identify in any creature. So we blow up the reef and we lose that piece of the puzzle. We'll never have a complete puzzle again as a consequence of our actions.

Or we poison the ocean with the chemicals that don't exist in nature. We've put into the ocean this avalanche of material: plastics, chemicals that we have synthesized and thrown into the ocean. We have altered the nature of the ocean largely because of old fishing gear, discarded or lost, and the plastic debris that has been allowed to flow into the ocean.

On the order of 300,000 marine mammals are killed every year as a consequence of entanglement or ingestion of these bits and pieces of plastic. A sperm whale came ashore in California a few years ago with 100 pounds of plastic inside. And they wonder why this animal died. Or the birds that you see on Midway Island that never get to fly because their well-intended parents go out and bring back cigarette lighters and toothbrushes and plastic toys and fragments of this and bits of that and stuff it down the goozle of the baby birds thinking that they're feeding them something nutritious. You see these pathetic piles of feathers surrounding a double handful of plastic that has so jammed up the intestinal tract and the stomachs of these creatures that they starve to death and die.

We are talking about tens of thousands of these birds that never get to reach maturity. It's a wonder any of them make it. And turtles eat plastic and die. And fish, even the fish, you could get really depressed thinking about the bad news, but the good news is we've got evidence. We can count the numbers, look at the depletion, look at the loss of sharks killed for their fins or killed for sport or killed for their cartilage, just killed, killed, killed.

Or grouper or snapper or tuna, oh my goodness. Tuna is an acquired taste. Fifty years ago, few people ate tuna. In Japan eating raw fish for sushi—the fine art of crafting beautiful dining experiences with raw animals from the sea—was a common practice but less common than it is today. Sushi doesn't have to be a seafood event; it can involve other kinds of food, especially plants. Vegetable sushi is delicious and nutritious, and not fraught with the dangers of eating wild creatures jammed with mercury and other things. And there's also the danger of killing the very last of these beautiful creatures.

The bluefin tuna—from the time when the large-scale extraction of tuna for luxury dining started in the 1980s to the present time—in the Pacific have been reduced to 2.7 percent of what was there in 1980. There are still some adult tuna out there, but they're smaller and less common. And the price goes up as the supply goes down. So it is still profitable to take the last bluefin tuna.

In the Atlantic the numbers are a little stronger. When I was the chief scientist at NOAA in 1990, 90 percent of the North Atlantic adult tuna population was gone; it had already been extracted. Although there are policies that restrict the number, when you're down to 10 percent, isn't it time to stop? Just stop, unless your goal is to exterminate them. If you really want to have an ocean without bluefin tuna, then kill at the rate that we're currently killing because there isn't a way for nature to keep up with the level of extraction.

But because of that wonderful characteristic that haunts humans called greed, we just can't resist. You see a swimming tuna, and you want to kill it because there's a market for it. The only hope is people who care, like Yao Ming in China, who said he'll never eat shark-fin soup. Just say, I will never eat tuna. I will never do it. First of all, say I don't need to do it. It's not sustenance for most people. For those for whom it is real sustenance, I say great, OK, native people for traditions, you catch the fish, you consume the fish locally, feed families. The social structure of your community is reliant on catching fish; that's different. That is not likely to deplete the ocean wildlife.

But when you catch fish to market to the other side of the world because they are going to pay hundreds of thousands of dollars for one fish—or like one beautiful bluefin, $1.8 million for one fish—that's not sustenance, that's luxury. We have a responsibility to not lose important pieces of the puzzle. Are we playing God to say it's OK if we lose bluefin tuna so that I can have this lovely taste on my lips for a moment. And then they're gone. I mean, that's playing God. That's actually saying that you know better than God, that you're more important than God's creation.

And we know from what we've seen on land that when you take away top predators—

What was there before: wolves, bears, big cats, eagles, and owls; that was the world that we inherited. We have to make space for ourselves, no kidding, but do we have to exterminate, annihilate, reduce to near extinction or total extinction other creatures because they don't happen to suit our view of what life should be like at this point in history? Let's figure out how to work together to have a planet where there's a place for ourselves within the fabric of life. Maybe we will regret losing some of the pieces we have deliberately caused to disappear over the ages. We're very close now with elephants, with rhinoceroses, with many of the large animals which miraculously have weathered the human storm in recent centuries and millennia.

Many of the big creatures in North America did die by our hand, the hand of humans, in the last 10,000 years. But we still have bison, why? Because we consciously took action to save the last ones. We almost exterminated sea otters; now they're coming back. There are still elephant seals—not because some people didn't try to exterminate the last ones, they really did—but a few managed to slip through, then a different attitude prevailed, and now we have elephant seals.

They've come back spectacularly on the California coast.

Only because we consciously gave them a break. We could kill every one. We now have the power to kill every blue whale, every gray whale, and every humpback, every whale period. We have the capacity to find and end the life of every one. But, cause for hope, we have determined they're more valuable to us alive than dead. And we are beginning to understand that forests, intact forests, intact coral reefs, intact nature, has a value that transcends products. Short-term use is not as important as our existence. The ocean has been the great stabilizing factor, and we are now destabilizing it, all at once. We're seeing the consequences in storms; we're seeing the consequences in warming; the place that has held the planet steady is now on shaky ground.

The very foundation of life itself is the ocean. *The living ocean*, it isn't just rocks and water; it's this amazing place. We had nothing to do with making it, but we are having a lot to do with destabilizing it. We are cutting great swaths through the fish: 100 million tons a year of carbon-based units that we're extracting from the ocean. Think of it as a big engine with the food chains that distribute nutrients. Whales poop, right, most living things do, and the nutrients that go back into the ocean power the phytoplankton that feed the krill that the whales eat.

You get this whole cycle of life going, and it's not that simple because along with the whales and the krill and the phytoplankton you've got gazillions of zooplankton every step of the way. They are channeling nutrients, taking but putting things back, creating this living soup that holds the planet steady. It's the circulatory system for the planet, and we are the beneficiaries. And all we think that the ocean is good for is a dump site and a place to take things that we want, whether it's sand, or minerals, or oil, or gas, or fish, or shrimp. Or we use the ocean to sail or for transportation or to wage war. But with every breath you take, the ocean matters to you, wherever you are.

Is that what you would say to someone in Kansas?

You bet. I do. You never see your heart either but you're glad it exists.

You've spoken about a fish called menhaden, that we use for fish oil supplements, and called it the "most important fish in the sea." We could get those same oils from plants, couldn't we?

Absolutely. The menhaden get the oil from plants, from microscopic plants, phytoplankton in the sea. They don't make the oils; they consume them and store them. So we can bypass the fish and go straight to the phytoplankton. We're not trying to synthesize the oils; we're trying to harness the power of very fast-growing algae, and instead of killing the fish and squeezing the oil out of them, we just grow the plants that make these little balls of oil and use that directly. And in a relatively small space, because it's cultivated in tanks inland, in Kentucky for heaven's sakes.

I know you don't eat fish. Do you eat meat?

I used to. I don't anymore. Once you know, a whole new world opens to you about being creative in terms of what choices are there. All of the basic foods that we require can be derived and are derived ultimately from plants. Broccoli is loaded with good stuff. A plant diet is the healthiest diet that a human can consume.

Are there responsible ways of occasionally eating fish and seafood?

Eat low on the food chain and give up wild animals. You get a pretty good ratio of conversion from sunlight to plants for tilapia, catfish, and carp.

So don't eat wild salmon?

That's worst of all. Wild salmon around the world have essentially been annihilated, right down to the point of being on the edge. A few places remain where the wild populations are pretty healthy: Alaska and parts of Russia. But here in California, you are so happy when you get three wild salmon coming back up the rivers. And the Atlantic salmon is greatly depleted in its natural habitat. Whether it's the European side or the Atlantic (North American East Coast), the natural streams are just a tiny trickle of what was there going back 100 years.

Part of it is dams, the upstream loss of what these creatures need to complete their life cycle. It's contamination of the rivers. It's straightening of rivers so that the kinds of places where the spawning is most favorable have been lost, and the rivers are warmed because of that re-channeling and the damming. We've really done a number on wild salmon. Nobody should eat them, except native populations with a long-term history and cultural needs. Give 'em a break.

How about traditional cultures that hunt whales?

Even a few people can eliminate what remains of these greatly depleted populations. When you get down to such low numbers, it's a choice they have to make of whether they can still maintain traditions in some way by honoring the whales and honoring their past, but to do so they should give up using exploding harpoons and fiberglass boats.

We live in a new era. There are many traditions people all over the world have sacrificed in favor of adopting new habits. They've made a choice, but they don't lose the knowledge or the respect for the past. It's brought them to a new place in their history. We can adapt to a new time. It was Darwin who said it wasn't the smartest or the cleverest or the fastest that succeeds. It's the ones that are the most adaptable to change.

We do have a choice. If we wait much longer, we won't have a choice, at least not the chance that we now have to take seriously the risky future we have arrived at. Now the ocean really needs us to take care of it, which means not managing fish but managing ourselves. I wish we could have made these choices 50 years ago. We are the luckiest people ever, to have the choice. Think about the doors that are closing, the species that are eliminated, the chemistry that is changing, the planet that is warming, the ice that is melting. It's getting harder and harder because we haven't responded fast enough to hold the planet steady. Now is the time.

I know you've often talked about going snorkeling or scuba diving.

Yes, get out there; get wet; no child left dry.

But can the oceans handle lots more people?

There's a carrying capacity to any place, but if you go with respect, the way you go into someone else's home, you don't wreck the furniture when you go to someone's home. Some go into the ocean deliberately causing harm. Let's go fishing—let's go kill something—let's go cause pain. Catch and release, doesn't that hurt your psyche somehow if you see an animal struggling for its life? Then you break its jaw getting the hook out and throw it back in the ocean. You release it, so you feel somehow self-righteous. Boy, where did that come from? I mean what is this, humans who want to go out and kill something for the joy of it. I never have quite understood that, even when I was a little kid. Their mind-set is: Let's go kill.

How about let's go live. This is good for me to go take a walk. I don't have to kill something to justify my taking a walk in the woods. My goal is to find a pileated woodpecker or to find a certain kind of mushroom, not to eat it but to respect it, to wonder how many millions of years have gone into creating that kind of mushroom. Ask questions: Does it glow-in-the-dark? What kinds of insects are living in the gills? This is a quest that should be never-ending because you find out one thing, and you want to know 20 other things. It's the joy of being a human: curiosity in a package with arms and legs.

Do you think you were born with this curiosity?

All kids are born with curiosity, and it's not just humans. Look at a kitten, look at a puppy, look at a young deer, look at baby fish; they're always looking around. Everything is new. Kids are natural scientists. They want to know everything about everything. Scientists never grow up, and no one ever should in the sense that you never stop exploring, never stop wondering what's next. Where is this beetle going when it flies off? Let's go find out. You should never ever, ever, ever be bored. Just look at a tree and ask yourself: What do I not know about this tree?

And you're still exploring, still searching?

I'm still breathing. I hope to continue doing so for a good long time.

Have you had any great dives recently?

I was just diving in Mexico, in the Yucatán. The most recent dive was a couple of weeks ago into a *cenote*; the entrance was at a cave. There were bats and swallows living up near the top, but it was filled with water. So we dived in there; we went into this tunnel and at various points you could see sunlight coming through, and we came out at another *cenote*. It was really extraordinary: stalactites were hanging down and stalagmites coming up from the bottom, but it was flooded so we were swimming through a cathedral. It was really lovely.

Could you tell me about a couple of successes?

I'll be going to one in October; it's called Cabo Pulmo. It's held up as a shining example. A family of fishermen, the Castro family, said the grandparents remembered when big fish were really common. You could just walk out to the shore and fish and get plenty for the family and to share. As the sons came along it was harder, and in recent years they have to go farther out to get just enough, not abundance. They work really hard, long hours, far offshore, to get fewer fish.

So they did what seemed like a crazy idea: Stop fishing and figure out other ways to generate income. They turned to tourism to get divers to come. This was a fishing village so they didn't have fancy hotels or the usual amenities to attract people, but they celebrated diving and used their fishing boats to take people out. Even without government mandates they decided among themselves to stop fishing this relatively small area. But then they worked with the government to officially designate it as a marine reserve. It's been 20 years now, and you can see the difference.

They actually have grouper. Most of the reefs that you visit in the Gulf of California and in coral reefs everywhere, grouper are the first to go because they're big, friendly, curious fish. Spear fishermen can just go up to them; it's like shooting a cow. They're looking at you, and then you kill them. There's nothing in their history that has prepared them for predation by smart primates that put bait in the water and use nets. We have just stripped the ocean of snapper and grouper and of course the sharks; shark fishermen have just demolished life in the Gulf of California and elsewhere around the world because of the global appetite for shark-fin soup.

But in Cabo Pulmo you actually see sharks. There's a giant tornado of jacks that has set up residence in this area. I've seen it every time, and I've been maybe a dozen times during the past five years. It's astonishing; you go five miles down the coast, nobody's home. They're just not there, and the corals are not as healthy as what you see within the reserve. The fish need the corals, but the corals need the fish too.

You see parrotfish inside Cabo Pulmo reserve. Parrotfish have become the latest fad, these parrotfish that once nobody would eat are now prime targets for restaurants. It's just sad; this is not a tradition. This is like: we've cleaned out the grouper, we've cleaned out the snapper, sharks are getting harder to catch, so what's left? The parrotfish, so let's go get the parrotfish. I've never eaten the parrotfish, but I'm told that they're not desirable as a food fish in the same way as a catfish or a tilapia or a carp.

In New Zealand, a scientist, Bill Ballantine, maybe 25 years ago, began with a very small area where he somehow convinced the local people to stop killing the fish and just have a little preserve. He documented it, went out there, talked to the people, and was able to demonstrate not just that that area recovered significantly, but that the areas immediately surrounding it had more fish too. So it was a safe haven that gave back outside the protected area, the spillover effect. That's not a good excuse for having marine protected areas, so you can have more fish to kill, but it does work. Most people don't even think at all about fish other than, mmm, delicious. But now we have come to other ways of understanding their value.

I think there's plenty of reason for hope. The Florida Keys [is] another great example. Billy Causey, who started out as an exotic fish collector for aquariums, has become one of the most ardent voices for conservation in the country, in the world, but he evolved from being somebody who was a fish catcher, catching little fish to sell to the aquarium trade. He likes to eat fish, still does, but he does not favor the large-scale extraction for luxury dining. Billy Causey proposed that there be safe havens within the Florida Keys National Marine Sanctuary, where sportfishing is encouraged inside the sanctuary. Even President George W. Bush said, "Why do they call them sanctuaries if you can fish inside?"

So some reserves aren't fully protected?

Papahānaumokuākea (in the coastal waters of Hawaii) is a monument, fully protected. That was the breakthrough. Monuments work—managed areas do not. What works is deliberate protection, safe havens. You just respect whatever's there: the lobsters, the shrimp, the poor beleaguered squid that have little protection wherever they exist, except in a fully protected area.

You've called for Hope Spots to preserve areas of the ocean.

Hope Spots, 30 percent by 2030. It's not just a nice number to resonate with the year, but an analysis of what it will take to restore what we've already lost. We can't just keep on killing, but because the momentum is so great, it's not realistic to think that we're just going to stop cold from fishing, although it would be much better if we could, even for the fishermen. If you want to have fish, you have to have fish, and we're down to 10 percent of many of the big fish that once were abundant. We're talking decades ago, not thousands of years ago, recent times, the lifetime of the fishermen.

For Hope Spots, you work with the top levels of government but also local people; you almost have to get them to buy into the concept, or it can't work even if you have a law. And even if you don't have a law, it can work if people understand they're protecting their livelihoods; more important, they're protecting their life, their existence. By keeping the natural systems safe they can prosper, as the people of Cabo Pulmo did, from looking at other ways, other values, whether it's tourism, fish-watching, or just a healthier, more vibrant community because the ocean is in good condition rather than dying.

We are fostering expeditions, working with National Geographic. We want to encourage people to visit these places, get the word out, make films, give talks, get people fired up. Make them want to be ambassadors and caretakers. Everyone can make a choice that will make the world a better place, every day.

Less than 10 percent of the ocean has been explored, but the best is coming, when you see what the Deep Rover images brought back from Antarctica this year of communities of life 1,000 meters down, or even just 100 meters down, along the edge of the ice in Antarctica. Think coral reefs, sponges, giant sea spiders, these crustaceans called arthropods, but instead of being the size of a flea, they're the size of your fist. Think about giant sea stars, not the size of your hand but the size of a washtub, giant creatures that are living where the water, if it were freshwater, it would freeze. This is so cold and dark, but it's thriving with life.

We are crippled when we think about the element of time because we live such a short time. Imagine being able to live as long as some of the deep-sea sharks. One Greenland shark has been aged at four centuries, 400 years. Think about what civilization was like four centuries ago, and they're still cruising around. How would you like to be as old as a redwood tree or some of the deep-sea corals that are thousands of years old? We are here and then we're gone, except for what we have brought with us from the past and what we can deliver to the future.

Armed with this brilliance that we have called knowing, we are able to determine, to some extent, our fate, our future, by making choices that deep-sea corals cannot, that even elephants cannot. Only we have that power. There is time, but I can't imagine facing my grandsons; they're just off to college yesterday. When their kids are off to college, what's the world going to be like? It depends on what we do or what we fail to do right now, the next 10 years. The next 10 years will be the most important of the next 10,000 years.

How deep have you gone in submersibles?

The last time was just a few months ago in Costa Rica. I have used more than 30 kinds of submersibles and have not yet been to the deepest part of the ocean, but it's on my bucket list. Maybe I'll have to build the submarine first. I have a passion for the ocean, snorkeling, holding my breath, scuba diving, rebreathers, submarines, remotely operated systems, living underwater, bring it on. I love it all. It's our world, it's mostly blue. What's holding anybody back?

ACKNOWLEDGMENTS

Completing a book is a monumental task, one that truly takes a community. First, I'd like to thank the creative people featured in this book: the writers, musicians, chefs, explorers, and other artists who make our world a richer place. All of them are tremendously busy people, yet they all had the generosity to spend some time with me discussing their craft, lives, and aspirations.

So many of these big-hearted people went above and beyond. I requested a half hour with Lucinda Williams; we ended up talking for an hour. Joan Rivers met my wife and me after her show at Napa's Uptown Theatre and was as kind and gracious as you could imagine. David Sedaris and I had not one but two interviews, about a year apart, and he made me feel as though he had all the time in the world. Sharon Jones, whose strength was sapped by cancer and chemotherapy, made the effort to speak with me on her final tour, just weeks before she died.

Jane Goodall, despite her packed schedule, consented to a follow-up interview after an editor asked for greater depth. And broadcaster Mike Krukow took time out from his gameday preparation to spend a half hour talking baseball in a booth overlooking the field at the Giants' ballpark. Author and documentarian Phil Cousineau and I had a lengthy conversation at San Francisco's Cafe Zoetrope; then we went to a Giants game following our interview.

The late Studs Terkel invited me to his home in Chicago when he was 93, and at the conclusion of our freewheeling conversation asked me if I'd like a shot of whiskey. And Dervla Murphy invited me to her home in southern Ireland to talk for hours while we drank cans of beer; then she prepared some lunch for us.

I'd also like to appreciate the editors who assigned the stories for which many of these interviews were originally conducted. Among them: Sy Safransky at The Sun magazine, John McMurtrie and the late David Wiegand at the San Francisco Chronicle, Drew Limsky who has offered me terrific assignments for a number of magazines, Dina Mishev at Inspirato, the team at The Explorers Journal, Ben Raker at Alaska Beyond, and Gretchen Giles, former editor of The Bohemian.

I'd also like to thank my colleagues at The Press Democrat, the Pulitzer Prize-winning daily newspaper based in Santa Rosa, California. It was arts editor Joanne Derbort who gave me a shot at music writing in 2008. Her successors, Linda Castrone and Dan Taylor, have continued to assign me profiles of musicians and authors. And thanks to Press Democrat managing editor Ted Appel, who gave me permission to use interviews I conducted for the newspaper.

It's been an immense pleasure to work once again with Travelers' Tales publisher James O'Reilly and executive editor Larry Habegger. Fifteen years ago we collaborated on my book of interviews with the world's top travel writers, *A Sense of Place.* So I knew that their sage counsel and thoughtful editorial suggestions would make *The Creative Spark* a better book.

I would be remiss if I didn't offer a shout-out to our local, independent bookstores. Here in the San Francisco Bay Area, we are blessed with thriving independent stores, such as Book Passage, Kepler's, Books Inc., and Copperfield's, humble palaces where a bookseller's recommendation can change a reader's life. Barbara Kingsolver calls these stores "the beating heart of intellectual and spiritual communities."

Naturally, it's my community of family and friends that sustains me. The friends are too numerous to name, but I hope they know I appreciate them. My brother, Andy Shapiro, my mother, Phyllis Shapiro, and my late father, Larry Shapiro, have since my earliest days offered me support and inspiration.

And my wife, Jacqueline Yau, is my unwavering companion. Her love, effervescent spirit, and kind-hearted encouragement keep me going and buoy my spirit. Thank you for believing in me.

CREDITS

Editorial Credits

Portions of the Jane Goodall interview appeared in The Explorers Journal, Earth Island Journal, and O, The Oprah Magazine.

Portions of the David Sedaris interview appeared in the San Francisco Chronicle.

Portions of the following interviews appeared in Inspirato magazine: Frances Mayes, Kyle Connaughton, Juan José Cuevas.

Portions of the following interviews appeared in The Sun magazine: Sylvia Earle and Studs Terkel.

Portions of the following interviews appeared in The Press Democrat newspaper: Amy Tan, Barbara Kingsolver, Dave Alvin, David Sedaris, Francis Ford Coppola, Graham Nash, Greg Brown, Ian Anderson, Jake Shimabukuro, Joan Rivers, Judy Collins, Kinky Friedman, Lucinda Williams, Lyle Lovett and Robert Earl Keen, Melissa Etheridge, Melvin Seals, Merle Haggard, Smokey Robinson, Warren Hellman.

Portions of the Sharon Jones interview appeared in the Santa Cruz Sentinel.

Portions of the Mike Krukow interview appeared in Alaska Beyond, the Alaska Airlines magazine.

Portions of the Richard Thompson interview appeared in the Sonoma County, California weekly, The Bohemian.

The following interviews were done expressly for *The Creative Spark*: Pico Iyer, Dervla Murphy, Phil Cousineau.

Photo Credits

Caterpillar and butterfly by Michael Shapiro
Pico Iyer by Brigitte Lacombe
Barbara Kingsolver by Steven Hopp
Lucinda Williams by David McClister
Robert Earl Keen and Lyle Lovett by Darren Carroll
Jane Goodall by Michael Neugebauer
Smokey Robinson courtesy of SmokeyRobinson.com
Dave Alvin by Beth Herzhaft
Melissa Etheridge by Lauren Dukoff
Francis Ford Coppola by Sofia Coppola
Joan Rivers by Charles William Bush
Graham Nash by Amy Grantham
Judy Collins by Brad Trent
Mike Krukow by Andy Kuno, ©2018 S.F. Giants
Dervla Murphy by Michael Shapiro
Greg Brown by Roman Cho
Richard Thompson by Tom Bejgrowicz
Melvin Seals by Kate Haley
Amy Tan by Julian Johnson
David Sedaris by Ingrid Christie
Merle Haggard courtesy of the Haggard family
Juan José Cuevas by Michael Shapiro
Studs Terkel by Nina Subin
Frances Mayes by Will Garin
Ian Anderson by Nick Harrison
Jake Shimabukuro by Coleman Saunders, Americus Studios
Warren Hellman by Peter Donaldson
Sharon Jones by Jacob Blickenstaff
Kinky Friedman by Hans Bauer
Phil Cousineau by Jo Beaton Cousineau
Kyle and Katina Connaughton by Roman Cho
Sylvia Earle by Kip Evans
Michael Shapiro by Catherine Karnow

ABOUT THE AUTHOR

In 1979, when Michael Shapiro was in high school, an exhibition called "A Celebration of Creativity in America and in You" opened at the California Academy of Sciences in San Francisco. The poster for it was a hand, rooted like a tree in the ground. The branches (made of the hand's fingers) were full of green leaves, and all sorts of colorful objects orbited the tree.

He had no idea that 40 years later he would compose a book about creativity, featuring many of the most inventive people of our time. Yet in high school, he already knew that creativity, and its root, curiosity, would be among the most important themes of his life. It was curiosity about the world that propelled him toward a career in journalism and the creative endeavor that is writing.

His features and news stories have appeared in The Washington Post, New York Times, Chicago Tribune, and Los Angeles Times. Shapiro's work has appeared in the following newspaper sections: news, sports, entertainment, business, real estate, home and garden, books, and travel. And from 2011 to 2018, Shapiro wrote the San Francisco Chronicle's weekly gambling column.

Among his travel assignments: Shapiro has bicycled down Mongolia's unmarked dirt roads for The Washington Post, tasted tequila in Jalisco for American Way, played baseball for a week at the San Francisco Giants fantasy camp for Lexus magazine, and tracked pumas in Chile's Patagonia region on a photo safari for a custom lifestyle magazine. He's written for magazines ranging from the Saturday Evening Post to The Sun to Alaska Beyond. He's even written for O, The Oprah Magazine.

His National Geographic Traveler cover story, about Jan Morris' corner of Wales, won the 2007 Bedford Pace grand award for best feature about Great Britain. His article about sustainable seafood in Vancouver earned the 2016 Explore Canada Award of Excellence. He's won the Lowell Thomas Award from the Society of American Travel Writers, the Solas Award for travel essays, and is a four-time winner of Travel Classics' top prize.

Shapiro's first literary book, *A Sense of Place*, is a collection of interviews with the world's leading travel authors including Bill Bryson, Jan Morris, Peter Matthiessen, and Paul Theroux. In 2008, he wrote the text for the pictorial book, *Guatemala: A Journey Through the Land of the Maya*, with photography by Kraig Lieb. In 1997, Shapiro published *NetTravel: How Travelers Use the Internet*, an early guide to online travel planning.

He co-directed and produced the 2017 documentary film, *Junkyard Alchemist*, about the artists Patrick Amiot and Brigitte Laurent, who turn junk into art. The film earned Best of the Fest recognition in the short film category at the Sebastopol Documentary Film Festival. That same year, Shapiro delivered a Sonoma County TEDx talk entitled "The Space Between" about how travel fosters understanding and can courage people to build bridges rather than walls.

hapiro lives with his wife, Jacqueline Yau, in Sonoma
v, California, just north of San Francisco. He volunteers

as a whitewater raft guide and sea kayak trip leader for Environmental Traveling Companions, a Northern California outfitter that takes special needs groups on outdoor adventures. In 2016, he co-led a 16-day raft trip down the Colorado River through the Grand Canyon, somehow rowing his wife without incident through the harrowing rapids of Lava Falls.

For more about Michael Shapiro, please visit his website: michaelshapiro.net.

For more information about this book, reviews, and author appearances, see thecreativesparkbook.com.